British Science Fiction Cinema

British Science Fiction Cinema is the first substan＿＿ ＿uy of a genre which, despite a sometimes troubled history, has produced some of the best British films, from the prewar classic *Things to Come* to *Alien* - made in Britain by a British director. The contributors to this rich and provocative collection explore the diverse strangeness of British SF, from literary adaptations like *Nineteen Eighty-Four* and *A Clockwork Orange* to pulp fantasies and 'creature features' far removed from the acceptable face of British cinema.

Through case studies of key films like *The Day the Earth Caught Fire*, contributors explore the unique themes and concerns of British SF, from the postwar boom years to more recent productions like *Hardware*, and examine how SF cinema drew on a variety of sources, from TV adaptations like *Doctor Who and the Daleks*, to the horror/SF crossovers produced from John Wyndham's cult novels *The Day of the Triffids* and *The Midwich Cuckoos* (filmed as *Village of the Damned*). How did budget restrictions encourage the use of the 'invasion narrative' in 1950s films? And how did films such as *Unearthly Stranger* and *Invasion* reflect fears about the decline of Britain's economic and colonial power and the 'threat' of female sexuality?

British Science Fiction Cinema celebrates the breadth and continuing vitality of British SF film-making, in both big-budget productions such as *Brazil* and *Event Horizon* and cult exploitation movies like *Inseminoid* and *Lifeforce*.

I.Q. Hunter is Senior Lecturer in Media Studies at De Montfort University, Leicester.

British Popular Cinema

Series editors: Steve Chibnall and I.Q. Hunter

De Montfort University, Leicester

At a time when there is a growing popular and scholarly interest in British film, with new sources of funding and notable successes in world markets, this series explores the largely submerged history of the UK's cinema of entertainment.

The series rediscovers and evaluates not only individual films but whole genres, such as science fiction and the crime film, that have been ignored by a past generation of critics. Dismissed for decades as aberrations in the national cinema and anaemic imitations of American originals, these films are now being celebrated in some quarters as important contributions to our cinematic heritage.

The emergence of cult genre movies from the apparently respectable lineage of British film emphasises the gap between traditional academic criticism and a new alliance between revisionist film theorists and extra-mural (but well-informed) cinema enthusiasts who wish to take the study of British film in unexpected directions. This series offers the opportunity for both established cineastes and new writers to examine long-neglected areas of British film production or to develop new approaches to more familiar territory. The books will enhance our understanding of how ideas and representations in films relate to changing gender and class relations in postwar Britain, and their accessible writing style will make these insights available to a much wider readership.

Books in the series:

British Crime Cinema
Edited by Steve Chibnall and Robert Murphy

British Science Fiction Cinema
Edited by I. Q. Hunter

Forthcoming titles:

British Horror Cinema
Edited by Julian Petley and Steve Chibnall

The British Historical Film
Edited by Claire Monk and Amy Sargeant

British Science Fiction Cinema

Edited by I.Q. Hunter

London and New York

First published 1999
by Routledge
11 New Fetter Lane, London EC4P 4EE

Simultaneously published in the USA and Canada
by Routledge
29 West 35th Street, New York, NY 10001

Routledge Ltd is a Taylor & Francis Group Company

Selection and editorial matter © 1999 I.Q. Hunter
Individual chapters © 1999 Individual contributors

Typeset in Palatino by Routledge
Printed and bound in Great Britain by Biddles Ltd,
Guildford and King's Lynn

All rights reserved. No part of this book may be reprinted or
reproduced or utilised in any form or by any electronic, mechanical, or
other means, now known or hereafter invented, including
photocopying and recording, or in any information storage or retrieval
system, without permission in writing from the publishers.

British Library Cataloguing in Publication Data
A catalogue record for this book is available from the British Library

Library of Congress Cataloging in Publication Data
British science fiction cinema / edited by I. Q. Hunter.
p. cm. – (British popular cinema series)
Filmography: P.
Includes bibliographical references and index.
1. Science fiction films–Great Britain–History and criticism.
I. Hunter , I. Q., 1964–   II. Series.
PN1995.9.S26B65   1999
791.43'615–dc21   98–50528

ISBN 0–415–16868–6 (pbk)
ISBN 0–415–16867–8 (hbk)

Contents

Illustrations

Notes on contributors

James Chapman lectures in Film and Television Studies at the Open University. He is the author of *The British at War: Cinema, State and Propaganda 1939–1945* (1998), and has published articles in the *Historical Journal of Film, Radio and Television* and the *Journal of Popular British Cinema*. He is currently writing his next book, *Licence to Thrill: A Cultural History of the James Bond Films* (1999).

Steve Chibnall teaches film at De Montfort University, Leicester. He published his first book, *Law-and-Order News* in 1977 and has recently written *Making Mischief: The Cult Films of Pete Walker* (1998), and co-edited with Robert Murphy, *Villains: The Underworld of the British Crime Film* (1999).

Ian Conrich lectures in Media and Cultural Studies at Nottingham Trent University. He is a member of the editorial board of the *Journal of Popular British Cinema* and has published in *Sight and Sound*. He has recently contributed to the following publications: *The British Cinema Book* (1997), *Trash Aesthetics* (1997), *Liberal Directions: Basil Dearden and Postwar British Film Culture* (1997) and *A Handbook to Gothic Literature* (1998).

John R. Cook is Senior Lecturer in Media Studies at De Montfort University, Leicester, where he has taught courses in TV drama and science fiction. He is the author of two editions of *Dennis Potter: A Life on Screen* (1995, 1998). Among his current research projects is a collected volume of new essays on TV science fiction, which he is co-editing with Peter Wright.

I.Q. Hunter is Senior Lecturer in Media Studies at De Montfort University, Leicester and co-editor of the British Popular Cinema series.

Peter Hutchings lectures in the Department of Historical and Critical Studies at the University of Northumbria in Newcastle. He is the author of *Hammer and Beyond: The British Horror Film* (1993).

Jeffrey Richards is Professor of Cultural History at Lancaster University. He is the author of many books on British cinema, including *Visions of Yesterday*

(1973), *The Age of the Dream Palace* (1984) and *Films and British National Identity* (1997).

Andy Sawyer is Librarian of the Science Fiction Foundation Collection at the University of Liverpool Library, which also holds the John Wyndham Archive. He is also Reviews Editor of *Foundation*, the International Journal of Science Fiction, and teaches on the University's MA in Science Fiction Studies.

Sue Short is a Ph.D. candidate at De Montfort University, where she is completing a dissertation on the cyborg as cultural myth. She has previously contributed an article on British science fiction television to *20/20* magazine. She is currently lecturing in Media Studies at City of Westminster College in London.

Paul Wells is Subject Leader in Media Studies at De Montfort University, Leicester. He has published *Understanding Animation* (1998) and *Art and Animation* (1997), and is currently working on books concerned with animation and cultural history in Britain and the United States. His six-part radio history of the horror film, *Spinechillers*, won a Sony Award, and his work on the genre is published in a short study, *Horror Films* (1999).

Linda Ruth Williams is Senior Lecturer in Film at Southampton University. She is the author of three books: *Sex in the Head* (1993), *Critical Desire: Psychoanalysis and the Literary Subject* (1995) and *D.H. Lawrence* (1997). She has written widely on cinema, psychoanalysis and feminism, and regularly contributes to *Sight and Sound*. She is currently completing a book on contemporary erotic thriller films.

Peter Wright lectures in SF, Utopian and Dystopian Writing, and Film Studies at Edge Hill University College and the University of Liverpool. He has published articles on Gene Wolfe and Edgar Rice Burroughs and numerous reviews. Current projects include an in-depth study of Gene Wolfe, a collection of essays on British television science fiction with John R. Cook, and an anthology of women's pulp stories.

Acknowledgements

I should like to thank my colleagues at De Montfort University's British Cinema and Television Research Group for their support during the editing of this book, and De Montfort's Research Committee for providing funds towards its completion. My thanks also to Rebecca Barden and Alistair Daniel at Routledge for their help, tolerance and commitment to the British Popular Cinema series.

Photo illustrations are courtesy of the British Cinema and Television Research Group archive at De Montfort University and the British Film Institute Stills, Posters and Designs. Every effort has been made to obtain permission to reproduce copyright material. If any proper acknowledgement has not been made, I would invite copyright holders to inform us of the oversight.

Thanks are due above all to my wife, Melanie, to whom this book is dedicated. It had to be you.

Introduction

The strange world of the British science fiction film

I. Q. Hunter

X the unknown cinema

Although British science fiction films have been intermittently produced since the silent era and include some of the genre's most celebrated examples, from *Things to Come* (1936) to *Alien* (1979), there has been little sustained critical discussion of their distinctive themes and approach. Isolated examples have been plucked out for praise, but often this has obscured the generic tradition to which they belong and their place within the history of British cinema. If, in Julian Petley's famous formulation – a weary phrase by now but unavoidable in this context – British cinema has a 'lost continent' of ignored films at odds with its dominant realist tradition, then science fiction must be one of the least explored areas of that large but increasingly well-mapped landmass (Petley 1986).

The writers in this book, the first to consider British sf in its own right, approach the films from a variety of perspectives, recognising that no obvious critical context exists for understanding their alien presence in British cinema. American sf films of the 1950s are typically seen as 'paranoid' and – depending on your point of view – reflecting anticommunism (Biskind 1983) or a horror of conformism (Jancovich 1996). British films of that era, by contrast, are less virulently anticommunist (Landy 1991: 395), and more concerned with tensions in postwar consensus than with metaphors of Red invaders. The most powerful critical contexts within which to view the genre's recent development in America, such as Vivian Sobchack's Jamesonian interpretation of postmodern sf as the house-style of late capitalism (Sobchack 1991: 223–305), are insensitive to British films' specific, often quirky, inflections of the genre, and smoothe over the differences between national versions of science fiction. Attempting to discover a more nuanced understanding of British sf, this book for the most part focuses on movies which have had little critical discussion other than their original reviews and a paragraph or two in histories of sf film. These trash films, pulp fantasies, creature features and low-budget exploitation movies collude with the least respectable pleasures of British cinema – its populism, openness to American influence, and refusal of seriousness and dull realism (see figure 1).

Figure 1 'The least respectable pleasures of British cinema': *First Man into Space* (1958).
Source: Courtesy of the British Cinema and Television Research Group archive

There have been some general surveys of the field, from the perspectives both of science fiction and the revival of Gothic horror in British film that began in the 1950s. John Baxter's pioneering *Science Fiction in the Cinema* (1970) devotes a chapter to British sf, but his conclusions are mostly negative. He points out that British science fiction films have been relatively rare and (not entirely accurately) that 'lacking the comic books and pulp magazines from which American sf film drew its inspiration, the English sf cinema has never developed the popular mythology that sustains the American field' (Baxter 1970: 90). Although admiring of several films, such as *Children of the Damned* (1963) and *The Man in the White Suit* (1951), he sees many of the better films as 'sf by accident, their real source lying in the serious novel rather than in popular fiction, as does that of almost all the science fiction film produced in the British Isles' (90). As later critics would conclude, he suggests that 'the field in Britain has never equalled in imagination the work of its writers, and attempts to emulate their successes have been compromised by commercial considerations or artistic lethargy.... The great British sf film has yet to be made' (101). Similarly John Brosnan in his chapter on British sf films in the 1950s in *Future Tense* sees the films, with exceptions like the *Quatermass* trilogy (1955–67) as lagging behind American ones, though following much the same direction: 'from 1956 onwards the cycle degenerated into ever cheaper and more perfunctory variations of the monster theme' (Brosnan 1978: 106).

David Pirie's *Heritage of Horror*, which initiated discussion of the hitherto overlooked contribution of Hammer's Gothic romances to British cinema, summed up the attitude to British sf that still obtains today (Pirie 1973: 131–8). Although the horror renaissance that began with Hammer's *The Curse of Frankenstein* (1957) emerged directly out of the success of sf-horror films like *The Quatermass Experiment* (1955), it was the 'imaginative mythic themes' of the Gothic tradition that found greater public response than the films' science fiction elements, which were adequately catered for by contemporary American movies (Pirie 1973: 131). Pirie sees the films of the 1950s as responding, like American films of the period, to anxieties about atomic radiation and the new encroachments of science; but, in an important move that links the films closely to events specific to this particularly nervous time in British culture, he suggests that the films rework themes of the Second World War against the background of 'Suez, of unrelieved tension, of a sharp rise in the crime rate and a sense of impending chaos' (Pirie 1973: 31), He singles out *Quatermass II* (1957) as most completely embodying this contemporary paranoia:

> Certainly there are grounds for speculation on the fact that the year in which Anthony Eden led England into his grotesque reprise of the Second World War (with himself cast in the role of Churchill and Nasser – 'the little Egyptian upstart' – as Hitler) should have seen the first of a series of sombre SF movies, in which the British Army and/or Quatermass stand fast to repel invaders from outer space (or the bowels of the earth).
>
> (Pirie 1973: 30–1)

Pirie is dismissive of most later sf films, including *The Day the Earth Caught Fire* (1961) ('particularly poor' (136)), which were made when it was clear that 'there was no automatic market and productions in the field consequently became highly sporadic' (134).

Detailed readings of individual British films are offered in the two volumes of Bill Warren's monumental *Keep Watching the Skies! American Science Fiction Movies of the Fifties* (1982, 1986), which despite its title also covers British films up to 1962, John Clute and Peter Nicholls's *Encyclopedia of Science Fiction* (1995), and the *Aurum Film Encyclopaedia: Science Fiction* (1995), edited by Phil Hardy, whose contributors reiterate Pirie's conclusion that the best British films are *Quatermass II* and *The Damned* (1961). The *Quatermass* films again represent sf in Peter Hutchings's *Hammer and Beyond: The British Horror Film* (1993), which focuses on their problematisation of masculinity in the aftermath of the Second World War. Robert Murphy's *Sixties British Cinema* (1992) considers the overlooked films of that decade, and actually has a kind word to say for some of them. He highlights the merits of the 'modest but attractive group' of alien invasion films made independently at the start of the 1960s: *The Night Caller* (1965), *Invasion* (1966) and *Unearthly Stranger* (1963) which have a 'nice sense of ordinary people reluctantly, almost indignantly, involved in unusual events' (Murphy 1992: 182). Lengthier analyses of specific films are to be found in Patrick Luciano's *Them or Us* (1987) – a Jungian reading of archetypal imagery in *Fiend without a Face* (1959), though scarcely referring to the British context – and in Leon Hunt's *British Low Culture* (1998), which explores *Prey* (1977) as a contribution to that most despised form of British cinema, the sexploitation film. Otherwise the British sf films that have received most attention have been those with firm auteurist credentials, which can be detached from the mass of low-budget productions, and indeed from the confines of national cinema itself, and seen as contributions to world cinema. On the one hand, there are those by emigré directors: Joseph Losey's *The Damned*, made for and heavily cut by Hammer; Truffaut's *Fahrenheit 451* (1966); and above all Stanley Kubrick's *Dr Strangelove* (1964), *2001: A Space Odyssey* (1968) and *A Clockwork Orange* (1971). On the other hand, there are one-off oddities like John Boorman's *Zardoz* (1973) and Nicolas Roeg's *The Man Who Fell to Earth* (1976), which as art-films by directors whose reputations were established outside the genre can be safely insulated from comparison with the exploitation side of the genre. Still other films, such as *Alien* and *Outland* (1981), which are British by virtue of the circumstances of their production, are rarely seen as British-influenced at all but rather integrated into the history of American science fiction – in the case of those two films, as attacks on the dehumanising effects of late capitalism (Franklin 1990: 19).

Even so, before one embarks on a defence of British sf films, it is worth pointing out that scholars have had good reason to ignore or dismiss them. As Baxter and Pirie point out, the films tended to be, especially during the sf boom period of the 1950s and 1960s, low-budget concoctions bordering on horror or juvenilia and often seemed compromised by their imitation of American movies. Their titles attest both to their pulp ambitions and their similarity to the least respectable American sf: *Devil Girl from Mars* (1954), *Fire Maidens from Outer Space* (1956), *The Gamma People* (1956), *X the Unknown* (1956). Embarrassingly cheap and marginal films, they are certainly far removed from sf's more serious literary tradition (though, equally, with rare exceptions such as *Devil Girl from Mars*, they have achieved little cult success). Moreover, there are few auteurs who obviously lend themselves for sympathetic reappraisal and canonisation (a good case, however, can be made for Nigel Kneale, Michael Carreras and Val Guest and, though his films are uniformly awful, Freddie Francis). Terence Fisher, who earned a somewhat inflated reputation for his Hammer horrors, made a number of sf films which might have been expected to draw critical interest: *Four Sided Triangle* (1952), *Spaceways* (1953), *The Earth Dies Screaming* (1964), *Island of Terror* (1966) and *Night of the Big Heat* (1967). But they have largely been dismissed as pot-boilers by a director bored by the genre (Pirie 1973: 134). (See figure 2.)

After *The Quatermass Experiment*, British sf cinema, insofar as it found a niche at all, found one as sf-horror and built on the international success of Hammer's gruesome output. Indeed many British sf films are more usually thought of as horror movies. Narratives about space-flight, utopias, visits to alien

Figure 2 Invasion on the cheap: Thorley Walters and Virginia Fields in *The Earth Dies Screaming* (1964).
Source: Courtesy of the British Cinema and Television Research Group archive

civilisations and so on are much less frequent than the monster-on-the-loose fantasies inspired by *Quatermass*'s tale of an astronaut infected by an alien organism. Sf as a cinematic genre is in any case difficult to distinguish from horror, since its roots lay in such Gothic works as *Frankenstein* (1818) and its themes, more obviously in films than in the more optimistic and techno-logically gung-ho literary tradition, often complement horror's fearful attitude to science and the future. As Susan Sontag put it, sf films are about disaster rather than science, and use the resources of cinema for the catharsis of spec-tacular destruction (Sontag 1965). It was horror of science and modern life rather than optimism about their possibilities that gave sf films their peculiar thrill. For that reason it is generally more productive to consider sf films, British as well as American, separately from sf literature. Discussion of sf films has been plagued by the critical assumption that while they are valuable insofar as they register social anxieties, they are otherwise years behind their written counterparts. Fortunately more recent work on sf disentangles cinema from literature and focuses on the specific sensual and kinetic pleasures of the films rather than on their shortcomings as intellectual prophecy (Sobchack 1991; Hunter 1999).

Considered as horror films, however, British sf lacks what has been most valued by recent critics. The films arguably have no 'organic' relation to the national culture. Pirie argued that Gothic horror was British to the core, 'the only staple cinematic myth which Britain can properly claim as its own' (Pirie 1973: 9), and that it emerged from a culture in elaborate sexual denial. But British sf does not lend itself so easily to critical recuperation. First, the films are often highly 'Americanised' and in a sense therefore inauthentic expressions of the national culture. Second, compared with the lush transgressions of, say, *Dracula* (1958), with its bloodletting and erotic symbolism, the sf films are reactionary; critics nowadays prefer a bit of subversion. As 'boys' films, too, which privilege male know-how and rationality, and in which women are either absent, marginalised or ruthlessly objectified, they are less suited to the enthusiastic critical revival of the kind afforded, for example, to Gainsborough melodramas, which at least have the virtue of offering the requisite 'subversive' images of women. The sf films treat their monsters − and monstrously eroticised alien women − with rationalistic disgust rather than barely suppressed fascination. Although British sf films have their fair share of sexy aliens, their more usual casts of grotesque blobs, squelchy extraterrestrials and victims of mad science are less alluring representatives of Otherness than Dracula and his brides.

The critical consensus remains, then, that British sf is a poor thing, responsive at periods to national discourses, but too often a shadow of its more ambitious, confident, expensive and expansive American counterpart. In a sense, however, this is a curious conclusion to draw. Why should the sf film not succeed in Britain? After all, British writers from Mary Shelley to H.G. Wells defined the early literary history of the genre and throughout the century writers like Arthur C. Clarke, John Wyndham and Charles Eric Maine (whose novels have been adapted into British sf films more frequently than those of any other writer) both reached a wide audience and engaged with the genre's key themes no less impressively than the dominant American authors. Moreover, the defining myths of the future were offered by mainstream British novelists: George Orwell's *Nineteen Eighty-Four* (1949) and Aldous Huxley's *Brave New World* (1932). In the sixties the rise of the New Wave authors such as J.G. Ballard and Michael Moorcock established Britain at the forefront of avant-garde science fiction that explored 'inner space'. British TV science fiction has managed to gain an even firmer foothold on the popular imagination. Such series as *Doctor Who* (1963–89), *A for Andromeda* (1961) and *Blake's Seven* (1978–81) combined an admirably straightfaced seriousness with the British tradition of whimsical fantasy. *Doctor Who, Thunderbirds* (1965–6) and *Blake's Seven* in particular have inspired tremendous cult affection for their irreverence and kitsch cheapness. In the 1950s and 1960s, reflecting the cautiousness of producers who were aware that no ready market existed for British sf in the cinema, sf films were frequently adapted from successful TV and radio programmes. *1984* (1956), *The Abominable Snowman* (1957), *The Strange World of Planet X* (1957), *The Trollenberg Terror* (1958), the *Quatermass, Doctor Who* (1965, 1966) and *Thunderbirds* (1966, 1968) films, *Night of the Big Heat,* and later, *Doomwatch* (1972) and *Whoops Apocalypse!* (1986) all began on the small screen. *Pace* Baxter, British sf cinema derives not so much from serious literature as from television series.

It is not apparent, therefore, why British film-makers should not also have had a close understanding of the genre, not least because such themes as invasion and utopianism strike chords in a British context as well as in any other. But the fact remains that British sf cinema is largely unknown, its origins and purpose still a total mystery.

Exploring the films that time forgot

In the 1930s, where this book takes up the story of the British sf film, literature was the dominant influence. It was what Jeffrey Richards calls the Wellsian decade. *Things to Come*, based on Wells's novel, remains the masterpiece of early British science fiction cinema, notable for its exquisite design and its prophecy of the Blitz, a significant anticipation of later sf films' obsession with images of London trashed and under siege. Richards notes that Wells's scientific socialism, his enthusiastic embrace of an antiseptically perfect future, now looks disconcertingly like an advertisement for fascism. Few sf films would be so naive again about the compatibility of science and reason.

British sf of this period was deeply influenced by the expressionistic style of German sf, such as Fritz Lang's *Metropolis* (1926), to whose celebration of capital reconciled with labour *Things to Come* was Wells's irritated response. This reminds us, first, that sf is an international language, as it were; and, second, that the impact of an sf film has to do as much with set design and special effects as with the value of its intellectual content. *Things to Come*'s ideas dated quickly, but its visuals remained influential on films such as *Logan's Run* (1976) – ironically, as a model of an authoritarian dystopia.

The box-office failure of *Things to Come* makes it seem in retrospect something of a sport or oddity, a one-off prestige film. Few sf films were made in the 1940s. This was true in America as well, where sf was limited to escapist juvenile pulp, and drew ever more distant from the ambitions of Wells and the developing literary tradition. In Britain, only *The Perfect Woman* (1949), based on a stage farce about the invention of a female robot, indicated the themes that would flourish in British sf of the 1950s: a whimsical disdain for scientific accuracy and a nervousness about women.

It was in the fifties, in Britain as in America, that the sf film took off as a popular film genre in response to fears of atomic war, the power of science and Red invasion. Inspired by a flurry of American space-flight movies such as *Destination Moon* (1950) and *Flight to Mars* (1951) Britain produced *Spaceways* and *Satellite in the Sky* (1956), which continued the emphasis of *Q Planes* (1939), *The Sound Barrier* (1952) and indeed *The First of the Few* (1942) on Britain's technological mastery in the sky. Amusingly, they take it for granted that Britain would lead the space race; as Michael Weldon remarks of *Spaceways*, it is 'strange to hear characters worry that Englishmen might not be the first to conquer space' (Weldon 1983: 648). British sf was soon disabused of such pretensions, and by the mid-1960s the British space-flight movie was rare indeed. Apart from in *Spaceflight IC-1* (1965) and *Doppelganger* (1969), the only Britons who would make it into space had been kidnapped by aliens, as in *They Came from Beyond Space* (1967), *The Terrornauts* (1967), *Zeta One* (1969) and *Toomorrow* (1970).

The key British sf film of the 1950s was *The Quatermass Experiment*, in which adventures in space led only to disastrous contamination. At a time when America had otherwise colonised sf, *Quatermass* established the direction British sf would take and by the end of the decade the films were predominantly sf-horror. Since the market for sf was dominated by American films, sf production in Britain was left to B-movie companies such as Merton Park and Anglo-Amalgamated. American stars were drafted to attract international distribution (Brian Donlevy in the *Quatermass* films, Gene Nelson in *Timeslip* (1956)) and the films often masqueraded as American productions (Pirie 1973: 133–4) – *Stranger from Venus* (1954) was a remake of *The Day the Earth Stood Still* (1951), with the same star, Patricia Neal; while *Fiend without a Face* and *First Man into Space* (1959) purported to be set in, respectively, Canada and the USA. These 'pseudo-American' films (Pirie 1973: 133) continued throughout the 1960s. The most eccentric was Hammer's *Moon Zero Two* (1969), the studio's last foray into the genre. Presented as 'the first space western', it offered such unlikely pleasures as a bar fight in low gravity and a 'Gunfight in Lunar Corral', complete with rayguns holstered like Colt .45s, which, as the American pressbook took care to point out, 'honors the western tradition of the solitary hero protecting the virtuous young lady against a gang of villains'.

After *Quatermass*, *X the Unknown* and *The Trollenberg Terror* the most common theme of British sf was alien invasion, or rather invasion by the one or two aliens the budget could afford (in fact mass invasion narratives are rare outside Japanese sf with odd exceptions like *The War of the Worlds* (1953)). The invasion narrative was perfect for exploitation purposes since it required no expensive set-building, and the films' themes, with the Second World War fresh in the memory and the Third seemingly just round the corner, tapped directly into contemporary fears. The important difference from the American films was that the British ones were rarely teen-pics (though *Konga* (1960) was rumoured to have the working title *I Was a Teenage Gorilla*). The films may have been directed at young people, but the casts were rarely teenage and very often led by imported middle-aged Americans. Peter Hutchings, in his chapter on the invasion films, notes the irony that Britain should have been the target of alien interest at a period when its influence was diminishing in the wake of Suez and the loss of Empire. To invade Washington as in, say, *Earth vs The Flying Saucers* (1956) made political sense, but to set up bridgeheads on isolated Scottish islands and in sleepy villages suggests that the aliens enjoyed a curiously nostalgic idea of the centres of earthly power. Typically, as in *Invasion*, *Village of the Damned* and *Night of the Big Heat*, aliens turn up in the most out-of-the-way places, and the action is often set in country pubs, cheap locations where a cast of British stereotypes just sit around, talk and react with various degrees of sang-froid to the disruption of their quiet lives by symbols of modernity and Otherness. Hutchings argues that while films like *Quatermass II* were 'paranoid' texts in the mode of the American *Invasion of the Body Snatchers* (1956), nervous at Britain's waning power and postwar decadence, the main source of fear in the invasion narratives was women, terrestrial as well as alien. Steve Chibnall explores the remarkable consistency of this terror of 'alien' women in films from 1950s pulp like *Devil Girl from Mars* and *The Strange World of Planet X* to big-budget exploitation of the 1980s like *Lifeforce* (1985). Whereas in US films of the 1950s, as Mark Jancovich has pointed out (Jancovich 1996: 52–4), women often represent an intuitive and emotional, in short human, counterbalance to male rationality, in British sf they inspire only eroticised horror. As working women they encroach upon the realm of the male scientist; while in *Devil Girl from Mars* and *Unearthly Stranger* they are literally alien invaders, who either kidnap men as studs to repopulate their planets, or reduce them to blubbering wrecks. As permissiveness dawned, films such as *Zeta One*, *The Body Stealers* (1969) and *The Sexplorer* (1975) made explicit the masochistic appeal of these women who both threatened men and were the product of male fantasy.

The alien women cycle consisted chiefly of pulp movies, but a more considered treatment of the invasion theme is to be found in the adaptations of John Wyndham's novels in the early sixties: *Village of the Damned*, *Children of the Damned* and *The Day of the Triffids* (1963). Andy Sawyer considers Wyndham's appeal to film-makers, who exploited his popularity outside the usual genre readership (his novels were even set as A-level texts). Being considered a 'mainstream' writer led to critics underestimating the bleakness of his central themes: that civilisation is precarious and that, as Britain discovered during the war, its defence might entail tactics as ruthless as those of the aliens who threaten its overthrow. The films, especially the classic *Village of the Damned*, are model low-budget sf movies which imagine middle-class England's response to 'cosy catastrophes' that challenge its conception of itself as stable, consensual and imbued with the spirit of the Blitz. The adaptation of *The Day of the Triffids*, however, emerges in Sawyer's account as a case-study of how the demands of the American market could compromise what Sawyer calls a 'quintessentially English story' and transform a subtle reflection on the fragility of British society into a lurid horror story.

Ian Conrich retrieves from obscurity a small group of films that were directly inspired by American successes. The colossal creature movies, *Behemoth the Sea Monster* (1959), *Konga* and *Gorgo* (1961) imitated *The Beast from 20,000 Fathoms* (1953) and were even, in the case of the first two, made by the same director, Eugène Lourié, to ensure close replication of the formula. But although the films crudely reworked their sources they also managed to articulate specifically British themes. Like *The Beast from 20,000 Fathoms* and indeed like *Gojira* [*Godzilla*] (1954), which preceded it, they were products of anxieties about atomic radiation and can be read as straightforward allegories of the primitive forces set loose by the Bomb. The Behemoth, for instance, is a massive radioactive dinosaur who tramples London to avenge Nature's misuse by science. But there are surprising subtleties in these films. The creatures are neither so easily vanquished as in their American equivalents nor so entirely unsympathetic. The Behemoth is killed but new reports immediately arrive of mutated beasts 'off the coast of California'. Gorgo and its mother are allowed to return to the Irish Sea unscathed, despite flattening every tourist spot in the capital, and the military are powerless to prevent them from marauding again. Like the remake of *King Kong* (1976) *Gorgo* is an attack on the commercial exploitation of Nature and, to the delight of children in the audience, it celebrates the virtues of mother love rather than greedy materialism. *Konga*, meanwhile, which is something of a camp classic because of its astonishingly bad special effects, might even be read as a bizarre racial fantasy in the manner of the original *King Kong* (1933), with Konga, a giant gorilla inflated from a chimpanzee, a symbol of white fears of the ever more visible black presence in Britain. Conrich, however, draws attention to perhaps the most important aspect of British sf in the 1950s and 1960s: the films rework motifs from the Second World War and in particular the Blitz. They look back to the war as a time of consensus, purpose and resistance, to London under siege, since when Britain has lost prestige and global influence. Britain's social landscape in the 1960s was as changed as surely as London after the visits of Gorgo and Konga.

In my chapter on *The Day the Earth Caught Fire* (1962) and John R. Cook's on the Daleks films the focus narrows to this imagery of the Second World War. *The Day the Earth Caught Fire*, made at the height of CND's influence, replays the discourses of the Blitz in its story of Britain burning up after nuclear tests have sent the Earth spinning towards the sun. It asks whether British pluck and resolve are sufficient in the face of the new realities of the nuclear age. Although the nation puts up a good show in the film and the Earth finally survives, the consensus of the war years is gone for good: science has run mad, the Establishment is complacent and sclerotic, and the alienated young riot and loot in orgiastic revolt. Cook sees the Dalek films too as replaying discourses and myths of the war. *Dr Who and the Daleks*, a more simplistic film than *The Day the Earth Caught Fire*, promotes a positively Churchillian enthusiasm for resistance against the Daleks. They represent not communism but a Nazi-like scientist authoritarianism offensive to the Doctor's 'English' eccentricity and individualism. The Doctor teaches the Thals, an alien race oppressed by the Daleks, to fight as the British did in the war. The film's anti-pacifism, provocative in a children's film, was an ideological education for backsliders in its youthful audience who might need reminding of the lesson of appeasement. Its sequel, *Daleks – Invasion Earth 2150 AD*, is an allegory of Britain occupied, and its references to a bombed-out London, weaselly collaborators and selfless heroism irresistibly recall the experience of the Blitz as well as anticipating its reprise in a future war.

Sf images became ubiquitous in the 1960s as symbols of the decade's commitment to modernism: sf seemed not so much futuristic speculation as a descriptive sociology of the present day. Its imagery was grafted onto films of all genres, notably the Bond spy thrillers, whose sf trappings usually stopped with the gizmos in Q's workshop but which increasingly came to resemble *Flash Gordon. Moonraker* (1979), made after *Star Wars* (1977), is the most obviously science fictional, though *You Only Live Twice* (1968), in which Blofeld has a private space programme, runs it a close second. Nineteen sixty-eight was the watershed year for sf cinema, when for the first time since the 1950s studios began to produce big-budget sf for a mainstream audience. In America *Planet of the Apes* was hugely successful, its satirical dystopianism setting a pessimistic tone that would last till the euphoric space opera of *Star Wars*. Britain produced *2001: A Space Odyssey*, which changed everything. Kubrick's masterpiece, the most interpreted and over-interpreted of all sf films, raised the stakes for the genre. Unprecedented in scale, cost, technical perfection and intellectual difficulty, it not only established the possibility of intelligent epic science fiction but also began the identification of the genre with expensive, special effects-driven spectacle; decisively confirmed by *Star Wars* and *Close Encounters of the Third Kind* (1977), this is taken for granted in action movies today. Although British films occasionally tried to compete with *2001*, budgetary restraints ensured that only a few, such as *Doppelganger* and *Moon Zero Two*, ventured beyond exploitation horror about monsters of science and prehistory (*Trog* (1970), *The Creeping Flesh* (1972), *Horror Express* (1972), *The Mutations* (1973) and, at a stretch, *Digby – The Biggest Dog in the World* (1973)). Throughout the 1970s, a period of decline for British cinema as a whole, sf production was more scattered even than in the 1960s. There was an interesting flirtation with psychedelic strangeness with *Zeta One*, an astonishingly peculiar sex film, *Zardoz* (1973) and *The Final Programme* (1973), an adaptation of one of Michael Moorcock's Jerry Cornelius novels (see figure 3). This last film, which Moorcock loathed, represented a small, wayward engagement with the New Wave of science fiction writing. Otherwise, apart from J.G. Ballard's screen treatment for Hammer's *When Dinosaurs Ruled the Earth* (1970), the key writers of the New Wave had little direct influence.

Even so, *Zardoz*, *A Clockwork Orange* and *The Man Who Fell to Earth*, each very different from the exploitation-horror that still accounted for most British sf, reflected the new 'art-movie' openness that entered all kinds of genre-film-making in the 1970s. James Chapman discusses *A Clockwork Orange*, Kubrick's version of Anthony Burgess's 1962 novel, as representative of these more ambitious, auteurist sf films of the period. Although the film is grounded firmly in a British milieu, Chapman notes that it is difficult to place it within the history of British sf cinema because it owes more to the dystopian tradition of mainstream novels like *Nineteen Eighty-Four* than to any specific film sub-genre or cycle. Like *The Man Who Fell to Earth*, *Fahrenheit 451* (1965), *The Damned* and *Zardoz*, it is best understood not as a genre film but within the *oeuvre* of a director whose reputation was made outside sf. The most productive tensions felt in the film are not with other contemporary British sf movies but between the warring authorial presences of Kubrick, the cynical pessimist, and Burgess, the Catholic moralist.

Figure 3 A flirtation with psychedelic strangeness: Jon Finch and phallic set-design in
        The Final Programme (1973).
Source: Courtesy of the British Cinema and Television Research Group archive

At the other end of the scale of ambition and achievement in the 1970s
were a handful of sf sexploitation films: *Zeta One*, *Percy* (1971), *Percy's Progress*
(1974), *The Sexplorer* (1975) and *Outer Touch* (1979). How far these are sf is
debatable; it's unlikely their original audiences regarded them as such. But, as
we've seen, British sf films tend to be hybrids and the sf content has often
been incidental to the major attraction for the audience – horror or, as in
these films, the very modest titillation permitted by British censors. Sexploitation was the staple of the British film industry throughout the 1970s till
the emergence of home video in 1982 (McGillivray 1992). The sf variants
took what advantage they could of the genre's pornographic possibilities. *The
Sexplorer* is the most intriguing, with its eroticised alien visitor incarnated as
one of those 'permissive' foreign girls who excited and alarmed the British
male imagination with the promise of voracious sex. By the end of the decade,
aside from the waning exploitation market, Britain's most notable contribution
to sf was its supply of world-class technicians to essentially American films
made at Pinewood and Shepperton. *Alien*, for example, which was written by
Americans but directed by an Englishman, Ridley Scott, was filmed for reasons
of economy at Shepperton, with special effects and model photography completed at Bray Studios, the former house of Hammer horror. It is meaningless

to extricate from the complex realities of international co-production the 'Britishness' of *Alien*, or of *Krull* (1983), *Outland*, *Slipstream* (1989), the *Superman* movies (1978, 1980, 1983) and *Saturn 3* (1980) (though it was written by Martin Amis); one simply notes the involvement of British personnel in a genre defined by American product. The 'nationality' of a film, however, is not in the end the one determining context for its significance and it would be misleading simply to conclude that British sf has been 'compromised' by its enforced dialogue with American sf. In fact, the most compromised sf films – low-budget exploitation – have often turned out to be the most consistently 'British' in their attitudes.

For instance, British exploitation fell with glee on *Alien*'s reinvigoration of sf-horror with sexual imagery, and what Peter Wright calls the 'post-*Alien* intrusion film' emerged as a remarkably coherent and psychoanalytically rich set of fantasies about women and motherhood. Although British sf could hardly compete with the extravagance of *Star Wars* – though it tried to, badly, with *Flash Gordon* (1980) and *Slipstream* – *Inseminoid* (1980) *Xtro* (1982), *Lifeforce* and *Split Second* (1991) found in *Alien* a useful and creative combination of alien invasion narrative, Gothic horror and outright misogyny. As Wright demonstrates, despite the gory novelties of their 'body horror' effects these films were in fact strikingly traditional British sf in their conservatism, thrilled disgust at female sexuality, and staunch but worried defence of the patriarchal order. Wright notes a change, however, with *Split Second*, in which generic hybridity gave way to incoherent pastiche, and suggests that this marked the exhaustion of the 'ideological project' of the intrusion films and their collapse into postmodern self-parody.

Linda Ruth Williams considers the most self-consciously postmodern British sf films: *Nineteen Eighty-Four*, made in the year in which it is set, and *Brazil* (1985), Terry Gilliam's ultra-bleak parody of Orwell's dystopia. In either case futuristic prophecy is subverted to reflect on Thatcherism: *Nineteen Eighty-Four* offers an alternative present which may or may not be an allegory of the real 1984, while *Brazil*, in true postmodern fashion, refuses to pin down its retro-future to any more precise time than 'somewhere in the 20th century'. Despite the films' stylistic differences – *Nineteen Eighty-Four*'s sepia realism, *Brazil*'s hyperkinetic cartoon pastiche – Williams finds similarities in their gender politics. In both films conventional female sexuality is a sign of utopian escape and, though *Brazil*'s deconstructive knowingness partly exempts it from unreflexive sexism, their utopian elements are equally grounded in male fantasy and desire.

Since the 1980s, British sf films have been more infrequent than ever. The revival of tensions with the Second Cold War inspired *When the Wind Blows* (1986), an animated feature about Britons being wiped out in a nuclear attack (a topic approached in documentary fashion by the BBC's *Threads* (1987)) and a comedy, *Whoops Apocalypse!*, which unevenly reworked *Dr Strangelove*. More energetic have been the occasional sf-horror exploitation films, such as *Hardware* (1990) and *Death Machine* (1993), which have a distinctive, American-influenced subcultural sensibility, and remind us once again that British popular culture often attempts to revitalise itself by stealing from the unrespectable depths of its American counterpart. *Hardware*, like *Death Machine* a co-production that manages to smother signs of its British origins, fuses the slasher film with cyberpunk. As Sue Short notes, its postmodern magpie aesthetic, salvaging scraps from *Mad Max* (1979), *The Terminator* (1984) and countless other sf films, echoes the opportunistic recycling whereby the film's heroine, herself an artist, reconstructs a killer droid from fragments and waste. This policy of cheeky opportunism, Short argues, is the solution to the current impasse of British sf film – return to exploitation film-making; make a virtue of subverting Britain's dominant realist and heritage cinema with punkish chutzpah and outrage; and, even at the cost of 'Americanisation', seek commerciality by judicious theft of the latest trends and clichés. This is certainly the formula of *Event Horizon* (1997), a US–GB co-production with a British director, which cannibalises *Solaris* (1972), *Hellraiser* (1987) and *The Shining* (1980) to powerful if sometimes incoherent effect. Although on a much higher budget than *Hardware* it is a similar aggressively populist assemblage of allusions, vicarious shocks and youth culture references. *Event Horizon* can hardly be said to articulate distinctive British themes – whatever they might be in the postmodern 1990s – but since it was designed to play to international audiences whose familiarity with sf derives exclusively from American films, it would be perverse to judge it by any such narrow standard of cultural authenticity.

British sf films have often failed, or lacked ambition, or suffered from inadequate budgets; frequently they are horror films rather than 'pure' sf; and never have they wholly emerged from the shadow of the American films which by turns they have imitated, subverted and worked variations on. Yet, as this book is intended to demonstrate, few countries, perhaps only America and Japan, have so rich a heritage of sf genre films, more diverse, more responsive to the cultural moment, and much stranger by far than their critics have ever allowed.

Bibliography

Baxter, John (1970) *Science Fiction in the Cinema*, London: Tantivy Press.

Biskind, Peter (1983) *Seeing is Believing: How Hollywood Taught Us to Stop Worrying and Love the Fifties*, London: Pluto.

Brosnan, John (1978) *Future Tense: The Cinema of Science Fiction*, London: Macdonald and Jane's.

Clute, John and Nicholls, Peter (eds) (1995) *The Encyclopedia of Science Fiction*, 2nd edn, New York: St Martin's Griffin.

Franklin, H. Bruce (1990) 'Visions of the future in science fiction films from 1970 to 1982', in Annette Kuhn (ed.) *Alien Zone: Cultural Theory and Contemporary Science Fiction Cinema*, London: Verso.

Hardy, Phil (ed.) (1995) *Aurum Film Encyclopedia: Science Fiction*, 2nd edn, London: Aurum.

Hunt, Leon (1998) *British Low Culture: From Safari Suits to Sexploitation*, London: Routledge.

Hunter, I.Q. (1999) 'From SF to sci-fi: Paul Verhoeven's *Starship Troopers*', in Jonathan Bignell (ed.) *Writing and Cinema*, London: Longman.

Hutchings, Peter (1993) *Hammer and Beyond: The British Horror Film*, Manchester: Manchester University Press.

Jancovich, Mark (1996) *Rational Fears: American Horror in the 1950s*, Manchester: Manchester University Press.

Landy, Marcia (1991) *British Genres: Cinema and Society 1930–1960*, Princeton: Princeton University Press.

Luciano, Patrick (1987) *Them or Us: Archetypal Interpretations of Fifties Alien Invasion Films*, Bloomington and Indianapolis: Indiana University Press.

McGillivray, David (1992) *Doing Rude Things: The History of the British Sex Film, 1957–1981*, London: Sun Tavern Fields.

Murphy, Robert (1992) *Sixties British Cinema*, London: British Film Institute.

Petley, Julian (1986) 'The lost continent', in Charles Barr (ed.) *All Our Yesterdays*, London: British Film Institute.

Pirie, David (1973) *A Heritage of Horror: The English Gothic Cinema 1946–1972*, London: Gordon Fraser.

Sobchack, Vivian (1991) *Screening Space: The American Science Fiction Film*, 2nd edn, New York: Ungar.

Sontag, Susan (1965) 'The imagination of disaster', *Commentary* October 1965: 42–8.

Warren, Bill (1982, 1986) *Keep Watching the Skies! American Science Fiction Movies of the Fifties*, 2 vols, Jefferson, NC: MacFarland.

Weldon, Michael (1983) *The Psychotronic Encyclopedia of Film*, London: Plexus.

1 *Things to Come* and science fiction in the 1930s

Jeffrey Richards

The Second World War broke out in 1940 when Poland attacked Germany, Italy invaded Yugoslavia and Central Europe was engulfed by war. Initially the other great European powers stayed out. Russia held to a non-aggression pact and Britain remained neutral. In 1943, however, France entered the conflict and thereafter the war was conducted mainly in the air and with increasing use of gas. Eventually war-weariness, rising social discontent with communist uprisings in – for instance – Glasgow and Hamburg, and the onset of pestilence across Europe forced the warring nations to agree to a suspension of hostilities in 1949. From then until 1956, a succession of savage epidemics swept across the globe, culminating in the so-called Wandering Sickness, which carried off half the world's population. By 1957 civilisation as we had known it lay in ruins. You will by now have guessed that I have not taken leave of my senses and garbled twentieth-century history in a sudden brainstorm. This *was* the future as forecast by H.G. Wells in 1933 in his book *The Shape of Things to Come*.

The Shape of Things to Come was nothing less than an imaginative history of the future, from 1929 to 2106. Unread today, like so much of Wells' polemical writing, it is in fact a bold, vigorous, prodigiously inventive and passionately committed treatise. It fits no recognised genre but is a veritable kaleidoscope of history, theory and pure imagination, part lecture, part manifesto, part satire, part drama, ranging widely over such diverse subjects as scientific research, architecture, fashion, climatology and sexual mores. The ideas Wells puts forward he had been advocating since before the turn of the century but in *The Shape of Things to Come* they achieved a grand synthesis. The classic elements of his utopian vision, as defined by Krishan Kumar (1991: 191–223), were a broadly socialist world state with extensive social and economic powers, ruled by a technological elite whose watchwords were efficiency, simplicity and system, science in the service of society, and an evolutionary dynamism rather than the static perfection of other utopias.

The Shape of Things to Come showed how this state of affairs might be brought about. The first step was the abolition of capitalism. The First World War, believed Wells, had been the product of competitive free enterprise capitalism and adversary nationalism. The Wall Street Crash and the Depression signalled the final crisis of capitalism. But before its definitive collapse, capitalism would inexorably drag the world into a second great conflict, whose outbreak Wells prophetically dated to 1940.

After the Second World War and the ensuing plague (a projection forwards of the influenza epidemic following the First World War), Wells foresaw social dislocation, political disintegration and technological regression, a soaring crime rate and the collapse of religion. In Wells's scenario, the Christian Church had ceased to function by 1965. Predatory warlords and their bands of armed followers roam at will. Cities decay – by 1958 New York is abandoned and in 1970 the ruins of London are consumed by fire and flood.

Then when society has been scourged and purified, the reconstruction begins. 'It is no good,' Wells says, 'asking people what they want. That is the error of democracy. You have first to think out what they ought to want if society is to be saved. Then you have to tell them what they want and see that they get it' (Wells n.d.: 202). So the intellectuals must define the problem and propound the solution – the socialist world state – and a surviving elite of technocrats, scientists and engineers must put it into effect. Thus in 1965 a conference of technocrats in Basra initiates that programme of action which leads to the world state. Private property and national sovereignty are abolished. A series of controls is set up to run transportation, research, education and supply. They are administered by a fellowship of like-minded men and women and co-ordinated by a central world council. A Thirty Year Plan is drawn up to effect the necessary transition from the old to the new world, and opposition is quelled by the Air Police with the aid of the new Peace Gas - Pacificin. An era Wells calls 'The Puritan Tyranny' follows in which the elite, characterised by rigid self-discipline, spartan austerity and total dedication to work effect the transformation. Finally in 2059 comes the declaration of Megeve dissolving the world council. There is no further need for rulership. War, want, inequality and ill health have been eliminated. The martyrdom of man is at an end and humankind is now free to transform the planet, extend life and fulfil its potential.

Soon after the book appeared, Alexander Korda, Britain's premier film producer, ever alert to a prestige project, commissioned Wells to turn it into a film script. Wells, who had long been fascinated by the potential of cinema for conveying the message of his books, leapt at the idea (see figure 4). He had no illusions about the medium, however, and when in 1935 he published his fourth draft script for the film under the title *Things to Come*, he made clear his aim in a preface:

> *The Shape of Things to Come* is essentially an imaginative discussion of social and political forces and possibilities, and a film is no place for argument. The conclusions of that book therefore are taken for granted in this film and a new story has been invented to display them.
>
> (Wells 1935: 9)

Figure 4 Things to Come (1936): H. G. Wells (left) on set with Margaretta Scott and
        Raymond Massey.
Source: Courtesy of the British Cinema and Television Research Group archive

The story Wells devised centres on the careers of two men: John Cabal, leader
of the technocrats who set up the world state, and his grandson Oswald
Cabal, who has to deal with a reactionary backlash.

Not surprisingly, given that the film industry was an integral part of the
capitalist system, the attack on capitalism that is central to *The Shape of Things to
Come* is omitted and the film concentrates more on attacking the horrors of
war, which in the book Wells made clear was a product of that system. But
Wells's screenplay was further streamlined and pruned by Korda and his script
editor Lajos Biró to eliminate a diatribe against religion and a debate about
the role of woman as love object or workmate. But otherwise the scenario
was faithfully translated to the screen by Korda's top flight production team.[1]
He imported the ace Hollywood designer William Cameron Menzies to direct
and commissioned Arthur Bliss to provide the score. Bliss came up with the
first great British film score. Wells believed that the musical score was 'an integral
part of the design' of the film and consequently insisted on Bliss being involved
at every stage of the production (Bliss 1989: 104). Much of the music was
written and some of it pre-recorded before the filming got underway. Wells
thought the music 'admirable' (1935: 13).

The art director was Alexander Korda's brother Vincent, who was inspired
in creating the city of the future by the latest in modernist design – Oliver

Hill's avant garde furniture, Le Corbusier's garden city designs and Norman Bel Geddes's futurist airliners. The Hungarian futurist artist Laszlo Moholy-Nagy worked on the rebuilding of Everytown sequence (see Frayling 1995; Albrecht 1986: 160–4).

The resulting film, which took a year to make and cost some £300,000, twice the average budget of a Korda epic, was released in February 1936. For all the obvious artificiality of some of the special effects, the cut-glass accents and impeccable upper-class English manner of the juveniles and the hamminess of some of the acting, it remains a classic of science fiction cinema, a visionary work of compelling power, awesome imagination and uplifting optimism. The critics were dazzled. Sydney Carroll called it 'a leviathan among films...a stupendous spectacle' (*The Sunday Times*, 23 February 1936) and Alistair Cooke, the film critic of the BBC, pronounced it 'as visually exciting a film as ever came out of a British or any other studio' (Cooke 1971: 126). Graham Greene, then film critic of *The Spectator*, who found the film's future-vision 'vague, optimistic, childlike', thought the first third 'magnificent,' particularly the surprise air raid, staged in 'horribly convincing detail' (Greene 1972: 54–5). But the public did not respond as enthusiastically. Michael Korda called the film 'an instant box office failure' and reported that the film did particularly poorly in America where one distributor was reported as saying 'Nobody is going to believe that the world is going to be saved by a bunch of people with British accents.' Michael Korda blamed the terrifying bombing scenes and the 'cold and inhuman' vision of the future (Korda 1980: 120–4). But I suspect that audiences were put off more by the absence of a conventional narrative structure and the doubling up of roles among the actors than by the central ideas, hatred of war and support for the concept of long-term planning, which were in the mainstream of thirties thinking.

The first theme is pacifism and hatred of war. The horrors of the First World War had led to the general expression of the belief that it must never happen again. The League of Nations was set up in 1920 with the aim of settling all international disputes by negotiation and working towards global disarmament. In 1928 fifteen powers signed the Kellogg-Briand Pact, which renounced war as an instrument of national policy. Pacifism was in the air, as much in Britain as elsewhere. In 1933 the Oxford Union passed the motion that 'This house will in no circumstance fight for its King and Country' and an antiwar candidate won the East Fulham by-election. Perhaps the peak of antiwar sentiment was reached by 1935 when a Peace Ballot was held and ten million people voted for all-round reduction in international armaments. In the same year Stanley Baldwin and the National Government won the general election on a programme which included a pledge to initiate no policy of 'great armaments'.

Prophetically choosing 1940 as its starting date and setting the action in Everytown, though it is obviously London and in particular Piccadilly Circus, the film opens with the bravura intercutting of carol singers, turkeys for sale and Christmas shoppers with looming headlines proclaiming the imminence of war. At the house of John Cabal (Raymond Massey), the prospects of war are debated and Cabal insists 'if we don't end war, war will end us'. The children play games with their toy armaments, until over the wireless it is announced that the fleet has been bombed without warning, the country is at war and enemy planes are heading for Everytown. There follows a superbly staged air raid, a graphic and chilling illustration of Prime Minister Stanley Baldwin's dictum: 'The bomber will always get through.' Motorcyclists surge across the screen, the roar of planes is heard overhead and although we never see the planes, their bombs bring destruction to the busy streets as searchlights vainly probe the sky. The panic and devastation ends with a slow and eloquent track in to the body of a child buried in the rubble. The child, symbol of hope for the future, is to be a recurrent image in the film.

The war drags on until 1966 and in its wake comes plague – the Wandering Sickness – and the collapse of civilisation. Victims of the plague are shot to prevent them spreading infection and the pestilence subsides. Amid the ruins of Everytown, a quasi-medieval village springs up, with buses turned into houses, cars pulled by horses and the community led by a warlord, the Boss (Ralph Richardson), who still leads armed raids on neighbouring settlements.

The Boss is challenged by the arrival of the white-haired, black-clad figure of John Cabal, who declares that he represents an organisation called 'Wings Over the World' which stand for 'Law and Sanity' and plans to restore civilisation from its advanced scientific base on the Persian Gulf. Although the Boss arrests Cabal, a great fleet of airships appears over Everytown, drops 'Peace Gas' bombs, knocking out the population and taking control. Everyone revives in time except for the Boss, who is found to have died.

Cabal declares that the work of rebuilding must go ahead with the creation of a new planned, technological society. So the second theme of the film – scientific planning – emerges. 'Planning' was the great panacea of the 1930s. It was based on faith in the efficacy of reason and science to tackle and overcome whatever problems faced the nation. Planning had worked during the First World War and the political and economic crises which broke out at the end of the 1920s prompted a return to it as the solution to them. Prominent thinkers both on the left and the right advocated planning, pointing with some justice to the comprehensive and successful economic and social policies embodied in Franklin D. Roosevelt's 'New Deal' in the United States and in Soviet Russia's 'Five Year Plan'. In Britain John Maynard Keynes's theories of a properly managed economy gained wide currency and the idea of planning lay behind many of the policies of the National Government: the abandonment of Free Trade and the introduction of protective tariffs, the rationalisation of depressed industries, the revival of slum clearance programmes, the passing of the Town and Country Planning Act and a massive reorganisation of local government.

The lengthy quasi-documentary sequence detailing the building of the new world is a celebration of technology. At the end of it, we see Everytown in 2036, a great new underground city of shining towers, white, clean, clinical, with artificial light and air, huge television screens and scientifically prolonged life. A child, being given a history lesson by her grandfather, declares happily: 'They keep on inventing things and making life lovelier and lovelier.' The latest invention is the space gun which will launch a projectile to begin the exploration of the universe. Oswald Cabal (Raymond Massey), John's grandson, and Raymond Passworthy (Edward Chapman) discuss the expedition, on which Passworthy's son and Cabal's daughter will be the crew. Passworthy is fearful and his fears are shared by the people. The symbol of reaction is Theotocopoulos (Cedric Hardwicke), sculptor, artist and individualist. He hates the cold, planned, technological perfection in which they live ('Arise, wake, stop this progress before it is too late'). He rouses the populace to destroy the space gun, but before they can reach it, it is launched. Passworthy asks if there is ever to be any rest and Oswald pronounces the Wellsian creed of evolutionary dynamism:

> Rest enough for the individual man. Too much too soon, and we call it death. But for Man, no rest and no ending. He must go on – conquest beyond conquest. First this little planet with its winds and ways, and then all the laws of mind and matter that restrain him. Then the planets about him, and at last, out across immensity to the stars. And when he has conquered all the deeps of space and all the mysteries of time, still he will be beginning. ('See figure 5.)

Viewed today, the second half of the film is replete with irony. For it is Theotocopoulos rather than Oswald with whom many people would now identify. Scientists, since they invented infallible means of destroying the world, have become bogeymen rather than saviours of humanity. The prospect of a clean, ordered, dehumanised future has come to be viewed with horror and the ecological movement, 'the small is beautiful' philosophy and the 'back to the land' groups have arisen to counter the effects of technological expansion.

There is also a *frisson* provided by the appearance of a blackshirted superman called Cabal, who talks about 'a new order' and declares, 'We don't approve of independent sovereign states; we intend to stop them.' Even more ironic that the master of Everytown should be called Oswald Cabal. There was at large in Britain in the 1930s another Oswald – Oswald Mosley, a blackshirted superman seeking a new order and preaching 'a union of modern Caesarism and modern science' for the transformation of society. He wished to plan Britain's way out of the depression. He also moved effortlessly from socialism to fascism.

But then fascism, Wells thought, 'was not altogether a bad thing. It was a bad good thing.' It was bad in its romantic nationalism and support for monarchy and church, bad in the violence of its methods, but good in its insistence on discipline and public service for its members and in its creation

Figure 5 'But for man, no rest and no ending': Oswald Cabal (Raymond Massey)
(right) pronounces the Wellsian creed of evolutionary dynamism to
passworthy (Edward Chapman) at the end of *Things to Come* (1936).
Source: Courtesy of the British Cinema and Television Research Group archive

of 'an organization with a purpose and a sort of doctrine of its own' (Wells
n.d.: 106). In the film *Things to Come* the superstitious and nationalistic warlord
the Boss represents the bad side of fascism – reactionary totalitarian government, militarism and obscurantism. Although explicitly intended by Wells not
to be 'a caricature of a Fascist or Nazi leader' (Stover 1987: 137) but a more
universal symbol, the role was performed – superbly – by Ralph Richardson
as a precise caricature of Mussolini (see O'Connor 1982: 82). The austere and
inspired Oswald Cabal, unforgettably incarnated by Raymond Massey, stands
for the good side of fascism with the blackshirted airmen ('The brotherhood
(or cabal) of efficiency, the freemasonry of science, the last trustee of civiliza-
tion'). The potential of the airmen for fascism is evidenced in reality by the
promotion of flying and the heroisation of air aces by the Nazi regime in
Germany and in fiction by Rex Warner in his powerful novel, *The Aerodrome*
(1941).[2] When fascism degenerated into autocracy, Wells lost sympathy with
it. Despite this, his view remains profoundly totalitarian.

It was George Orwell, that beacon light of sanity and clear-headedness,
who exposed the basic flaw in the idealistic Wellsian view as expounded in
book after book over forty years. Writing in 1941, Orwell pointed out that:

> Unfortunately the equation of science with common sense does not
> really hold good. Modern Germany is far more scientific than England

and far more barbarous. Much of what Wells has imagined and worked for is physically there in Nazi Germany. The order, the planning, the state encouragement of science, the steel, the concrete, the aeroplanes are all there but in the service of ideas appropriate to the Stone Age. Science is fighting on the side of superstition.

(Orwell 1971: 170)

When one reads in Wells of the suppression of dissidents and the greatest good of the greatest number as defined by a technocratic oligarchy, it is evident that it is but one short step to Orwell's Big Brother and the thought police.

Several critics compared *Things to Come* to Fritz Lang's *Metropolis* (1926): Sydney Carroll in *The Sunday Times* (23 February 1936) called it 'an elaborated *Metropolis*'. This comparison would have infuriated Wells, who had described *Metropolis* as 'the most foolish film. I cannot believe it would be possible to make a more foolish one' (Eisner 1976: 84). He wrote in the preface to his published treatment of *Things to Come* that he wanted his film to be the opposite of *Metropolis*. He explicitly did not want 'all the balderdash one finds in…*Metropolis*' – robots, a skyscraper city, the elimination of individuality, the dominance of servitude and uniformity (Wells 1935: 13). Nevertheless there are striking similarities between the two films. The opening sequence of *Metropolis*, a montage of machinery in operation, is paralleled in the sequence of the building of the new Everytown in *Things to Come*; a rioting mob streaming along elevated walkways figures in both films. But there are broader parallels too. Oswald Cabal resembles Joh Fredersen, the austere, remote, autocratic master of Metropolis. The workers of Metropolis are roused by the robot Maria ('Destroy the machines') just as the people of Everytown are roused by Theotocopoulos ('Destroy the Gun'). In *Metropolis* Rotwang the 'mad' inventor and magician in his little medieval house dwarfed by skyscrapers is out of step with the times and pursuing his own mad schemes. In *Things to Come* the 'mad' sculptor Theotocopoulos (first seen garbed like Rotwang in a long dark medieval gown) is another who is out of step with the times and opposed to progress.

It is clear why Wells would have hated *Metropolis*. For one thing, Lang envisaged the city of the future as the ultimate capitalist society with the workers enslaved and oppressed by a luxury-loving ruling class and dehumanised by their machines. But far from celebrating revolution against this state of affairs, Lang shows that when the workers rise up and destroy the machines, they flood their own homes and endanger their children. The final message is one of reconciliation between management and labour.

A second source of annoyance for Wells would have been the strongly religious imagery of *Metropolis*. Freder Fredersen is explicitly the Saviour of Metropolis, a Christ figure who with the aid of the Virgin Maria, reconciles the people and their divine ruler Joh (Jehovah) Fredersen. Freder has religious visions throughout the film: exploding machinery turning into the gaping idol Moloch devouring chained slaves; the statues of the seven deadly sins leaving their places in the cathedral to wander through the city. Maria preaches to the workers in catacombs, surrounded by candles and crosses, and tells the story of the tower of Babel. The finale takes place in and around the cathedral with Rotwang hurled to his death by Freder as he menaces Maria and the reconciliation taking place on the cathedral steps.

Ironically, it seems likely that Lang and his scriptwriter Thea von Harbou derived some of their ideas from two earlier novels by Wells, *The Time Machine* (1895) and *The Sleeper Awakes* (revised edition, 1910). From *The Time Machine* come the ideas of the beautiful, idle, pleasure-loving Eloi and the brutalised subterranean Morlocks, ideas given precise visual expression in *Metropolis*. From *The Sleeper Awakes* come the ideas of a future society dominated by a proto-fascist superman Ostrog, who rules the workers in a slave state and arranges for the idle elite to disport themselves in pleasure cities, and of the revolt of the workers after the Sleeper, alerted to what is happening by a young woman, goes among them in disguise. All these elements are present in *Metropolis*.

If Lang was deriving ideas from Wells, then the makers of *Things to Come* were not unaware of the visuals of *Metropolis* which had made a tremendous impression on critics. If in Wellsian terms the religious imagery, capitalist society and consensual message of *Metropolis* were retrograde, Lang was ahead of Wells in his concept of a spaceship. In his science fiction epic, *Woman in the Moon* (1929), Lang used leading German rocket scientists Oberth and Ley to design his spaceship and the result was much more authentic than Wells's Space Gun, an idea borrowed from Jules Verne's *From the Earth to the Moon* (1865) and dismissed by scientists as impractical.

The links between *Things to Come* and *Metropolis* emphasise the extraordinary symbiosis between British and German science fiction films in the interwar period. The visual imagery of *Metropolis* was one lasting influence. The other influence was thematic: the recurrence of the ideas of the celebration of technology, the heroic role of the engineer and the airman and the sinister machinations of international financiers. All these elements feature classically in Bernhard Kellermann's best-selling novel *Der Tunnel*. First published in 1913, it had sold 358,000 copies by 1940. It charted the construction of a transatlantic tunnel, linking Europe and America. Significantly it was published the year after the *Titanic* disaster and was the product of a time when many plans for tunnels were coming forward (Straits of Gibraltar; Siberia–Alaska etc.) as a way of avoiding maritime disasters (Segeberg 1987: 173).

The visual and thematic influence of *Metropolis* can be seen throughout Maurice Elvey's *High Treason* (1929). Based on a preachy pacifist play by independent M.P. Noël Pemberton-Billing, it prefigured *Things to Come* with its setting of a futurist London and the prediction of war breaking out in 1940 with a surprise aerial attack. It coincidentally featured an uncredited but unmistakable Raymond Massey as a member of the Peace League. The futuristic setting and the key role of women in organising opposition to war did not feature in the original play but were added for the film version, almost certainly under the influence of *Metropolis* (Aldgate 1997: 261).

The visual inspiration of *High Treason* was quite clearly *Metropolis*. The intricate model shots of the skyscrapered city, with planes darting between buildings and transportation provided by monorails, submarines and helicopters, immediately recall Lang's masterpiece, as do scenes of workers shuffling, heads bowed, into tunnels, and the sequence in which Evelyn Seymour (Benita Hume), like the robot Maria in *Metropolis*, incites the workers to revolt.

High Treason postulates a future in which tension exists between the United Atlantic States and the United States of Europe. This tension is being exacerbated by the machinations of the President of the International Armaments Corporation, a fat, monocled, cigar-chewing plutocrat, a key figure in interwar demonology. In New York, the Atlantic Council calls for military preparedness and there is a vision of an unprovoked aerial attack on New York.

The Paris–London express is blown up in the Channel Tunnel by agents of the International Armaments Corporation; the United Atlantic States are blamed; and the President of Europe orders immediate mobilisation. Dr Seymour, head of the World Peace League, which has twenty million members, and his daughter Evelyn work desperately to avert war. Evelyn leads the women munitions workers, all singing the peace anthem, to immobilise the planes of the European airforce. When the European president insists on proceeding with the war, Dr Seymour shoots him dead and broadcasts an announcement that Europe will submit its differences with the Atlantic States to arbitration. The Atlantic Council accepts the offer of arbitration and war is averted. But Seymour is tried for murder and executed. He goes willingly to his death because he has taken a life but he dies a martyr to the cause of peace.

The Times (9 August 1929) was impressed, praising the 'admirable acting' and Maurice Elvey's mastery of the technique of sound film. Indeed, the reviewer thought the film was more ambitious than Hitchcock's *Blackmail* for 'Mr. Elvey has endeavoured to visualize the London of 1940':

> And a strange London it is, with a double-decker bridge at Charing Cross, with television in daily use, with the newspapers entirely superseded by the broadcasting service, with airships flying overhead, with helicopters rising vertically from the roofs of city buildings, and with the blowing up of the Channel Tunnel. The 1940 age is evidently to be a purely mechanical one. Even in the night clubs the dancers are little more than automatic figures, and the jazz music is provided by mechanical means.

The Bioscope (14 August 1929) actually thought *High Treason* better than *Metropolis*. But it is in retrospect crude and naive pacifist propaganda, wholly lacking the power and drive of *Metropolis* or *Things to Come*.

Kellermann's novel *The Tunnel* was filmed in Germany in 1933, directed by Kurt Bernhardt. The leading figure is the dedicated engineer Alan MacAllan (Paul Hartmann) who spends nearly twenty years building the Transatlantic Tunnel. He is continually hampered by the sinister, effete and slightly unbalanced financier, Mr Woolf of Wall Street (Gustaf Gründgens), who buys up shipping company shares and employs agents to sabotage the tunnel. In the book, which contains a nasty strain of anti-semitism, Woolf is explicitly a Hungarian Jew, born Samuel Wolffsohn. He is described as 'a corpulent gentleman of an oriental cast of feature – sullen lips, a strong, crooked nose, short, dark, crisp hair and a short dark beard' (Kellerman 1915: 97). He is motivated totally by greed. This is played down in the film, though the suave cosmopolitan image Mr Woolf is given was one that Nazi propaganda often associated with international Jewish financiers.

MacAllan, on the other hand, emerges as a proto-*Führer* figure. When the workers are incited to strike by Woolf's paid agitator, MacAllan addresses them in a Hitlerian speech ('I am a worker like you…all labour is struggle…all I ask of you is – faith') wins them over and they march off singing. He later denounces Woolf, who eventually kills himself to avoid arrest, with similar Hitlerian rhetoric. After his wife has been killed in an accident, MacAllan is encouraged by his friend Hobby to carry on ('Work – there is nothing else for you') and he completes the project, the dedicated, celibate, single-minded leader whose success with the tunnel prefigures Hitler's construction of the Autobahn system.

A French-language version of *The Tunnel* starring Jean Gabin was made simultaneously with the German version. But two years later it was completely remade in Britain by Gaumont-British. Costing £200,000, it was the most expensive Gaumont-British production to date. It was directed by Maurice Elvey and featured guest appearances by George Arliss and Walter Huston as the British Prime Minister and the American President. While it shared the *Things to Come* commitment to technology and peace, it also suffered the same fate at the box office, a failure which hastened the end of Gaumont-British as an active producer.

While the central plot strand, the triumph of the tunnel builders over natural disasters, human failings and financial chicanery, remains constant, there are substantial differences between the German and British versions. Whereas the German *Tunnel* is set in the present, the British *Tunnel* is set in the future, unspecified but from internal evidence the 1950s when there are televisions, videophones, futuristic cars and planes. There is no sabotage in the tunnel and the villain is not the American (and implicitly Jewish) financier Woolf but a French armaments tycoon Grellier, who manipulates the stock exchange in order to gain control of the tunnel company. The hero, rechristened Richard MacAllan, who is both engineer and airman, is no *Führer*, but the tough, go-getting, American professional familiar from Hollywood films and associated with Richard Dix, who played the role in this version. Far more time is devoted in the British version to the romantic, family and marital complications of the characters than in the German version. In the latter MacAllan's wife Mary sits patiently at home waiting until, hastening to the scene of the latest tunnel disaster, she is run over by a train. In the book, MacAllan's wife and daughter were killed by an enraged mob of relatives of workers killed in the tunnel. MacAllan eventually marries tycoon's daughter Ethel Lloyd. In the German film version he remains single. In the British film version, MacAllan's obsession with the tunnel leads to his estrangement from his wife Ruth, who goes blind after contracting tunnel sickness; MacAllan and his best friend Robbie fall out over his treatment of Ruth; tycoon's daughter Varlia Lloyd falls for and pursues MacAllan in vain; finally his son Geoffrey joins the tunnel workers and is killed in an accident. *The Times* (12 November 1935) rightly complained that all this 'takes up too much time when one might otherwise be enjoying the curious machinery or the simple excitements which admirers of Jules Verne will expect, and will quite often find, in this film'. But the effect of these additions to the plot was to soften and humanise the characters by comparison with their German counterparts.

The other major difference from the German version is the strong pro-peace message. In 1929 *High Treason* had postulated for 1940 a United States of Europe opposed to a United States of the Americas, perhaps a long-range reflection of the postwar isolationism of the United States. But by 1935 *The Tunnel* was proposing an alliance of Britain and the United States against the threat from unspecified 'Eastern powers', probably to be understood as communist Russia. This perhaps reflects a situation where the rise of Hitler had made a united Europe less likely and an Anglo-American alliance was deemed sensible in the face of mounting European uncertainty.

The Gaumont-British screen adaptation of *The Tunnel* was undertaken by the German writer Kurt Siodmak and he provides a major link between British and German science fiction. Siodmak also wrote a novel directly inspired by *The Tunnel*, *FPI Antwortet Nicht* (*FPI Does Not Answer*). The similarity of the two stories (technological triumph; visionary engineer; sabotage and workers' unrest) was emphasised by the casting of the same actor, Paul Hartmann, as the engineer in the German film versions of *The Tunnel* and *FPI*. The film version of *FPI* was produced in Germany in 1932 by Ufa and directed by Karl Hartl. It was made in three simultaneous versions with different casts: a German-language version starring Hans Albers, an English-language version starring Conrad Veidt and a French-language version starring Charles Boyer.

The engineer Droste designs and builds a floating platform which is moored in mid-Atlantic to allow transatlantic planes to refuel. When the agents of a shipping line seek to sabotage the platform, dashing round-the-world aviator Elissen flies to the platform and helps to save it. The film celebrates both the engineer and the airman, shows the building and operation of the platform but, as in Siodmak's version of *The Tunnel*, spends too much time on the romantic triangle of engineer, aviator and shipbuilder's sister. Despite an attractive Allan Gray score, excellent photography and special effects and stylish star performances, the film emerges in all its versions as slow-moving and portentous. It is, however, historically fascinating as evidence of the then current interest in floating aerodromes to facilitate transatlantic flights. Lufthansa had three of them moored in the Atlantic and some scenes for the film were shot aboard a prototype in the Baltic.

Ironically *The Tunnel* and *FPI* celebrated means of crossing the Atlantic which were almost instantly obsolete. In 1927 Charles Lindbergh flew the Atlantic non-stop and in 1939 regular non-stop transatlantic flights were initiated jointly by Pan-American and Imperial Airways. To his credit, Kurt Siodmak spotted this and in 1937 co-scripted the thriller *Non-Stop New York*, set aboard an airliner on a non-stop transatlantic flight, anticipating reality by two years. It was made by Gaumont-British which less than five years before had released both *The Tunnel* and *FPI*.

The Anglo-German technological epics shared with Wells the celebration of the engineer, technology and progress. But with their international capitalist conspiracies and heroic leaders, they also looked forward to the ideology of the Nazi era. In science fiction terms, the 1930s were undoubtedly the Wellsian decade. Hollywood produced the definitive versions of *The Island of Dr Moreau* (filmed as *The Island of Lost Souls* in 1932 but banned in Britain till 1958) and *The Invisible Man* (1932). Britain produced *Things to Come* and *The Man Who Could Work Miracles* (1936). The latter was a characteristically Wellsian social comedy in which the gods give miraculous powers to a meek draper's assistant but he overreaches himself, causes cosmic disaster and wishes the powers away. It proves the truth of the dictum that 'absolute power corrupts absolutely'. But, like *Things to Come*, it was not a box office success.

The description 'Wellsian' was applied by the critics to a delightful little film, *Once in a New Moon* (1934), directed by Anthony Kimmins at Sound City (*Picturegoer* 28 May 1935; *Kine Weekly* 20 December 1934). Based on a 1929 novel by Owen Rutter, this film is a political allegory in favour of 'good old British liberal democracy'. Although Wells had indeed written *In the Days of the Comet* (1906) about the effects of the approach of a comet on the inhabitants of the Potteries, this story resembles rather more Jules Verne's *Hector Servadac* (1877), in which a chunk of the Earth is swept up by a comet and carried off into space. In this case, it is the piece of the Earth containing the Essex village of Shrimpton-on-Sea. When the full extent of the catastrophe is revealed, the emergency committee set up under lord of the manor, Viscount Bravington, turns itself into the cabinet of Shrimpton-in-Space and names Bravington president. But social tensions arise. Sid Parrot the butcher takes the lead in denouncing the ruling clique (squire, stockbroker, colonel) for hoarding food, fuel and wine, while everyone else is on short rations ('What people want is equal rights'). Bravington's son, Hon. Bryan Grant, takes the side of the people ('They only want fair play') but Lord and Lady Bravington reject his views ('You give these people an inch and they take an ell'). Lady Bravington describes the proposal for equal shares for all as 'rank socialism'. Socialist agitator Edward Teale now proposes storming the manor house, seizing the food and fuel and overthrowing capitalism and aristocracy ('This is the age of the worker'). But the villagers reject violence and seek a general election and a democratic constitution rather than rule by a dictator. They nominate postmaster Harold Drake as their candidate for president and he wins a decisive victory in the polls against Lord Bravington. But Lady

Bravington refuses to hand over the food and fuel and aided by armed servants and gamekeepers, repulses a raid on the manor house. War is declared between the two sides. But at this point the comet hits the Earth again and Shrimpton lands in the North Sea as an island. War is averted, Drake and Bravington reconciled and the villagers gratefully evacuate the island to settle on the mainland.

The film rejects both the conservative snobbish/autocratic option of Lady Bravington and the sour revolutionary socialism of Edward Teale who wants to burn down the manor house and shows himself a cad by forcing his attention on Harold Drake's daughter Stella. Instead it settles for democracy and the election of decent, bookish, mild-mannered Harold Drake as president, with consensus ensured by the union of the Bravington's democratic son Bryan and Drake's daughter Stella. Although the film generally follows the narrative line of the book, it is worth noting that the character of Teale does not figure in the book and has clearly been added by the film-makers in the interests of balance to counterpoint Lady Bravington who is a diehard conservative and a convinced supporter of dictatorship.

Despite the dominance of a Wellsian vision in 1930s science fiction cinema, the most popular future vision of the decade was not Wellsian at all. It was propounded in a book published in the same year as *The Shape of Things to Come* by the British author James Hilton. Wells noted disparagingly of the 1930s that 'There was an abundant production and consumption of reassuring and deliberately "cheerful" books, a movement towards religious mysticism and otherworldliness' (Wells n.d.: 92). He might have been writing of James Hilton's *Lost Horizon*. On the face of it, no one could have been more different from Wells than James Hilton. A self-confessed sentimentalist, mystic and romantic, the celebrant in *Goodbye, Mr Chips* of the virtues of the public school and of heroic individualism, he declared, 'I dislike regimentation of any kind', and he wrote with regret of the vanishing preeminence of the British Empire, with its traditions of liberalism and parliamentary democracy, freedom of speech, thought and belief (Hilton 1938: 52–61).

Lost Horizon was Hilton's fifth novel, winner of the Hawthornden Prize and a bestseller on both sides of the Atlantic. Part mystery, part adventure, part romance, it was four-square in the Rider Haggard tradition of lost races and eternal women. The hero is no Wellsian technocrat but a classic imperial mystic, the fictional counterpart of Sir Francis Younghusband, soldier, diplomat, explorer and sage. He is Hugh Conway, nicknamed 'Glory' Conway, His Britannic Majesty's Consul in Baskul. Tall, charming and good looking, his background is unimpeachable – public school and Oxford, a rowing blue at college and a DSO in the war, a spell as a don teaching oriental languages. The book tells of his kidnapping, along with three others, and their transportation to the lamasery of Shangri-la in the Tibetan Valley of the Blue Moon. There Conway learns he has been chosen as successor to the 200-year-old High Lama. Hilton acknowledges the fairy-tale nature of his story by naming the High Lama Father Perrault after the celebrated French fairy story writer and setting Shangri-la in the Valley of the Blue Moon ('once in a blue moon').

The book's central core is a discussion of the philosophy of Shangri-la, a simple blend of Christianity and Buddhism. The Lamas, drawn from all nationalities, find their lives extended by the miraculous climate of the valley. Each pursues an individual programme of research into a self-chosen topic and above all they gain time – to think, to meditate, to study and to grow. They will preserve the best of civilisation and when the World War comes, as it must, Shangri-la will be a haven of learning and wisdom, as the High Lama explains:

> Here we will stay with our books and our music and our meditations, conserving the frail elegances of a dying age, and seeking such wisdom as men will need when their passions are spent....Then, my son, when the strong have devoured each other, the Christian ethic may at last be fulfilled and the meek shall inherit the earth.
>
> (Hilton 1953: 128)

This speech provides a key moment in the American film version of Hilton's novel, directed in Hollywood in 1937 by Frank Capra. Capra expanded Hilton's philosophy to embrace a simplified populist 'good neighbourliness', stressed the element of escape from the rat race of modern life and summed it up in the simple command 'Be Kind'. But he provided the perfect interpreters for Conway (renamed Robert for the film) and the High Lama in Ronald Colman and Sam Jaffe, a stunning Art-Deco Shangri-la and a compelling final sequence in which we see Conway, a speck on a snowy vastness, struggling back towards Shangri-la where he has realised his true destiny lies. The film's success led to Hilton's departure for Hollywood where he became one of the highest-paid scriptwriters, his genteel brand of essentially middle-class escapism fitting the mood of the films of that era perfectly. Eloquent testimony to this is to be found in the fact that all over Britain suburban bungalows and semis began sporting 'Shangri-la' name plates, the latest addition to the world of 'Chez Nous', 'Mon Repos' and 'Dunroamin'. The Capra film was more popular than the Korda, just as the Hilton book outsold the Wells. For in the end it was easier to relax into a truly escapist world than to build a new one.

The basic rules of Shangri-la are moderation in everything and good manners to all. The philosophy anticipates that of Mr Chips – 'A sense of humour and a sense of proportion' as the recipe for life. Indeed Chang, the Lama who acts as Conway's guide, notes that their philosophy is somewhat akin to that of the public school and Conway compares Shangri-la only half-jokingly to an Oxford college. This is the key to understanding Hilton's paradise. It is a sort of super-public school, presided over by a sacerdotal Chips and devoted to academic study. In its own way it is as elitist as Wells's, though Hilton's elite are donnish Lamas rather than thrusting technocrats.

Indeed curiously the two utopias have much in common. Both arose from disillusionment with society as it was: for Hilton it was changing too fast and for the worse, and for Wells not fast enough. Both systems explicitly reject democracy and can be traced back directly to Plato's Guardians, the philosopher-rulers of the ideal Republic. Both authors detest war and foresee the inevitability of a great conflict which would be followed by a new dark age. Both authors reject the selfish materialism of modern capitalist society. Both authors foresee a prolongation of life and the elimination of passion.

Both authors also detected the source of opposition and personified it. Mallinson, Conway's Vice-Consul and fellow prisoner (transformed in the film into his brother), persuades him to leave the valley and return to civilisation, rejects the serene passionless existence of the Lamas, demanding 'a short life and a gay one'. Theotocopoulos in *Things to Come* uses almost the same words to call for a return to the days when life was 'short, hot and merry'. Both are seen as reactionaries, throwbacks to an outlook which gave emotion primacy over reason. They are both in the end overtaken by events.

Despite the similarities, the two utopias are at bottom irreconcilable. Oswald Cabal explicitly rejects the moderation and the Christianity that are at the heart of Hilton's vision. For in the last resort, Wells's utopia is Fabian socialism writ large and Hilton's is liberal individualism writ small.

Both utopias have their attractions: Hilton's mystical intellectual bolt-hole, a sort of multi-national All Souls College in the Himalayas, and Wells's austere creed of work, discipline and planning. But events have overtaken them too. Although mystical religion and scientific perfectionism have dedicated minority followings, the idea of either a scientific elite or an intellectual elite, however meek, inheriting the Earth would not find general favour today. More seriously for these visions, the predicted Second World War was not followed by a new dark age. For the forces of democracy triumphed and civilisation as we know it was preserved more or less. If there is another worldwide holocaust, no one at all may survive it, even in the Himalayas.

Acknowledgements

I am indebted to my colleagues Dr Thomas Rohkramer and Dr Bob Bliss for help and advice.

Notes

1 Some scenes were shot but cut before release, in particular all those scenes with Rowena, the estranged wife of Oswald Cabal, debating with her husband their rival philosophies of life. Rowena was played by Margaretta Scott, who also played the role of Boss's mistress, Roxana. In addition, all Theotocopoulos's scenes, originally filmed with Ernest Thesiger in the role, were reshot with Cedric Hardwicke, who gave a more robust and less eccentric performance as the artistic agitator.

2 On the Nazis and flying, see Fritzsche 1992 and Paris 1995: 76; and on the ambivalent image of flying in interwar British literature, see Cunningham 1988: 155–210.

Bibliography

Albrecht, Donald (1986) *Designing Dreams: Modern Architecture in the Movies*, London: Thames and Hudson.

Aldgate, Anthony (1997) 'Loose ends, hidden gems and the moment of "melodramatic emotionality"', in Jeffrey Richards (ed.) *The Unknown 1930s*, London: I.B.Tauris.

Bliss, Arthur (1989) *As I Remember*, London: Thames.

Cooke, Alistair (ed.) (1971) *Garbo and the Nightwatchmen*, London: Secker and Warburg.

Cunningham, Valentine (1988) *British Writers of the Thirties*, Oxford: Oxford University Press.

Eisner, Lotte (1976) *Fritz Lang*, London: Secker and Warburg.

Frayling, Christopher (1995) *Things to Come*, London: British Film Institute.

Fritzsche, Peter (1992) *A Nation of Flyers: German Aviation and the Popular Imagination*, Cambridge, Mass.: Harvard University Press.

Greene, Graham (1972) *The Pleasure Dome: Collected Film Criticism 1935–40*, London: Secker and Warburg.

Hilton, James (1938) *To You, Mr. Chips*, London: Hodder and Stoughton.

—— (1953) *Lost Horizon*, London: Pan.

Kellermann, Bernhard (1915) *The Tunnel*, London: Hodder and Stoughton.

Korda, Michael (1980) *Charmed Lives*, Harmondsworth: Penguin.

Kumar, Krishan (1991) *Utopia and Anti-Utopia in Modern Times*, Oxford: Basil Blackwell.

O'Connor, Garry (1982) *Ralph Richardson*, London: Hodder and Stoughton.

Orwell, George (1971) *Collected Essays, Journalism and Letters*, vol. 2, Harmondsworth: Penguin.

Paris, Michael (1995) *From the Wright Brothers to Top Gun: Aviation, Nationalism and Popular Cinema*, Manchester: Manchester University Press.

Segeberg, Harro (1987) *Literararische Technikbilder. Studien zum Verhältnis von Technik und Literaturgeschichte im 19 und frühen 20 Jahrhundert*, Tübingen: Max Niemeyer Verlag.

Stover, Leon (1987) *The Prophetic Soul: A Reading of H.G. Wells's Things to Come*, Jefferson, NC and London: McFarland.

Wells, H.G. (n.d.) *The Shape of Things to Come*, London: Hutchinson.

—— (1935) *Things to Come*, London: Cresset.

2 'We're the Martians now'

British sf invasion fantasies of the 1950s and 1960s

Peter Hutchings

An astronaut infected with an alien organism stumbles across London (*The Quatermass Experiment* (1955)); alien-controlled humans construct a sinister refinery in the English countryside (*Quatermass II* (1957)); a Martian space-craft is unearthed at a tube station (*Quatermass and the Pit* (1967)); an extraterrestrial masquerades as a housewife (*Unearthly Stranger* (1963)); aliens take over a country hospital (*Invasion* (1966)); a visitor from one of Jupiter's moons kidnaps young women and returns them to his planet for breeding purposes (*The Night Caller* (1965)).

In reality Britain has rarely been invaded. In its fantasies the opposite is true. It is perhaps fitting that a nation with such an expansive imperial past should have developed a rich tradition of narratives about itself being invaded, whether this be in the thriller, horror or science fiction genres. All the exam-ples of invasion referred to above come from British science fiction movies of the 1950s and 1960s, an especially active time as far as imaginary invasions are concerned. Sometimes dismissed as lesser versions of or adjuncts to the better known US science fiction invasion films of the 1950s, these British films actually have a distinctive character of their own and this chapter will seek to identify the nature of this distinctiveness. It will focus on the ways in which the films engage with issues to do with national identity that are quite different from those addressed by their American cousins. Also discussed will be the changes that occur in the British invasion fantasy as it moves from the 1950s to the 1960s.

Before embarking on this, however, it is worth considering some of the broader issues associated with the subject of imaginary invasion. A useful starting point is perhaps the most famous fantastic invasion of all.

Fears of invasion

> No one would have believed, in the last years of the nineteenth century, that human affairs were being watched keenly and closely by intelligences greater than man's and yet as mortal as his own; that as men busied themselves about their affairs they were scrutinised and studied, perhaps almost as narrowly as a man with a microscope might scrutinise the transient creatures that swarm

and multiply in a drop of water. With infinite complacency men went to and fro over this globe about their little affairs, serene in their assurance of their empire over matter. It is possible that the infusoria under the microscope do the same.

H. G. Wells, *The War of the Worlds* (1898)

These resonant opening lines from *The War of the Worlds* – with the matter-of-fact sense they give of humanity being caught in the gaze of another race – constitute a founding moment in the history of the science fiction invasion fantasy, just as the novel in which they feature has proven to be something of a model for alien invasion narratives. It is also true to say that while Wells has secured a place for himself (albeit a marginal one) in the literary canon as the writer of 'popular classics', twentieth-century fantasies about alien invasion have generally received a bad critical press. It is as if the intelligence of Wells's anti-imperial work – with its full-scale assault on British complacency – has been betrayed by a pulp tradition which has assimilated only the sensational qualities of the story and discarded its more serious elements. Bug-eyed monsters wielding death-dealing ray guns and, more recently, the increasing public fascination with UFOs and alien abductions have all been insistently associated with a credulous, juvenile point of view. This has been so regardless of whether one is concerned with real life – and the alleged actual presence of extraterrestrials amongst us – or merely with fictions about alien assault and invasion. The audiences for the latter, it is assumed, are content, keen even, to see any culture that is different from their own presented as threatening simply because of that difference. Matters are made worse by the association of this us/them attitude with a politically reactionary point of view – whether this be the anti-communism of 1950s America or the gung ho nationalism of the recent *Independence Day* (1996). The imperatives remain clear in all cases – *we* are good, *they* are bad, destroy *them* before they destroy *us*.

Film historians writing on 1950s American sf cinema – notably Peter Biskind (1983) and Mark Jancovich (1996) – have sought to dispel this prejudicial outlook through identifying a set of ambiguities and ambivalences apparent in a range of American invasion fantasies. In particular they have drawn our attention to the ways in which these films are as much about anxieties internal to America as they are about real or imagined fears of communist infiltration and invasion. As Jancovich notes, 'the concerns with the Soviet Union were often merely a displacement or a code which different sections of American society used in order to criticise those aspects of American life which they feared or opposed' (Jancovich 1996: 17).

While this is certainly true, the stress laid in many of these accounts on films which are especially distinguished and insightful in their exploration of the collective national psyche – *Invasion of the Body Snatchers* (1956) and the films of Jack Arnold – tends to cover over the fact that the alien invasion fantasy as a generic format is less straightforward than might be imagined. The transformation presented in *The War of the Worlds* of what were once transcendent and immutable values into a set of relative, contingent beliefs is actually a property of alien invasion fantasies in general, even (perhaps especially) those which seek most rigorously to deny it. This is because the mere imagining of an alien culture always involves an acknowledgement of Otherness and this in turn unsettles a certain complacency and racial self-centredness. Humanity's imaginary dominion, its sense of itself as being at the centre of things, is wounded – and the extraterrestrial origins of this means that the wounding is especially traumatic, inflicted as it is against humanity in general rather than any circumscribed section of it. Once it is realised that, to use a phrase firmly associated with the science fiction genre, 'we are not alone', and once humanity is forcibly made aware of the boundaries or frontiers between it and an Other, then humanity becomes limited and is rendered fragile and perpetually vulnerable.

Alien invasion fantasies rely on what might be termed a relativisation of culture and cultural values. The instabilities and anxieties inevitably involved in this are managed in a variety of ways. In Wells's case, for example, the day is saved via the intervention of germs, 'the humblest things that God, in His wisdom, has put upon this earth'. Thus God – God in man's image, so to speak – is restored to the centre, although this turns out only to be a provisional conclusion, for mankind is left in expectation of further possible attacks. Many readers might well be left suspicious that those helpful germs could in the end prove just as dangerous to humanity as they were to the Martians. One thing should be clear, however: there can be no going back to a life led in blissful – and, as far as Wells is concerned, complacent – ignorance of something which exists 'out there'. Bearing this in mind, it does seem that the Martians' lasting achievement is not their temporary occupation of Earth but rather their forcing humanity to acknowledge the existence of an alien culture and in effect to make mankind return the gaze directed against it at the novel's beginning. Inasmuch as they succeed in doing this, the Martians have won, for they have effectively destroyed once and for all a particular human-centred way of existing in and making sense of the universe. It does seem that this destructive mechanism, by which humanity is presented with an overwhelming sense of its own limitations, is constitutive of all invasion fantasies. Regardless of the narrative outcome, the war is always over before the invasion even begins simply because the mere existence of an alien culture is sufficient to do the damage. It could further be argued that the articulation of such fantasies is dependent on a social and cultural context which has become relativised and less sure of itself. Hence the 1950s was a prime decade for invasions, not only because of the tensions associated with the Cold War, but also because of a number of shifts and new trends in the west, most notably a growing affluence and materialism coupled with a widespread sense that traditional values were increasingly being brought into question. Importantly, these various changes did not manifest themselves uniformly across the western world. Consumerism, for example, meant something different in America from what it did in Britain (where it was often associated with anxieties about the alleged undue influence of American culture on the British way of life). It follows that any account of British sf, while needing to preserve a sense of the generic character of the alien invasion fantasy and how all such fantasies, regardless of their country of origin, share certain qualities, must at the same time take account of the socially and historically specific pressures exerted upon the fantasies by the context within which they were produced.

Quatermass and the aliens

Alongside the best-selling novels of John Wyndham (including *The Day of the Triffids* (1951), *The Kraken Wakes* (1953) and *The Midwich Cuckoos* (1957)), probably the best-known invasion stories to emerge from 1950s Britain featured the character Professor Bernard Quatermass. Making his first appearance (played by Reginald Tate) in *The Quatermass Experiment*, a highly successful BBC Television serial from 1953, he subsequently featured in two more serials, *Quatermass II* (1955, played by John Robinson) and *Quatermass and the Pit* (1958/1959, played by André Morell). All three were written by Manx writer Nigel Kneale (also responsible for the celebrated television adaptation of Orwell's *1984* (1954)). Each of them presents a narrative in which an alien threat to the Earth gradually escalates to a point of absolute crisis at which time the knowledgeable Quatermass acts decisively in order to save humanity. In 1955 Hammer released its film version of *The Quatermass Experiment*. Directed by Val Guest with the American actor Brian Donlevy in the title role, it proved to be the company's first major box-office hit and in many ways was a forerunner to the Gothic horror cycle that was shortly to follow. Film adaptations of *Quatermass II* (again directed by Guest with Donlevy as the scientist) and *Quatermass and the Pit* (directed by Roy Ward Baker with Andrew Keir as Quatermass) appeared in 1957 and 1967 respectively. (A fourth Quatermass television serial appeared in 1979. Known both as *Quatermass* and *The Quatermass Conclusion*, it featured John Mills as Quatermass. There was also a radio serial – *The Quatermass Memoirs* – in 1996.) Hammer's film versions are better known today than the original television serials, if only because the serials are much harder to see. In writing about Quatermass, however, it is necessary to consider both versions of each story. This is not only because the television versions often contain significant sequences omitted from the films, but also because film and television programme alike display a considerable media awareness. Each contains comments about the medium in which it appears as well as about other media, and this in turn has implications for the way in which the alien invasion itself is presented.

The film version of *The Quatermass Experiment* concludes with the monster being discovered in Westminster Abbey by a live television outside broadcast team who promptly cease transmission, thus cutting off the television audience – but not the cinema audience – from the sight of Quatermass dealing with the threat. Charles Barr has linked this break in transmission with other attempts by 1950s British cinema to distance itself from television, its main rival, by presenting itself as 'a more autonomous and full-blooded experience' (Barr 1986: 214). This insistence on the difference between the two media is also apparent in the film being sold on its initial release as *The Quatermass Xperiment*, a marketing device designed to draw a prospective audience's attention to its status as an X certificate film. The X certificate, denoting a film for adults only, had been introduced in 1951 and had rapidly become associated with a growing explicitness *vis-à-vis* the representation of sex and violence. As Barr notes, there is a certain irony attached to this given that the film had itself been adapted from a television serial. The irony is compounded when one realises that the 1953 television version of the story contains a sequence set in a cinema during a screening of an absurdly juvenile, pulp-like science fiction film. Here the television drama, with obvious aspirations to be a mature treatment of pre-existing generic themes, seeks to differentiate itself from what it perceives as the mindlessness of the mainstream, conventional science fiction product. One might add here that the television version of *Quatermass and the Pit* also contains a scene not unlike the film version of *The Quatermass Experiment* in which a television outside broadcast is interrupted. In the case of *Quatermass and the Pit*, this takes place at a press conference in front of the recently uncovered Martian spacecraft and is witnessed mainly from the viewpoint of some people watching television in a nearby pub. Yet again television is shown as inadequate as a means of representing some appalling alien threat, although it is noteworthy that this time it is the television version of the story itself which is announcing its own shortcomings.

In fact the more one looks at the Quatermass stories, the more one sees how both television and film versions exhibit a sense that the material with which they are dealing is not easily assimilated into traditional forms and mechanisms of representation. Hence all the distancing references in both television programmes and films as well as the fact that the camera on board the original Quatermass rocket in *The Quatermass Experiment* (a device meant to provide a reassuringly objective account of the space journey) is broken in the crash which initiates the story. Hence too the presence in both versions of *Quatermass and the Pit* of a new type of recording device which picks up brain waves and translates these into images which can then be projected and viewed by others. Such a device abolishes the distinction between the prosaic mundanity of the television broadcast and the vapid escapism of the space opera shown in the TV *Quatermass Experiment*, engaging instead with private mental processes. In *Quatermass and the Pit*, the knowledge this provides finally enables Quatermass to discover the truth about the Martian invasion of the Earth that took place five million years previously. What the use of this radically new device suggests is that a new way of seeing is required in order to counter the alien threat, one that goes beyond what is currently available in 1950s British society. More generally, such moments of modest self-reflexivity – where, if only for a few sequences, a particular technology of vision and/or representation is foregrounded in the narrative – point to a widespread sense in these stories of they themselves being something new and strange within

British film and television culture, something which is in many respects quite alien to the pre-existing norms of representation and storytelling.

These narratives about alien invasion, and indeed the aliens themselves, are defined in their strangeness against what for 1950s Britain passes for reassuringly familiar contexts. This means that while many of the conventional trappings of the science fiction genre – rockets, extraterrestrials and the like – are present, they are invariably located in relation to a reasonably accurate approximation of the real, even humdrum, world. The opening of the film version of *The Quatermass Experiment*, in which a rocket crashes near a cottage in the country, neatly dramatises a much more widespread collision that takes place throughout this and the other Quatermass narratives between the fantastic regime of science fiction and the 'realism' of British everyday life. The climactic sequence in Westminster Abbey would have had a particular resonance in this respect, especially for the television audience who only a few months previously had witnessed the same location on their screens during the Coronation of Queen Elizabeth II. There is a kind of iconoclasm here, a furtive pleasure in seeing the Queen supplanted by a deadly alien monster about to reproduce, just as there is in *Quatermass II* (film), where the Shell Haven Refinery in Essex is transformed into an alien base, and in *Quatermass and the Pit* (TV), where the Martians and the surgically altered apemen are discovered in, of all places, Knightsbridge. One consequence of this mixing of the familiar and the strange, with the strange often concealed within the familiar and close to home, is that audiences are invited to look at their own world in a different light, seeing it to a certain extent as itself an alien world.

A comment made by Kim Newman in a discussion of US anti-communist movies offers a useful way of thinking about the view of 1950s Britain found in the Quatermass stories. Newman states that unlike their American counterparts, British sf invasion films of the 1950s seem to be 'still fighting World War Two' (Newman 1996: 79). It is certainly true that the Quatermass television programmes and films are replete with distancing references to a Cold War conflict. As the avuncular Inspector Lomax (played by Jack Warner) puts it in *The Quatermass Experiment* (film), 'No one wins a Cold War', an attitude fully endorsed by the discrediting of the views of the hawk-like militarist Colonel Breen and his cronies in *Quatermass and the Pit* (TV and film). It is also true that the Quatermass stories show Britain as a nation still bound to the experience of the Second World War. This manifests itself in a number of ways: examples include the workers at the alien factory in *Quatermass II* who seem to have been transplanted directly from a morale-boosting Second World War film and whose social club contains a poster boasting the war-like slogan 'Secrets Mean Sealed Lips'; the concern with wartime unexploded bombs in *Quatermass and the Pit* as well as the way in which the destruction visited upon London at the conclusion of that story very clearly re-enacts the Blitz. It does not follow from this, however, that these stories are simply nostalgic or backward-looking. Instead this attachment to a collective memory of the Second World War needs to be connected with another distinctive feature of the Quatermass stories – one which further separates them from the US invasion fantasy – and that is their marginalisation of romance and sexual desire and their general suppression of domestic matters.

In the 1950s Quatermass stories, Quatermass himself is someone who, while working to protect the nation, remains a curiously isolated figure, bereft of anything resembling a meaningful relationship. (In the 1979 *Quatermass*, he has acquired a granddaughter; possibly connected with this is the fact that here he seems a much weaker figure who can only defeat the aliens through the sacrifice of the lives of both himself and his granddaughter.) The standard, if not clichéd, figures of the clean-cut square-jawed hero and his girl, which are present in some form or other in most US sf films of this period and parodied in the film-within-a-TV-programme in *The Quatermass Experiment* (TV), are absent. The most likely candidates for such roles are Victor Caroon, the surviving astronaut in *The Quatermass Experiment*, and his wife, but in both film and television versions their relationship remains marginal to the main narrative and Caroon himself ends up converted into an alien monster. In addition to this, families – another notable signifier of normality in many US sf films – are few and far between in the 1950s Quatermass stories.

While US science fiction invasion fantasies generally proceed in the direction of a heterosexual and/or familial resolution, the Quatermass stories have a tendency to view individuals as existing primarily within and in relation to groups, institutions and collectives. In the world of Quatermass, there are scientists, soldiers, policemen, politicians, journalists, workers, but few lovers or families and, to a certain extent, no free-standing individuals either. What one finds instead is a mode of social existence that bears more than a passing resemblance to a notion of the people developed and circulated in Britain during the Second World War. This pervasive ideal of national identity was presented in a range of propagandistic material in which the people as a national collective absorbed and superseded the individual, where romance and desire were expendable, even frivolous, given Britain's troubled circumstances, and where the nuclear family that had been disrupted by war was replaced by the group as the prime site of interaction and mutual support. The crucial difference between this wartime notion of the people and the Britain of Quatermass is the populist and hegemonic nature of the former. In the late 1930s the population, and especially a working class alienated from ideas of national unity after the experience of the Depression, had to be won over to the war and the accompanying need for sacrifice. This led to the propaganda for this position having a persuasive, concessionary quality to it, the constant message being that Britain would be a better, more just and integrated nation after the war than it was before (Hurd 1984).

The nation as it exists for Quatermass in the 1950s is certainly unified in that, initially at least, there seems to be no internal dissent or conflict (apart from that occasionally articulated by Quatermass himself). However, the nation in the films lacks any sense of a wartime urgency to bind it together; its unity – with everyone having a place in the collective – is superficial. On one level this registers in a mass complacency where the people seem unconcerned about the dire threat with which they are faced. So in *The Quatermass Experiment* (film), rubbernecking crowds stand idly by at both the beginning and the end while the police's only advice is for everyone to go home (where, presumably, they would all watch television until something disturbing appeared on screen, at which point transmission would be terminated) (Hutchings 1993: 41–50). Similarly in *Quatermass II* the community at Wynerton Flats seems extraordinarily blind to the weird events going on around them, while the nation in general is complacent to the point of culpability in not noticing that aliens have established a firm foothold in Britain. On another, more disturbing level, the superficiality of unity and consensus is apparent in the violence that suddenly – shockingly in the context of the 1950s – tears apart the social order. One thinks here of the worker uprising in *Quatermass II* where the managers and their agents are machine-gunned and the workers themselves fed into the factory machinery, and the riot that concludes *Quatermass and the Pit*, in which a kind of race war breaks out on the streets of London. In each case, the violence can be related to underlying social tensions to do with class and race conflict apparent in Britain at this time; but because these tensions have only been faintly articulated within the respective dramas (for instance, there is a passing reference to a race riot in a radio news broadcast heard near the beginning of the TV version of *Quatermass and the Pit*) the violence has a frighteningly spontaneous, irrational quality to it.

Within such a context Quatermass himself tends to be viewed ambivalently. On the one hand, he is a boffin-like protector of a society which generally seems incapable of protecting itself. On the other, as a 1950s scientist he is also, more disturbingly, associated with advanced technologies that register as strange and alien in the 1950s world and which on occasion parallel the technologies used by the alien invaders. So in *The Quatermass Experiment* it is the scientist's own failed experiment, and the Frankenstein-like hubris embodied in it (emphasised, not surprisingly perhaps, in the Hammer version) which brings the alien infestation to Earth while in *Quatermass II* Quatermass's design for a moon colony is turned against the human race when it appears fully realised in the English countryside as the initial home for the invading aliens. In part this ambivalent treatment derives from a broader uncertainty at this time about the role of the scientist in the nuclear age, as someone who deals with a mysterious power that is both wonderful and immensely destructive. However, typical of the idiosyncratic slant taken on such matters by the Quatermass stories is the fact that the narrative most explicitly about the nuclear age – *Quatermass and the Pit* – is also the one where Professor Quatermass is at his most dove-like and socially responsible and where, for once, he is not made complicit with the alien invasion (this role is taken instead by Colonel Breen).

It should be clear by now that lurking beneath the appeal of the Quatermass stories to the virtues of the wartime collective is a sense that something is wrong with Britain and that this predates any alien invasion. To a certain extent the function of the aliens is to reveal and clarify something that is already there, with their subsequent destruction a means of dealing, if only temporarily, with internal social tensions. It is interesting in this respect that, on a superficial level, the Quatermass aliens tend to be associated with a particular sort of modernity – especially shiny, streamlined artefacts such as the rocket in *The Quatermass Experiment*, the Wynerton Flats complex in *Quatermass II*, and the Martian spacecraft in *Quatermass and the Pit* (in which, ironically, the most modern-looking object turns out to be five million years old). However, once these smooth, futuristic surfaces are penetrated, the aliens themselves are revealed as ultra-natural, defiantly organic, even primordial. So in *The Quatermass Experiment* the alien infestation is a primitive biological organism that absorbs human bodies and eventually transforms Victor Caroon into a plant-like creature; in *Quatermass II* the aliens are yet again relatively primitive, jellyfish-like objects nourished by an ammoniacal substance; while in *Quatermass and the Pit* the spacecraft not only contains the insect Martians and the genetically altered apemen but itself seems to have organic qualities.

When seen in this way the aliens do not merely inaugurate a Darwinist struggle of the species but also raise the possibility of an evolutionary regression, whether this be characterised by the primordial creatures in the first and second Quatermass stories or the apemen in *Quatermass and the Pit*. (A more appropriate Wells reference than *The War of the Worlds* here might be *The Island of Dr Moreau* (1896).) Significantly, these aliens are often also associated with a contaminating dirtiness – for example, the black slime in *Quatermass II* which nourishes the aliens but which besmirches everything else it touches, or the mud from which the spacecraft is dug in *Quatermass and the Pit*. This filth, and the disgust and revulsion that go with it, makes the invasion/possession of the body which precedes the attempted full-scale invasion in all three 1950s Quatermass stories especially traumatic. The polluting experience of bodily invasion is thereby equated with the messy eruption of biological processes, with this taking place in a society whose adherence to a collective unquestioning mode of existence and general censoriousness and conservatism render it singularly ill-equipped to deal with something quite so vulgar and shockingly physical.

Within this situation Professor Quatermass mounts a holding operation. Associated himself with an alienating modernity, he nevertheless works to protect the existing social order from both external and internal threats. Yet Quatermass's Britain is visibly weak and vulnerable, caught as it is in a kind of collective postwar doze. Clearly this state of affairs cannot continue indefinitely. Change must be recognised and assimilated while Quatermass, who in combining traditional and progressive qualities is very much a figure of transition, will have to step aside. Britain faces a different sort of invasion.

Closer to home

In a sequence near the beginning of John Krish's *Unearthly Stranger*, a scientist invites a male colleague home to meet his new wife. The scientist is concerned about his wife, because, as strange as it might seem, she never blinks. Everything seems normal, even clichéd, in this early 1960s household with the partially domesticated husband willing to do a share of menial chores while the sexy wife manages the major tasks in her smart kitchen. Then the husband's friend sees the wife remove a red hot casserole dish from the oven with her bare hands. Understandably shocked, he retreats without comment but during the meal he cannot help staring at her. She chides him gently for this. Then she blinks (see figure 6).

The housewife is an alien, of course, sent to interfere with the scientist's attempts to project humanity out into space. Unlike the earlier Quatermass invasions, however, the principal site for this alien invasion is the domestic household and the face the alien wears is that of the female. The refocusing apparent here on both domesticity and gender is a general characteristic of many of the post-Quatermass invasion fantasies (see Chibnall, this volume). A consequence of this – in films such as *Unearthly Stranger, Invasion, The Night Caller, The Earth Dies Screaming* (1964) and *Night of the Big Heat* (1967) – is that invasions take on a smaller-scale, more intimate quality. The aliens are merely passing through (*Invasion*), have relatively limited strategic aims which do not include a full-scale invasion (*The Night Caller, Unearthly Stranger*) or are encountered in isolated settings that are never integrated into a national or

Figure 6 Domestic alien: the unblinking gaze of Gabriella Licudi in *Unearthly Stranger* (1963).
Source: Courtesy of the British Cinema and Television Research Group archive

international whole (*Invasion* again, *Night of the Big Heat*). To a certain extent the aliens' limited ambitions in these films might be assigned to low budgets and a consequent restriction to small casts and few sets, although the fact that the hardly high budget Quatermass television programmes and films still managed to convey a sense of the whole nation being under threat, suggests that something other than financial constraints is at stake in these 1960s films. Arguably connected with this disappearance of an idea of the nation as an integrated whole is the foregrounding in these films of notions of sexual difference – whether this be female invaders (*Unearthly Stranger*, *Invasion*), male aliens seeking out human females (*The Night Caller*) or, more generally, the alien invasion highlighting gender divisions and tensions within a particular group of humans (most spectacularly, *Night of the Big Heat*).

Quatermass-like elements are still undoubtedly present, especially in the films' opening sequences. *Invasion* begins with an ominous failure in a military radar system; *The Night Caller* with the descent of a mysterious extraterrestrial object to Earth and its subsequent investigation by a team of scientists (with both of these decidedly reminiscent of *Quatermass II*); and *Unearthly Stranger* with the unexplained death of a scientist working on a top secret government space project. Yet these various inaugural mysteries never really demonstrate the possibilities for escalation and proliferation found in all the Quatermass stories. Thus in *Invasion* the aliens are only interested in recapturing a fellow alien and once they have done this they leave; while in *The Night Caller* the alien escapes to Soho where instead of planning for an invasion he advertises for women in the improbably titled magazine *Bikini Girl*. More prosaically, *Unearthly Stranger* focuses its attention on an extremely bizarre marriage. Even those figures who appear most Quatermass-like – notably the scientist played by Maurice Denham in *The Night Caller* – turn out to be ineffective, compromised by their personal relationships or, in the case of Denham's scientist who is killed by the alien, just plain weak.

The view of the nation that emerges from this is also quite different from that offered by the Quatermass stories. Perhaps inevitably given the context within which they were produced, these invasion fantasies all register a general diminution in British national identity consequent upon the visible decline of Empire after the Suez affair in 1956. The idea that Britain had a world-wide sphere of influence – a precarious enough notion in the 1950s – was clearly no longer tenable in the 1960s and one gains the sense that underlying the 1960s invasion films is the strategic question of why anyone would bother to invade Britain at all. As far as internal matters are concerned, it seems from these films that Britain has lost its centre and become fragmented, its population scattered in isolated groups and its institutions and hierarchies no longer as efficacious as they once were. So, for example, the hospital in *Invasion* is a far cry from the hospitals that feature prominently in a whole range of 1950s films – including *White Corridors* (1957), *No Time for Tears* (1957), *Doctor in the House* (1954) and its sequels – and which there act as a kind of microcosm of the caring Welfare State. *Invasion*'s hospital, by contrast, is beset by internal squabbles and is eventually sealed off from the outside world by an alien force field. More comically, the unsuccessful attempts of the army officer in *The Night Caller* to explain over the phone the situation to his obviously less than intelligent superiors yet again points to the inadequacy of any higher authority.

Connected with this is the films' fascination with and anxiety about gender, and especially the changing role of the woman, something that hardly concerned Quatermass at all. In a sense, particular notions of femininity are central to the increasingly consumerist society that was Britain in the 1960s. On the one hand, the woman as embodied in the figure of the housewife is the prime organiser of domestic consumption; but on the other hand, she is also often presented as the sexualised object of male consumption (most notably in this period in the James Bond films). The kidnapped women in *The Night Caller*, which in many ways is the most reactionary of the films being discussed here, seem to fall into the latter category. Defined entirely by their physical appearance and their sexual attractiveness – their abductor presents all his victims with a photograph of them as if to underline their objectification – they are throughout the film completely under the control of the male alien. Surprisingly, they are not even rescued at the end. It is interesting in this respect, if also disturbing, that the most intelligent, self-assured and independent woman in the film, the scientist Ann Barlow, is identified by the alien as especially threatening and is brutally killed.

More complex in their treatment of women are *Invasion* and *Unearthly Stranger*. In the former, all three aliens – two women and one man – are played by oriental actors. At first glance this might be seen as invoking fears of Chinese communist subversion, but *Invasion* also needs to be located in relation to a wider orientalist strain in British cinema in the 1960s – including the *Fu Manchu* movies starring Christopher Lee, *Battle Beneath the Earth* (1967) and even *Dr No* (1962) – which in their stress on warlord villains seemed to be more about nostalgia for a lost imperial age than more contemporary fears and anxieties. *Invasion* is certainly not nostalgic, but its treatment of race is far from straightforward. While it might use the race of its oriental actors in an arguably racist sense to accentuate the otherness of the aliens, it also features another oriental female as a nurse at the hospital. What this produces is a kind of racial ambiguity about the identity of the aliens so that they are not fully or easily distinguishable from the humans in the hospital, or, to be more precise, from the hospital's 'resident alien', i.e. non-white human (see figure 7). This ambiguity is carried over into the gender roles adopted by the aliens as well for while there is a good deal of evidence in the film to support the female aliens' account of themselves – namely that they are extraterrestrial police in search of an escaped male criminal – the male alien's claim that he is a dissident on the run from what presumably is a female-dominated society is never fully discounted. The authoritative identification and containment of the aliens that is enacted throughout the 1950s by Quatermass is clearly no longer

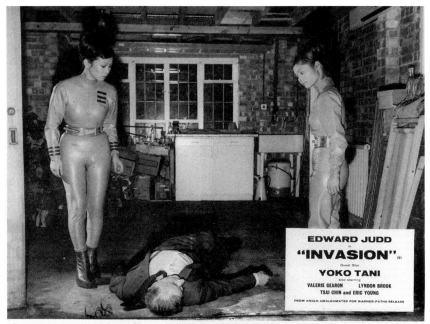

Figure 7 An alien race: the 'oriental' visitors of *Invasion* (1966).
Source: Courtesy of the British Cinema and Television Research Group archive

achievable and what one is left with instead are some unanswered questions and a sense that the truly important drama is taking place elsewhere.

This failure to name and control the alien threat is developed further in *Unearthly Stranger* with particular reference to the figure of the housewife. The film works systematically to make the image of the housewife appear strange, so that in effect it becomes a surface beyond which some otherness may be lurking. It does this through stressing the performativity of the role, the way in which housewifery seems to be defined via the carrying out of a series of actions – such as preparing the evening meal – under the benign gaze of the husband. Once this performance is recognised for what it actually is – as is the case in the kitchen scene – then immediately the woman becomes a threatening enigma for the male, who can no longer trust the evidence of his own eyes. Hence the film's stress on the transformation of the male gaze at the woman into something troubled and fearful; hence too the mounting male paranoia of its hero – such a traumatic revelation obviously puts male identity itself in a state of turmoil. *Unearthly Stranger* concludes in true paranoid style with the scientist discovering that not only his wife but the helpful secretary at his office are aliens. He is last seen surrounded by a group of women, any or all of whom might be aliens too. The cool gaze of the Martians at the beginning of *The War of the Worlds* has been transformed into the female gaze, a gaze that dispels male complacency. The scientist's self-confidence, which in the Quatermass stories saved the nation from disaster, has gone and all that is left is a state of perpetual uncertainty.

Quatermass revisited

Hammer's 1967 version of *Quatermass and the Pit* is something of an anachronism. Of all three film versions, it is the most faithful to the television original and yet the view of Britain it conjures up, with all its wartime resonances, surely belongs more to the 1950s than it does to the 1960s. Nevertheless there is something about the story it tells which has a significance that goes beyond the immediate circumstances of its original production and which clarifies some of the more general qualities of the British invasion fantasy. In the story it is discovered that five million years ago Martians mounted a successful invasion of Earth by proxy through altering selected humans to instil Martian-like behaviour in them. The consequences of this are startling for it means that, as one of Quatermass's associates remarks, 'We're the Martians now'. This statement of fact is also, of course, a statement of defeat, for how can one change the very essence of the human when it is revealed as being partly alien?

As was suggested at the beginning of this chapter, the invasion fantasy generally can be seen as a narrative of defeat. In a sense, aliens always win. What is apparent in *Quatermass and the Pit*, however, and indeed in all the British sf invasion films discussed here, is how close to the surface this realisation actually is, certainly more so than in most of the contemporaneous American sf films. It is as if Britain, displaced from an imperial history and the glories of the Second World War and caught up in a series of bewildering social changes, is more open to self-doubts and an accompanying acknowledgement of its own limits. That such an acknowledgement is always fearful — and viewed in films such as *Unearthly Stranger* and *Invasion* as a kind of collapse — is hardly surprising given that the identities of both the nation and the individual are at stake. Yet the dispelling of a self-centred complacency can in itself be seen as a positive experience for, as Quatermass finally comes to realise in *Quatermass and the Pit* and as H.G. Wells understood all along, to know the alien more clearly is to know oneself as well.

Bibliography

Barr, Charles (1986) 'Broadcasting and cinema: 2: Screens within screens', in Barr (ed.) *All Our Yesterdays: 90 Years of British Cinema*, London: British Film Institute.

Biskind, Peter (1983) *Seeing is Believing: How Hollywood Taught Us to Stop Worrying and Love the Fifties*, London: Pluto.

Hurd, Geoff (ed.) (1984) *National Fictions*, London: British Film Institute.

Hutchings, Peter (1993) *Hammer and Beyond: The British Horror Film*, Manchester: Manchester University Press.

Jancovich, Mark (1996) *Rational Fears: American Horror in the 1950s*, Manchester: Manchester University Press.

Newman, Kim (1996) 'Are you now or have you ever been…?', in Stefan Jaworzyn (ed.), *Shock*, London: Titan.
Wells, H.G. (1898) *The War of the Worlds*.

3 Apocalypse then!

The ultimate monstrosity and strange
things on the coast...an interview
with Nigel Kneale

Paul Wells

Nigel Kneale has been critically acclaimed for the TV serial adventures, *The Quatermass Experiment* (1953), *Quatermass II* (1955), *Quatermass and the Pit* (1958), all of which were subsequently filmed by Hammer, and *The Quatermass Conclusion*, featuring Professor Bernard Quatermass; his screenplays for film adaptations of John Osborne's *Look Back in Anger* (1959) and *The Entertainer* (1960); and his own television dramas *The Road* (1963), *The Year of the Sex Olympics* (1968) and *The Stone Tape* (1972). Though Kneale has consistently denied that he is a science fiction writer, his work in the genre possesses wit, intelligence and originality. Highly distinctive and memorable, his *Quatermass* stories, for example, reflect the times in which they were written, communi-cating postwar social angst, Cold War fears and public concerns about the space age. Kneale's knack for creating engaging characters and unusual scenarios within ordinary contexts has made his science fiction work both emotionally tense and intellectually challenging. His preoccupation with the supernatural, the paranormal and mythology mixes with the cultures of 'hard' science to re-define the terrain of speculative fiction. The claustrophobic intensity of almost pre-destined doom in Kneale's work speaks to a belief in humankind's inevitable move towards its own destruction. Though never didactic, his texts are often prescient, insightful and leavened by comic touches, half-driven by the mystical, half-inspired by the everyday surreality of common lives.

PAUL WELLS: Before you became a screenwriter, I understand that you wrote short stories.

KNEALE: That's right. One particular collection, *Tomato Cain*, which came out in 1949 actually won the Somerset Maugham prize. A number of the stories were set in the Isle of Man, where I am originally from. Some were quite funny; others were trying to be mildly creepy. It was quite hard to consider yourself a writer, though, because there wasn't anybody else actu-ally writing. I made no money out of the book at all. I realised at that point that I could not earn a living so I tried the BBC, which was just reviving television production after the war. They had been wiped out during the war and were just ticking back into life. They had the equipment, of course, but very little money, yet it seemed to be the infant medium I was looking for. It was a good time to get involved.

WELLS: What sort of work did you do at first?

KNEALE: I met up with Michael Barry, who had become Head of the Drama department at the BBC. I knew of him from our time at RADA [Royal Academy of Dramatic Art]. He took me in on the strength of having written this book, which had done well in review terms, if not anything else, but they had no money to pay me at all! I think I had five pounds a week out of petty cash. In order to bump it up, I did odds and ends for the Children's Department, the Music Department and Light Entertainment, so I covered a fair field. Basically, I worked on scripts for a year or two – there were two of us in the script office – making adjustments, writing adaptations of plays and novels, but mostly trying to make stage plays a little more like 'television', although nobody really knew what that was. One producer thought that a television drama ought to be staged like a radio play with each actor approaching the microphone to say their lines. Or there was the other extreme, with everything being done in close-up with endless cutting from face to face. I tried to turn stories into something that looked more like a screenplay than a stage production. Stage plays were divided up into acts, so you could have an act-break when people could make the tea and go to the lavatory; you could have an 'interval'. Very famous those intervals. They were often the best things on the air!

WELLS: What do you think you contributed as a writer to these programmes?

KNEALE: A lot of film companies were closing, so they gave the BBC a lot of their props, and the easiest thing to do was look around and make a story out of what was there. I tried to make a story a bit more fluid and to look a bit more like a film because I've always liked films. I knew I could never be a director, although I would have liked to have been. I have a skin allergy which means I can't last more than ten minutes in the sun, so that ruled me out as a director. So, it was writing or nothing. In my early writing years I went to the cinema about twice a week and was really influenced. I wanted to make my work more visual: less making points in verbal terms and more paying off through images, which you tended not to get then. Most of the stuff was designed for actors to make a big point with a big verbal display in a speech instead of what one would try to do in a decent screenplay, which was to let the camera tell the story. A big visual point, which may or may not involve actors, enables you to get a kind of pace in the work, which again, you would not get if you were 'wordstruck'. In a way, this has been a tendency through all television drama. The pundits say, 'Oh, this is too much like a television play', when they wish to condemn something as too 'wordy' or insufficiently visual. Of course, they also complain when it is too visual because then it is 'too shallow'. Obviously you can't win, but when a screenplay is working you know that you're telling the story the right way. I think now that I can write a screenplay straight on to the typewriter and know it is all working.

WELLS: How did *The Quatermass Experiment* come about?

KNEALE: I had written a whole lot of 'odds 'n' sods', and one day in 1953 the BBC suddenly discovered that they had a gap in the schedule, a slot for a serial, and nothing even remotely planned. It was a mid-summer slot, and the summer schedule is the rottenest time of the year for programming. Someone said, 'For God's sake, can somebody do something?', and given that there was only two of us, it didn't leave many options. As the other fellow was going on leave, I wrote it. I churned it out fairly fast; in fact, I was still writing it while it was being transmitted. There were six episodes, and I was still working on the last one when the second one went out. I saw it as an opportunity to do something different – an adventure yarn, or something that wasn't people talking in drawing rooms. I wanted to write some strong characters, but I didn't want them to be like those horrible people in those awful American science fiction films, chewing gum and stating the obvious. Not that I wanted to do something terribly 'British', but I really didn't like all the flag-waving you got in those films. I tried to get real human interest in the stories, and some good humour.

WELLS: What do your remember about the production of the series? [See figure 8.]

KNEALE: The first episodes were made at Alexandra Palace with very old cameras, but *Quatermass II* was made at Lime Grove in the new studios. I think *Quatermass and the Pit* was made at Riverside. We did some filming on location to link in with the studio stuff – streets, parks and places like that – but they weren't really as much part of the story as I would have liked. We shot in oil refineries for *Quatermass II* and that was much more part of the general tone of the piece.

WELLS: The television series were ultimately made into film versions, of course. How did that come about?

KNEALE: By the time we'd finished the first series, it had had a certain success, and was really very different from what people generally saw on a television screen. In a way I don't like to regard it as science fiction because I think science fiction is a kind of cult thing. It has its particular adherents, its own fans, whereas I was writing stuff for the general audience. You don't really write science fiction for a big audience, though Spielberg has since done this, but I'm not sure you can actually call things like *E.T.: The Extraterrestrial* [1982] science fiction. The thing was that *The Quatermass Experiment* did have very high viewing figures, and afterwards various film companies wondered if they could make a version of it. I remember Sidney Gilliat was interested. I wish that he had made it because he was obviously an excellent person to do it, but he was frightened by the new 'X' certificate. All the companies were convinced that if a film had an 'X' certificate, nobody would ever go to it, even if it got past the censor properly, and that it would end up in the rather 'rattier' kind of cinemas. Of course,

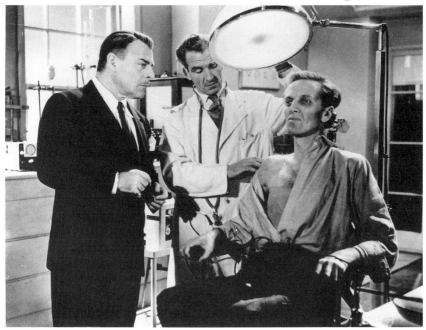

Figure 8 'Something horrid had happened': Professor Quatermass (Brian Donlevy)
(left) face to face with Victor Caroon (Richard Wordsworth) in *The
Quatermass Experiment* (1955).
Source: Courtesy of the British Cinema and Television Research Group archive

Hammer came in, and far from being frightened of the 'X' certificate, they
gloried in it. In fact, they produced this horrible title of *The Quatermass
'X'periment*, which was very vulgar. They took it off later, but that's how it
started. That was the film version [1955], with which I had nothing to do.

WELLS: Clearly, you weren't very impressed with the film.

KNEALE: No, it wasn't nearly as good as the television version. I think that
there were one or two good performances. A man called Richard
Wordsworth was a marvellous actor and played the unfortunate at the
centre of the story. Brian Donlevy played the scientist and I thought he
was terrible, mainly because he wasn't interested and was drunk most of
the time. It was well directed by Val Guest in a brisk style. I was not asked
to do the script. At the time I was 'a television writer', and television writers
didn't count for much, so they got an American to do it. They planned to
have an American star and an American screenwriter so that they could sell
it in the States, and they did. Because all the action was around London,
and all the other characters were notably English, the main problem was
the way that Donlevy played it because he couldn't understand what the
other characters were saying. He *had* been a very good comic actor in the
days of Preston Sturges, but he had rather given up, and the very fact that
he was available should have told them not to use him.

WELLS: The central character played by Wordsworth contracts a terrible virus. Where did the idea for that come from?

KNEALE: There had never been any rockets in space at that time, and the fictional films that were made addressing such a thing were really dire. It was still a very 'fictional' idea that a rocket would fly off of the surface of the Earth and go somewhere in particular. I simply took the idea that one did go somewhere, but it did not come back happily. All the men climbed out, but something horrid had happened, something completely different. I didn't want a man in a rubber suit. For one thing, we couldn't afford a man in a rubber suit. We had nothing remotely as grand as a rubber suit, so the whole thing had to be told entirely in terms of people on Earth, and the horror fundamentally *suggested*. It was dictated purely by the medium of television. We had no choice. It led logically to a story in which an invisible entity entered the rocket and came back with it. It wasn't anything as literal as a virus, but something able to spread itself into all living forms on the Earth: animal, vegetable, microscopic, everything. You've got the ultimate and unclassifiable monstrosity. It could be big, small, anything. It was a total monster. In the film they reduced the idea very considerably to a kind of waddling octopus – not unlike Mr Donlevy when you think about it!

WELLS: Why did you decide to have the story climax at Westminster Abbey?

KNEALE: Westminster Abbey was a very familiar concept to the audience. The Queen had been crowned there a few weeks earlier and it was quite easy to suggest that we were showing the audience Westminster Abbey, when in fact it was just a bit of studio with a few columns and props. There is an academic lecturer talking about the inside of the Abbey, and suddenly, lo and behold, on camera three is the monster. It was television about television, which was new I think. They had shots of outside broadcast apparatus and in the end it had the sense of a show within a show.

WELLS: The image of the 'monster in the abbey' has rich connotations which relate it to the Gothic romance. Was this part of your thinking for the story?

KNEALE: There wasn't time for any real consideration of theme, but in the end if you're working class you draw on things that are in the back of your mind. Of course, I'd read *Frankenstein*, and probably some of that became part of *Quatermass*. I couldn't read the old Gothic novels, though. I can't read Gothic science fiction. Page one sees me off. The terrible struggling to be impressive. It's usually rather humourless, or with a pseudo-humour where characters chuckle at themselves. For the most part, writing a screenplay was simply a matter of getting on with a lively story which would be actable. I was thinking purely in dramatic terms and not so much about how it would look on the screen. For one thing, you could not depend upon anything looking very good. You had to make it 'camera-proof' in a sense, so that even if the vision had been turned off it would still work. I was fortunate in the end because I got a good director in Rudy Cartier, who, even though he was at the mercy of some rather primitive equipment, added a visual quality to it. To give you an example of how bad it was,

I remember one script, a year or so earlier than *Quatermass*, which required that a character produce an egg for some purpose – needless to say it wasn't for a cookery programme; rather it was concerned with a scientific experiment – and it was necessary to add the line 'This egg' because you couldn't tell that it was one! There wasn't a hard enough line around the thing to be sure that it was an egg, or a stone, or something else. We were always at the mercy of that, so you could not be fancy and say, 'We're going to have an extraordinary ending for this', because the 'low-tech' that was available wouldn't have supported it – it was unimaginably terrible.

WELLS: The film versions clearly demonstrate some technical advances at least. You were screenwriter for *Quatermass II* [1957] – what was your feeling about that film?

KNEALE: I wrote that about a year or two after the original *Quatermass*, and the script of that changed a good deal. Mr Donlevy had had two more years of soaking up a lot of Scotch every lunchtime. By the afternoon he couldn't remember what the story was, so it had to change to deal with that, which pretty well sank it as far as I was concerned. Having said that, I did have a lot more time to think about it, and I very much enjoyed dealing with a conscious theme. It was a period when a lot of mysterious radar establishments and places of that sort had been built across the counties, and if anything it was done with even greater secrecy than it would be now, because there was a great nervousness in the country. People were frightened of what might drop from the skies, and they didn't want to ask too much about what was going on. People just hoped everything would be all right, but rumours did circulate: 'What's this thing being put up on the coast?', 'Who put it there?', 'Is it really to keep the Russians away, or is it something else?' I decided my story would be about the 'something else', some large mysterious thing put on Earth by alien things from a long way off. Then it was a matter of dressing the idea up and exploring what you could do with it. The first problem was to try and find some huge set which would seem 'high-tech' for 1955, and which the audience would totally believe in. We were given great assistance by the Shell Oil Company and used their refinery down on the coast. It looked very good and was used in both the television and film versions. Once you suggested to the audience that it wasn't Shell at all but something very different, then that was enough. It looked so advanced that it was easy to suggest that it could not have been built by human hands but was the work of aliens. Such an idea was in the general consciousness of people who read the newspapers or took a general interest in what was going on around them, so I knew it would be responded to and the audience would get the implication. You didn't need to go into enormously elaborate explanations of things because these were basically very 'Earth-bound' stories which did not stretch the imagination about 'rockets-in-space'. Recognisably human characters in recognisable places and situations, especially familiar bits of London, suddenly became suspicious and scary.

WELLS: How did you imagine 'the creature' for *Quatermass II*?

KNEALE: Certainly the creature was different from the monster in the abbey. There was a certain amount of pattern-making, though. The first story was about a contemporary small-scale but spreading invasion of the Earth. The second was about something that had happened some time before, so that the spread had already happened and had become much more dangerous. It was completely established. A take-over was happening at various points on the Earth's surface and had a year's start on us before it was discovered. The third one, *Quatermass and the Pit*, when I came to write it, involved something that had happened millions of years before, so the take-over was completely established. There wasn't a sense of repetition, of saying, 'Oh, here comes the rocket or the flying saucer; it is going to land and then we get the story'. Rather, by going back in time, the story becomes about identifying and chasing a long-established enemy. I like this historical aspect to story-telling.

WELLS: Were you satisfied with the treatment of this theme in the film of *Quatermass and the Pit* [1967]?

KNEALE: Again, it suffered from shrinkage. On that occasion, I did do the script entirely without other hands involved, but I don't think it was as good as the BBC's version, which is now available on video. The central performances were more memorable and the extended story enabled you to play with the idea more. For instance, you can get away from melodrama, which is probably the curse of this sort of story. If you're presenting a moment of action which is dangerously close to melodrama you can immediately correct it by saying, 'Ah, but wait a minute…', and then introduce something fresh or funny or which appears to contradict the moment which has just occurred. Film storytelling is cruder. You don't have the time to make changes.

WELLS: You suggested earlier that you don't like to think of the *Quatermass* stories as purely science fiction, but do you think that there are ingredients which make a successful science fiction or horror story?

KNEALE: I think that it's a matter of suggestion. It's always far more horrible to let something happen in the audience's mind – or the reader's mind if it's a book – than to come straight out and show it. A lot of Hammer's stuff, certainly after I had my dealings with them, veered off into the 'bucket of guts' horror which sought 'effect'. The effect is to try and produce a squeamish reaction in the audience – the 'Urghh' factor – which I can't go along with, because that isn't 'horror'. It's just like visiting an abattoir, and that isn't horrifying, it's just sickening. Horror is much more basic. It is what you might feel if you went, for example, into a jungle or a place where you had lost all your bearings and were no longer sure of anything. You begin to suspect that there is something dangerous present which you wouldn't be able to identify. You're not seeing anything visually horrible at all, but you know there is something that may endanger or kill you. That is a feeling that I think we all have. We have very ancient instincts to escape from danger. I suppose that's partly why people like to go and see science fiction or horror films: it tickles some ancient instinct and stirs it into activity. Maybe that's why younger people go more than the elderly, because their reactions to it are sharper, quicker. Another factor is that the strangest things ought to happen in the most ordinary of places. If a monster appears in an everyday place, it's much more frightening than in some Gothic castle where you would expect it to be. Actually, these were the very things that they *didn't* want when I came to write a script for John Carpenter's film, *Halloween III: Season of the Witch* [1983].

WELLS: I understand that you had considerable problems with that project.

KNEALE: A director called John Landis, who made *An American Werewolf in London* [1981], was planning a 3D version of *The Creature from the Black Lagoon* [1954] and asked me out to Hollywood to write the story. While I was there I met John Carpenter, and he asked me to write a script for the third *Halloween* film. I wasn't really interested because I didn't like the first two films. I didn't like the single idea of the chase and the kill in those movies, so he agreed that I could explore some other situations, concentrating on suggestions of magical and supernatural elements. I specifically tried to write it not in terms of 'squeam', but Carpenter said he was under orders from his distributors to put all the squeam back. So, you've got the gouging of eyes, the drilling of heads – all those terrible horror clichés which are not worth watching. His producer, Debra Hill, seemed to think that audiences needed to be amused by seeing the same as the first movies, but I'm not in the business to amuse them. I had my name removed from the project. By the way, *The Creature from the Black Lagoon* was never made. Another *Jaws* [1975] movie came out of the water, and that was that.

WELLS: Returning to your work specifically in science fiction, how did you approach the adaptation of H.G. Wells's *First Men in the Moon* [1901] in 1964?

KNEALE: I've always loved H.G. Wells; he's a wonderfully visual writer – *The Invisible Man* [1897], 'The Man Who Could Work Miracles' [1898], *The Shape of Things to Come* [1933] – all full of striking images. Funnily enough, *First Men in the Moon* was more about the other side to Wells, which is the humour. Wells is an historian, a science fiction writer, and a domestic comedy writer – it was the domestic comedy that appealed to me. The comic characters really dominate the story. I had what I thought was quite an amusing idea to reverse the ending of *War of the Worlds* [1898] to end the film of *First Men in the Moon* (1964): a scientist from Earth gives the Selenites on the moon a cold. Everything that's happened since in space makes it all seem ridiculous.

WELLS: *Quatermass* returned in the late 1970s as a television series starring John Mills. How did you envisage this final instalment?

KNEALE: I was quite unhappy about it really. Though it was interesting to write about a future society in near collapse, the rest of the story was a little disappointing. An alien culture is taking human beings, but once this is discovered there is not as much suspense as I would have liked. I tried to have the older generation saving the young people, but I'm not sure if the young people were worth saving. They weren't that interesting, and they were a bit out of date: flower children instead of punks. Also, by then Quatermass had had his day, I think.

WELLS: Do you think that there are any consistent preoccupations that inform your science fictional works?

KNEALE: I always look for an idea that seems to contain contradictions. In *The Quatermass Experiment*, for example, the contradiction is that we go into space, making *progress*, but bring something back which takes us backwards. Another of my stories, *The Road*, is about a haunted wood in the eighteenth century. Some proto-scientists are poking about trying to investigate the nature of the haunt, but when it manifests itself it isn't a haunt from a previous time but from our time now. It is a terrible vision of the atomic holocaust. It certainly involved a lot of contradictions between what these people in 1770 thought might happen compared with what we know in our terms did happen. Apocalypse then!

4 Alien women

The politics of sexual difference in British sf pulp cinema

Steve Chibnall

There is often less danger in the things we fear than the things we desire.
Four Sided Triangle (1952)

There's a whole new breed [of women] that feel they're just as smart, just as courageous, as men, and they are. They don't like to be over-protected. They don't like to have their initiative taken away from them.
It Came from Beneath the Sea (1955)

Like the Western, war and gangster stories, science fiction developed as a male genre. Although its writers were occasionally female (C.C. Moore, Judith Merril and Marion Zimmer Bradley, for example) its audience was overwhelmingly male (Warner Jr 1969: 24–6; Merrick 1997: 59–61). This may be partly explained by sf's emphasis on male-coded technology – space ships, robots, time machines and all the other 'boys' toys' which distanced the genre from the domestic and feminised sphere (on the gendering of scientific knowledge and discourse, see Keller 1985). It was indeed the relationship between man and machine rather than between man and woman that was key – not simply, or even necessarily, to the popularity of an sf text, but to its status within the genre. The consideration of technological progress and its implications for social arrangements became a distinguishing characteristic of 'serious' science fiction.

But as fast as the genre pressed its claims for legitimacy as serious discourse on the future, it was undermined by a less cerebral sub-literature of 'pulp' sf which traded as non-scientific sensation and fantastical space opera (Harbottle and Holland 1992; Nicholls 1979: 485, 559–60). By the early 1950s this pulp literature was becoming a repository for male imaginings which went well beyond technological speculations to sexual fantasy of the most exotic kind (Harrison 1977; Nicholls 1979: 536–9).

It would have been easier for the legitimisers of the genre if 'serious' had been easily distinguishable from 'pulp', but as the mass commodification of popular literature gathered pace much the same iconography and garish design were used to ensure the marketability of both generic strands (Aldiss 1975).

When the generic conventions of sf began to be employed in the construction of films in the early postwar years it was primarily the pulp tradition that was drawn upon. The predominance of invasion narratives among this wave of films is conventionally attributed to the preoccupation with the twin threats of communism and nuclear war (Warren 1982/86; Biskind 1983: 102–44; Sayre 1982: 191–214). However, when we examine pulp sf cinema in Britain we discover that a third threat dominates its narratives – the threat from women.

Although British cinema can offer no representation of this threat on the scale of Allied Artists' *Attack of the 50 Ft Woman* (1958), a significant number of films combine female monstrosity and otherness with male erotic spectatorship. These 'sexy alien' movies clearly mix fear of female sexuality with excitement about its possibilities.

'A woman! you must be joking'

Britain's fledgling sf cinema of the 1940s was quick to seize upon the potential of technology as a solution to male sexual frustration. In Bernard Knowles's fantastical comedy *The Perfect Woman* (1949), a dotty professor (Miles Malleson) models a female robot on his niece (Patricia Roc) and hires Nigel Patrick and Stanley Holloway to try out the machine. Malleson insists that 'she must be put through the most rigorous tests' to prove that she is indistinguishable from the real thing. 'I call her the perfect woman,' he tells the expectant road testers, 'she does exactly what she's told, she can't talk, she can't eat, and you can leave her switched off under a dust sheet for weeks at a time.' Olga the Robot appears to have no domestic function and is designed as a decorative toy for the male. Her fetishistic underwear clearly signifies her erotic promise and renders her creator's assertion that, strictly speaking, she has 'no sex' entirely unconvincing. The implicit fantasy of a fully compliant sex machine is intensified when niece Penelope decides to impersonate Olga, provoking Nigel Patrick to remark that 'if he makes them as well as this, there won't be a single home without one' (see figure 9). In the end, however, the film only flirts with transgression. While Olga the proto-sex machine runs amok at the mention of the word 'love', Penelope, the real woman, wins a marriage proposal and, in spite of playing the obedient robot, remains in control of the situation.

As well as giving expression to male domination fantasies *The Perfect Woman* indexed anxiety about the growing assertiveness and expanded expectations of women since the Second World War. Attempts to remake women as compliant love objects were again evident in two films made by Terence Fisher in the early 1950s. In *Stolen Face* (1952) a Harley Street plastic surgeon (Paul Henreid) remodels the face of a female convict to the likeness of his lost love, a concert pianist (Lizabeth Scott), with predictably disastrous consequences. Like *The Perfect Woman*, the film gives a technological twist to the Pygmalion myth, this time adding fears about class mobility to its anxiety about female independence (Rigby 1995). *Four Sided Triangle* is more unequivocally a science fiction film. Here, Fisher reworks the *Frankenstein* fable as a three-way love story. Two scientific prodigies grow up loving the same girl, Lena

Figure 9 'A fully compliant sex machine': Miles Malleson adjusts Patricia Roc's
fetishistic garb in *The Perfect Woman* (1949).
Source: Courtesy of the British Cinema and Television Research Group archive

(Barbara Payton). As children, the boys pay homage to Lena and compete for
her approval, but as adults only one can marry her. When Robin (John Van
Eyssen) finally wins Lena's favours on her return from a spell in the United
States, Bill (Stephen Murray) becomes determined to harness his scientific
brilliance to his erotic obsession. His and Robin's masculine science has already
usurped the feminine role by creating a 'reproducer' to duplicate matter; now
Bill adapts a machine designed to 'transform the world into a place of peace
and plenty' to replicate Lena for his own use. The replicant's body is Bill's to
possess, but ironically her romantic memories, like Lena's, are of Robin. Bill
cannot control or colonise the mind he has created and the Lena duplicate
dies in the attempt to empty her memory of past attachments.

Based on a novel by William F. Temple, *Four Sided Triangle* is a complex
discourse on science, humanity, religion and gender which, like *Frankenstein*,
warns against men's attempts to use science to flout the God-given laws of
biology. Less obviously, the film associates the blasphemies of science and
gender transgression with transatlantic influences. The strongly Americanised
Lena, played by a notoriously promiscuous Hollywood actress (Payton 1963;
Johnson and Del Vecchio 1996: 78), returns as a sex bomb to the humble barn
in rural England where Bill and Robin conduct their experiments and it is
her desirability which perverts the altruism of the British scientists. But ultimately *Four Sided Triangle* shows not so much the perniciousness of American

possessive individualism as the futility of attempts to control and manipulate the new postwar woman.

This independent postwar woman was to reappear in Fisher's next science fiction picture *Spaceways* (1953). In *Four Sided Triangle*, platinum-blonde Lena had acted as a laboratory assistant, donning trousers to occupy the male work space. In *Spaceways* the arrival of dark-haired Dr Liza Frank in her fully-fashioned white overall is heralded by the concern of the male scientists that if they use up any more hydrogen hyparoxide 'there may be no blondes in the world'. But if Barbara Payton's Lena was primarily an object of others' desires, Eva Bartok's Liza is very much an agent of her own. Although General Hays greets her with 'a more charming mathematician I could hardly imagine' she not only quickly proves herself a capable scientist and a full member of the lab team, but also eventually demonstrates her bravery, keeping her cool as her space rocket careers out of control. Admittedly, her devotion is ultimately more to her beloved colleague Stephen (Howard Duff) than to her profession, but her decision to risk death to help the man she loves lifts her into the heroic category usually reserved for men (on representations of female scientists in American sf films, see Bansak (1996) and Smith (1996)).

The character of Dr Liza Frank may have incorporated aspects of conventional femininity, but she remained a disturbing presence in the male preserve of experimental science. An even greater disturbance is apparent when Michelle Dupont (Gaby André) is introduced to her new colleagues in *The Strange World of Planet X* (1957). They already have very definite expectations:

Brigadier: I forgot. I was to tell you that your new assistant is a woman.
Dr Laird: A woman! You must be joking.
Gill: He has to be joking.
Brigadier: I'm afraid not. There's no one else available to operate this computer of yours.
Dr Laird: But a woman, this is preposterous. This is highly skilled work.
Brigadier: She's very highly qualified, Doctor.
Gill: Yeh, I know the type, frustrated angular spinster, very dedicated to her calling, without a sense of humour, bossy and infuriatingly right every time.

Their expectations are quickly disrupted, however, first by the sight of Michelle's legs as she enters the frame and then by the realisation that she is French. 'Is there anything beside your name?' Gill (Forest Tucker) asks her. 'Oh yes,' she replies 'Bachelor of Science (beat) and Mademoiselle.' The Otherness of female scientists like Liza and Michelle is further emphasised by the casting of European actresses, just as the desirability of *Stolen Face*'s and *Four Sided Triangle*'s love objects had been underlined by the casting of Hollywood stars. *The Strange World of Planet X* struggles to manage the contradictions embodied in a mademoiselle whose knowledge can supply vital technological breakthroughs and who can as easily turn scientific discourse into sexual innuendo: 'Oh I see you don't understand this machine,' she taunts Gill. 'Each circuit is capable of use over and over again, if it has a few micro-seconds to clear itself. That means you can have as many surges as you like in banks of three.' But Gill, as a male scientist largely impotent in the face of the threats created by his own experiments as well as Michelle's sexual voracity, is unlikely to be able to handle her circuits successfully. When, at the end of the film, she is trapped in the web of a mutant spider for which an arrogant male science-in-the-service-of-the-military is responsible, her salvation (and humanity's) relies on the intervention of an extraterrestrial benefactor. Smith, the alien, makes it clear that the *Strange World* of the title is the one created by unscrupulous scientific 'progress', but it might equally apply to the increasingly strained realm of gender relations in postwar Britain.

In each of the films discussed so far, problems for male protagonists stem from their inability to exercise full control over the women who are introduced into their environment. From *The Perfect Woman* to *The Strange World of Planet X* the space that women occupy becomes increasingly public, reflecting the growing presence of women in the British labour force during the 1950s. Over that period, the ratio of women to men in paid employment increased from approximately 1 in 4 to 1 in 3 in spite of strong cultural pressures in favour of domesticity (Hill 1986: 16). The tensions created by this contradiction are apparent in these films just as they are in the contemporary *Quatermass* television series (Leman 1991). Like the work of Richard Matheson in the period (Jancovich 1996: 129–66; Wells 1993: 181–99), these are texts which highlight the inadequacies of a male-coded scientism, questioning its assumptions of superiority and recognising that deepening crisis of masculinity which has often been noted by writers on postwar film culture (Biskind 1983; Krutnik 1991; Thomas 1992). If none takes its scepticism about masculine power as far as Matheson's *The Incredible Shrinking Man* (1957), each in its own way acknowledges both the confusion created by female independence and the intractable Otherness of women from the male perspective.

UFO: unearthly female obsessions/ultimate fetish object

The impossibility of containing women within the domestic sphere and their ascribed categories of wife and mother supplies an important source of tension in British sf film; but the unconstrained woman was more than a challenge to masculine control. She was also the object of sexual interest. However, as Vivian Sobchack (1985) has argued in relation to American sf films, these fantasies of sexual desire untempered by the disciplines of marriage and domesticity and their concomitant fears of impotence are frequently displaced onto non-human objects. But we are not talking about bug-eyed monsters here. Taking their inspiration from literary works like Catherine Moore's *Shambleau* (1933) and Philip J. Farmer's 'The Lovers' (1952), and from American space movies like *Flight to Mars* (1951), Britain's pulp sf films of the mid-1950s began to feature humanoid extraterrestrials with all the signifiers of femininity and desirability. Jacqueline Pearson, commenting on the Otherness of the female in male-authored sf has remarked that, when it comes to sex, men and women 'meet as aliens' (Pearson 1990: 17). British films like *Devil Girl From Mars* (1954) and *Fire Maidens from Outer Space* (1956) offer literal examples of inter-planetary miscegenation.

The Danzingers' *Devil Girl from Mars*, directed by David Macdonald from a screenplay by James Eastwood and John C. Maher, is by far the more entertaining of two alien encounter films released in 1954. The other, Burt Balaban's *Stranger from Venus*, a low-rent reworking of the seminal American film *The Day the Earth Stood Still* (1951) and featuring the same leading actress (Patricia Neal), has a male alien visiting Earth, the 'delinquent planet', to maintain the peace of the galaxy. Where he visits is not entirely clear. It may well be some Poverty Row vision of Canada imagined by the German screenwriter and American director, but it hardly matters as the action is claustrophobically confined to a small inn. The best that can be said for the film is that its threadbare *mise-en-scène* and sloppy writing give it a strange feeling of dislocation; but if we want to see what pulp pleasures it is really possible to wring from an isolated inn and a mysterious alien we need look no further than *Devil Girl from Mars*. It has a greater sense of the kitsch and the bizarre than any other British film of its decade. Even the reviewer for the *Monthly Film Bulletin* (June 1954), in a remarkably early piece of camp criticism, was captivated:

> Settings, dialogue, characterisation and special effects are of a low order; but even their modest unreality has its charm. There is really no fault in this film that one would like to see eliminated. Everything, in its way, is quite perfect.

The essence of the narrative is as simple as it is preposterous – a Martian woman and her robot visit a remote Scottish inn and attempt to abduct healthy male specimens – but the film's sub-plots, sub-texts, S & M iconography and hilarious dialogue make *Devil Girl* a triumph of trashiness (see figure 10).

With tongues firmly in their cheeks, the film's scriptwriters assemble a cast of broadly drawn 'types' to await the arrival of their Amazon Queen from outer space. The men are all standard genre figures – McDermott the tough American newshound, Professor Hennessey the objective scientist, Jamieson the Scottish innkeeper, Tommy the plucky little boy, and Albert, who, with a nod towards *It Always Rains on Sunday* (1947), is an escaped convict being harboured by a barmaid. In addition there is the faithful disabled retainer, who exists presumably to demonstrate to visiting aliens what an unhealthy specimen looks like and is first in line for vaporisation in their eugenics programme. But it is the women who really run this show which, as *Kine Weekly* (6 May 1954) noted, combines 'ingenious stunt offering and artful women's stuff'. First there is Hazel Court's Ellen, a sleek metropolitan model who is renouncing her corrupt city ways and getting back to nature. 'I'm

Figure 10 'A triumph of trashiness': Nyah (Patricia Laffan) terrorises Scottish men
with her raygun and S&M gear in a cult film *Devil Girl from Mars* (1954).
Source: Courtesy of the British Cinema and Television Research Group archive

twenty-six,' she tells Michael, 'and in all these years I haven't done a single thing
I really wanted to do.' She is 'just a stupid girl from the big city, dazzling the
natives with clothes she gets for nothing'. And what does she want now? –
'spend more time in the country, find the right man, have children'. As a
prodigal daughter Ellen is one custodian of the film's conservative values, the
other is the redoubtable Mrs Jamieson (Sophie Stewart). Largely unfazed by
the arrival of a spaceship in her back garden, believing that 'the proper
authorities will be here directly to take it away', she has 'trust in the Lord' and,
in the great tradition of British cinema's matriarchs, absolute faith in the
restorative properties of a cup of tea.

As other authors note in this volume, one can read British alien invasion
films as re-runs of the Second World War, and Mrs Jamieson certainly rekin-
dles the indomitable spirit of the Blitz. When McDermott introduces her
latest guest as 'Miss Nyah, she comes from Mars', her response is the stoical
'Oh, that'll mean another bed'. The centre of the film, however, is the Devil
Girl herself. Patricia Laffan cuts a magnificent figure as the cruel dominatrix
from the planet of war. Her obedient robot may look like a fridge on legs, but
Nyah has stepped straight from the pages of a fifties fetish magazine. All
leather cap and cowl and stiletto boots she is a creation of kinky costumiers

'Atomage' as much as a creature of the atom age. As simultaneous cultural nightmare and erotic fantasy she embodies all the threats and possibilities of ascendant female power. 'What do you know of force?' she taunts the men who are obliged to submit to her mind control. 'Force as we use it on Mars... I can control power beyond your wildest dreams.' A fascist femme fatale, she has come to turn the men of Earth into sex slaves and she will brook no opposition. She imperiously declares that she 'will select some of your strongest men to return with me to Mars'. 'And if they don't want to go with you?', asks Carter. 'There is no "if"', she replies. It is clear that what she represents is nothing less than the extinction of patriarchy. A Martian future would see men's phallic power reduced to the mere servicing of matriarchal needs. Like the telescopic phalli on which Nyah's spaceship rests, men's importance would be purely functional. Nyah's account of Martian history is a prophecy for Earth:

> Many of your Earth years ago, our women were similar to yours today. Our emancipation took several hundred years and ended in a bitter, devastating war between the sexes. Women became the rulers of Mars, but now the male has fallen into decline. The birth rate is dropping tremendously, for despite our advanced science we have still found no way of creating life.

The arrival of Nyah is a revelation, not simply of extraterrestrial life, but of the quiet revolution of morals, mores and gender relations in Britain. Like Klaatu in *The Day the Earth Stood Still*, she reveals to men the parlous state they have fallen into – losing their religion, putting too much faith in science, failing to reject violence and allowing the erosion of sexual difference. When repentant murderer Albert sacrifices himself in blowing up Nyah's spacecraft on its way to London, he rescues a patriarchy strengthened by the realisation of danger.

If Nyah is a product of patriarchal anxiety, her eroticisation is a function of repressed desire. She selects young Tommy for abduction because 'his mind is clear of all your emotions and fears'; that is, he has not yet experienced the sexual repression that fuels the melodrama of *Devil Girl*. The consequences of desire and repression are again evident in Cy Roth's cod-Freudian epic *Fire Maidens from Outer Space* in which the paranoid masochism of the earlier film is turned into dreams of sexual plenitude centred on the thirteenth moon of Jupiter. When an expedition of cockney scientists and their American colleague (Anthony Dexter) land on the planet after some of the most unconvincing space travel ever seen in low-budget film-making, they discover the survivors of the lost continent of Atlantis – sixteen toga-clad maidens ruled by an aged patriarch (Owen Barry), all conveniently English-speaking. The thirteenth moon is a paradise that looks remarkably like the Home Counties and the astronauts are ecstatic to find alien women 'with all the necessary ingredients' displayed to their best advantage in an exotic fire dance to the music of Borodin. The only serpent in this garden of Eden is 'The Creature', an atavistic monster of the id, half-man half-beast, who prowls the countryside of New Atlantis. The creature is a personification of the astronauts' own lustful desires, a surrogate Oedipus who slays the patriarch and releases the libidos of maidens and astronauts alike before perishing in purifying fire. The death of the patriarch, however, means not only a release from the bondage of sexual restraint (the astronauts are tied up while they watch the fire dance) but the establishment of a matriarchy in New Atlantis, as if the latter were a corollary of the former.

Like earlier American visions of plenitude-in-space such as *Flight to Mars* and *Cat Women of the Moon* (1953), *Fire Maidens* is an essentially juvenile fantasy of penetrating the society and the bodies of women. New Atlantis is described as 'impregnable' and the symbolism of virginity is taken further as the astronauts and creators struggle to break into the garden of the Fire Maiden's palace. It is hardly surprising that *Kine Weekly* (5 July 1956) assessed its appeal as mainly to 'the satchel club trade'. But it remains a rare example of a British film about alien encounters in outer space. As the pace of cultural change began to quicken with the onset of the sixties and the taboos on the free expression of sexuality began to weaken, the politics of sexual difference in British sf remained earthbound, even though its female antagonists continued to hail from space.

John Krish's *Unearthly Stranger* (1963) and Alan Bridges's *Invasion* (1966) are easily the most accomplished films in the alien women cycle. Each uses the skills of lighting cameramen Reg Wyer and Jimmy Wilson respectively to create an atmosphere of dislocation and tension which is unusually effective for a British low-budgeter. *Unearthly Stranger* is the most explicit treatment of the Otherness of women in all British sf films, a male-voiced *I Married a Monster from Outer Space* (1958). Rex Carlton's knowing script plays interestingly with four types of alienness from the point of view of the English Establishment: the Otherness derived from class, gender, nationality and planetary origin. The procedures of civil service vetting are cleverly used to expose the discriminatory practices which perpetuate the public schoolboy club of science and politics. Major Clarke (Patrick Newell) has the job of vetting the wife of scientist Dr Davidson (John Neville). 'She's an alien, isn't she?,' asks Clarke. 'She was born in Switzerland,' replies Davidson. He is bitter that Clarke does not find it necessary to investigate his boss's wife because 'she's from a nice respectable English family'. Suspicion and mistrust of women, however, run deep in this male bastion. Their secretary Miss Ballard (Jean Marsh) is dismissed as hopelessly irrational. 'She relies on the unknown, what she can't see but can only fear deep down,' remarks Davidson despairingly. 'She's like a lot of women,' adds his boss Sir John. But their attitudes to women still fall short of the open misogyny of the sweet-munching Major: 'As a confirmed bachelor, I'd rather face the unknown than a face covered in cold-cream at night and pin-curlers over breakfast.'

Davidson spends the film trying to break free from male bonding and the masculine-gendered 'bureaucratic mind'. At the office he is constantly reminded of his wife (Gabriella Licudi) by small signifiers of her existence, and during his time with her in her domestic sphere he is feminised, swapping suit and tie for sports shirt and soft sweater. But the femininity of Miss Ballard and Mrs Davidson is largely illusionary. Both are extraterrestrials, part of a twenty-year mission to sabotage man's – or rather men's – attempts to discover the secrets of space travel. The infiltrators' impersonation of the human female is imperfect – they have no pulse, they are impervious to heat and they sleep with their eyes open – but it seems to take men a long time to notice, unlike children who instinctively shy away. The real clue to the alienness of these women, however, is that they have no blink reflex and it is their unblinking, interrogative appropriation of the male gaze which is the key metaphor of *Unearthly Stranger*. As Peter Hutchings (this volume) also notes, it is men and male society who are the objects of critical scrutiny in this film, and alien women who are ultimately in the ascendant. But their experience of earthly gender relations leaves them confused and torn between Julie Davidson's embrace of human (and not simply feminine) emotions of love and the desire for children, and Miss Ballard's proto-feminist dismissal of romance as ideology: 'You call it strong to give yourself to someone else for this so-called "love". You talk a lot about love – the love of freedom, for example – but do you have it, do you really have it? It's an illusion and we have learned to live without illusions.'

Although *Invasion* cannot match the complexity of *Unearthly Stranger's* allegorical approach, similar themes emerge in a more muted form to join the concern with sexual repression found in earlier films. Skilfully directed by Alan Bridges, who was already responsible for the highly accomplished B thriller *Act of Murder* (1964), *Invasion* generates a mood of menacing tension and sweaty sensuality. Although the film features the arrival of three E.T.s and the mobilisation of troops there is never any suggestion of an alien 'invasion' force. But beyond the sinister visit of representatives of an advanced species, there are invasion threats of a more earthly kind – the possibility of a Russian nuclear strike and the challenge to conventional moralities posed by the spread of sexual permissiveness. The insistent bleeping of a radar screen, a squaddie reading *The G-String Murders*, an adulterous couple in a car, and the fetishised rubberwear of the strange visitors are all woven by Jimmy Wilson's restless camera into a glittering *noir* tapestry of decadence, perversity and danger. Like the hospital which the visitors seal off with their force field, Britain has become a pressure cooker, an overheating society waiting for the steam to blow, just as it is in *The Day the Earth Caught Fire* (1961) and *Night of the Big Heat* (1967) (see Hunter, this volume). Heat in these films signifies both a challenge to British *sang froid* and the presence of alien emotional states.

Once again, the glimpses of extraterrestrial gender relations in *Invasion* offer a prophecy for human society. On Lystria women appear to be responsible for administering the law. 'Our justice is a poor thing, often conducted by women,' complains the male Lystrian (Eric Young). He is surprised to find that on Earth men retain positions of authority. 'You tell her what to do?' he inquires incredulously as Dr Vernon (Edward Judd) instructs his nurse, 'and she obeys you?'The Lystrian is an escaped murderer (or dissident?) who is pursued by two policewomen from his planet, the exotically oriental and rubber-clad Yoko Tani and Cali Raia. That human society has equally capable women waiting to assume positions of power is emphasised by the roles of Valerie Gearon as Dr Harland and Tsai Chin as Nurse Lim. The nurse has a close physical resemblance to the Lystrians which enables one of them to impersonate her (swapping one fetishised uniform for another). Dr Harland's is the increasing confident voice of the woman professional. When her male colleague excitedly speculates that the Lystrians could be 'years ahead of us', her response – 'They still have prisoners' – may be read as a sardonic comment on the position of women in her own society. Whatever their competencies, women lie outside the circle that encloses the patriarchal English Establishment, a circle that is as invisible but as real as the alien force field around the hospital. To those within the Establishment circle like the senior consultant Carter, who has friends in high places and who dies (ironically) when he tries to drive through the force field, those outside are alien and interchangeable. It might be the Chinese nurse substituted by a Lystrian or Private Morgan, the Welsh soldier who is addressed as 'Jones' by his commanding officer because it is 'the same thing'.

The girls from Starship Venus

In its concern with difference and permissiveness *Invasion* points towards the final phase of the alien women cycle. John Gilling's *The Night Caller* (1965), based on a novel by Frank Crisp, shifts *Invasion's* anxieties about fragmenting moralities into the realm of full-blown paranoia, tempered only by a subtle sense of self-parody. This really is sf *film noir* located in sin-drenched Soho at night with all the signifiers of temptation and corruption. Gilling and *Unearthly Stranger's* cinematographer Reg Wyer use all the classic elements of expressionist cinema to construct a Festival of Light fantasy of moral decline. 'We mustn't let our imaginations run riot,' Professor Morley (Maurice Denham) cautions at one point, but this is superfluous advice in a film that has an extraterrestrial operating from a mucky bookshop and abducting wayward women via advertisements in *Bikini Girl* magazine. The film seems fully aware of its own absurdity – the E.T. runs 'Orion Enterprises', is called Medra (an anagram of 'dream'), and is humanoid apart from one mutant arm which looks as if it was bought in a joke shop.

Although *The Night Caller's* E.T. is male, there is a strong suggestion that Earth faces a crisis because its women are becoming alienated from their 'natural' state of simple domesticity. Not only are they disappearing into the Bermuda triangle of Soho to become victims of genetic experiments, but they are also developing intellectual pretensions. These sexual and intellectual transgressions are conflated in the character of Ann Barlow (Patricia Haynes), a scientist from a military research centre who 'poses' as a model to trap Medra. Before killing her in the film's most shocking scene, he gives a voice to patriarchal paranoia:

'I fear what I cannot control, and I cannot control an intelligence which is almost equal to mine. A mind such as yours searches and destroys.' His account of the catastrophe on Ganymede has all the hallmarks of the destructive war of the sexes on the Devil Girl's Mars, and is a call for physical and emotional restraint:

> We interfered with the laws of the Universe just as you are attempting to do now. We found it impossible to suppress the emotions of love and hate, so we slipped into the dark abyss. The problem of life is that there is always an enemy who will kill or be killed. There is always someone to fear!

In the British science fiction film that 'someone to fear' is just as likely to be wearing an apron, a bikini or a fully fashioned lab coat as a red star and an astrakhan hat.

There are more female scientists under threat from aliens in Amicus's pedestrian *They Came from Beyond Space* (1967) and Tigon's *The Body Stealers* (1969). *They Came from Beyond Space* offers the usual evidence that Freddie Francis's talents lay in cinematography rather than direction, but even a Hitchcock would have struggled to make much from Milton Subotsky's tired script based on, but hardly inspired by, Joseph Millard's *The Gods Hate Kansas* (1941). With more wit and imagination, Subotsky's script might have been salvaged as an episode of *The Avengers* but instead it was left to founder as a tale of a scientist who, protected from alien mind control by a silver plate in his head, rescues his colleague and lover from possession by an unearthly parasite. The film is fuelled by the same paranoia as the American *Invasion of the Body Snatchers* (1956), but in turning its fifties pessimism into simplistic sixties optimism it manages only to squander any claims to cultural relevance.

Like Francis's stale offering, Gerry Levy's *The Body Stealers* is a rehash of the established themes of British sf film. Patrick Allen plays randy Bob Megan, a rugged troubleshooting 'alpha' male hired to solve the riddle of abducted parachutists. Megan brings his no-bullshit individualism to the bureaucratic worlds of the military and science where his testosterone is stirred by dedicated researcher Julie Slade (Hilary Dwyer). However, his lecherous gaze is quickly distracted by exotic femme fatale Lorna Wilde, described in the film's publicity as 'the beautiful face from outerspace', whom he discovers moon bathing on a beach at midnight and quickly seduces. But in the spirit of the wham-bam-thank-you-ma'am liberated sexuality of 1969 she disappears in her lurex mini dress after a quick post-coital smoke. Like most advanced civilisations from space which visit these shores, Lorna's has a population problem to which humans are seen as the solution. Her patriarch has a rational plan to use the bodies of Earthmen whose attachment to 'sentiment' keeps them 'backward', but Lorna has been humanised by her association with Bob and protects him by slaying her father figure. As in *They Came from Beyond Space* the Earthman volunteers to organise an expedition to help the troubled aliens in the *Zeitgeist*'s spirit of love and co-operation. The bodies of men and women are once again their own, no longer 'stolen' by regimes of repression.

The dream of carnal liberation and sexual plenitude is taken a stage further in *Zeta One* (1969), a bizarre psychedelic concoction of sexploitation and feminist fable and a high-point of British cinema's flirtation with weirdness in the late 1960s. Again commissioned by Tigon, *Zeta One* was the first film to be made at Euroscan's Camden Studios, a half-converted wallpaper factory in north London owned by *Zeta*'s producer George Maynard and director Michael Cort. Like 1968's box-office success *Barbarella*, it was based on a graphic narrative, in this case a story from Michael Glassman's 'photo fantasy' magazine *Zeta* (Jones 1968). The film offers quite a faithful adaptation of one of the magazine's tales of the three-sided contest between a Bondian secret agent James Ward, a villainous bourgeois patriarch Major Bourdon, and the Angvians, an all-female community who inhabit a parallel dimension.

Early publicity described *Zeta One* as a 'space-age-strip-girlie-thriller' (*Kine Weekly* 1 February 1969), but the film is really a satirical sex comedy which lampoons both the science fiction and secret agent genres, turning James Bond into a male bimbo who is easily outwitted by women and using sf's lost race tradition to develop a light-hearted allegory of the struggle for female liberation. The result may be 'quite preposterous illogicality and silliness' (David McGillivray, *Monthly Film Bulletin* March 1971) but it is much more than the 'parade of sub-standard pin-ups in sado-masochistic array' described in *Today's Cinema* (17 April 1970). Its style is deliriously unhinged with fractured narrative, uneven pacing, and the sort of wacky casting policy that results in Charles Hawtrey playing a sadistic heavy called Swyne. Martin Gascoigne's art direction further emphasises the film's spaced-out qualities with some wonderfully tacky psychedelic effects apparently generated with a kaleidoscope, light filters and some heavy-duty tinfoil.

But it is *Zeta One*'s gender politics that are significant within the alien women cycle. The Angvians (or angry ones) under Zeta's command may be 'beautiful girls who are out of this world', but they are also shock troops for the emergent women's liberation movement of the late 1960s. Zeta abducts politically unaware women, raises their consciousness by memory erasure, mental conditioning and meditation, and converts them into an Amazonian 'fighting force' (see figure 11). In his tweed deerstalker hat and plus fours, their antagonist, the sadistic Major Bourdon, represents the British 'squirearchy' at its most chauvinistic. His manor house misogyny is contrasted with the masculine cool of the more woman-friendly James Word. When Bourdon is finally defeated by Zeta's half-naked storm troopers, it is Word who is selected to fulfil the audience's fantasies of plenitude in the Angvians' 'insemination room'. Feted like an Arab potentate Word lies back while feminists in baby-doll nighties gyrate before him and prepare a meal of oysters and stout.

A critical and commercial failure on its release, *Zeta One* is easy to dismiss as a piece of crazed nonsense, but its significance lies in its eroticisation of collective feminist ambitions and its joyful welcome of a sexually rapacious matriarchy. The film links the permissive revolution to women's liberation in a way that would become familiar in the two sf sexploitation comedies of the

JAMES ROBERTSON JUSTICE   with BRIGITTE SKAY
CHARLES HAWTREY   and guest star DAWN ADDAMS
ROBIN HAWDON   ANNA GAEL   PRODUCED BY TIGON BRITISH FILM PRODUCTIONS
                             RELEASED BY TIGON PICTURES LTD

Figure 11 'Shock troops for the emergent women's liberation movement': the Angrian
       alien women of *Zeta One* (1969), Michael Corr's 'bizarre psychedelic
       concoction of sexploitation and feminist fable'.
Source: Courtesy of the British Cinema and Television Research Group archive

seventies. The first of these, Derek Ford's *The Sexplorer* (1975), originally titled
The Girl from Starship Venus, takes a wry look at human sexuality and gender
relations through the eyes of a female scientific investigator from another
planet (Monika Ringwald). By setting the investigation in London's Soho, the
centre of Britain's sex industry, Ford takes the opportunity to satirise the
superficiality of 'permissiveness'.

Much of the film's humour depends on the alien's misreading of everyday
human activity on what she refers to as 'Planet Dom' (a reversal of 'Mod').
Showers become 'cooling processes', porn films are 'instructional holo-plays',
traffic lights are 'opportunities for meditation', while cigarette smoking is
taken as a sign of overheating. When it comes to gender politics, however, our
alien 'surveyor' provides an ingenuous perspective on sexual attitudes and
mores. She assumes that men must be mutations. They appear scared by both
her appearance as a beautiful blonde and her frank investigation of sexuality.
Their fear is reduced by alcohol but 'most of them prefer to passively watch
others doing something'. Men's sexual liberation appears to be largely
confined to voyeurism and fantasy – a liberation of pornography rather than
libido. On the other hand, women, she observes, 'smile more' and 'obviously
they are the happy ones'. Their sexual potential, however, remains constrained

by patriarchial prohibitions. As a 'bag lady' she meets in a launderette tells her, 'one day, when you've been a good girl and not done all those things you wanted to do, you die'.

The humans encountered by the 'sexplorer' seem as alienated from their own bodies as she is from the form she has adopted for her investigations. But, lacking their inhibitions, she is able to get in touch with her new carnality. Her attempts at heterosexual intercourse are initially frustrated by the disconcerting tendency of her vagina to discharge electric shocks – prompting her seducer to exclaim, 'Women's Lib, they put you up to this, didn't they?'— but once she discovers her own sexuality, her desire is insatiable. She abandons her role as scientist and remains on Earth for a life of pleasure with considerate and loving Alan.

The Sexplorer may be a hand-me-down *Barbarella* in Soho, but its celebration of female sexual potential is just as joyful. Although the naiveté shared by Ringwald's alien scientist and Fonda's earthly astronaut is exploited for male titillation, they each open a space for more assertive and independent forms of femininity.

The casual eroticisation of female power and independence is again evident in Norman J. Warren's *Outer Touch* (1979). (Miramax released a revised version in America as *Spaced Out* (Brown 1995: 27)). Shot on a shoestring at Twickenham Studios, the film was Warren's second examination of the alien invasion theme. His previous film *Prey* (1977), a dark Darwinian fable which elevates the law of the jungle into the organising principle of a universal eco-system, is endearingly eccentric and sometimes unintentionally humorous, but ultimately offers a serious discourse on the predatory nature of masculinity. *Outer Touch*, on the other hand, is a 'spaced out', disco-driven *Carry On* which abandons any pretence at seriousness and largely reverses *Prey*'s ordering of gendered power. Even before the alien women land their spacecraft in the local park, the film's trio of ineffectual human males is already under the dominance of womankind. Diffident Oliver (Barry Stokes) cannot unlock his fiancée Prudence's icy virginity; would-be playboy Cliff (Michael Rowlatt) is obliged to walk his mother's poodle; and nerdy adolescent Willy (Tony Maiden) is in thrall to the busty sirens in his masturbation mags. The aliens come from a world in which men are extinct and are impressed neither by Earth, which 'calls itself a planet' and is 'full of aggressive, carnivorous life-forms', nor by Earthmen, the 'flat-chested specimens' which they, like the Sexplorer, assume to be mutations. The Space Amazons are quick to denounce men as inferior in intelligence and combat skills and to declare women the 'normal life-forms' and the 'superior species'. 'I will tolerate no resistance,' the Amazon skipper (Kate Furguson) tells her startled male captives. 'Behave badly and I will terminate you in an obscure and painful fashion.' Her status as an inter-galactic dominatrix is signified by her ray gun, Betty Page bob, and *Devil Girl* penchant for black leather boots and fighting suit.

The aliens hope to sell the humans to an intergalactic zoo, but become distracted by the delights of miscegenation. Many of the jokes depend on small bespectacled Willy being mistakenly identified as both a sexual athlete and 'the most superior being in the universe'. But, once again, the human male is unable to match the sexual capacity of the female alien.

Norman J. Warren has described his film as 'dreadful in a nice sort of way' (Brown 1995: 28), and the same might be said of the movie that closes Britain's alien women cycle. Although *Lifeforce* (1985), directed by Texan Tobe Hooper but shot at Elstree for London Films, enjoyed a budget around one hundred times bigger than *Outer Touch*, it is barely more convincing as a drama. The film is virtually a pastiche of pulp sf-horror which (as Peter Wright argues elsewhere in this volume) takes the alien women theme to new extremes of misogyny in its defence of the patriarchal order.

Lifeforce returns us directly to the first film in the cycle in its depiction of 'the perfect woman'. Although this time the alien may appear to be an independent creation, she is in fact another product of the male imagination – 'I am the feminine in your mind', she declares. When she is discovered in deep space entombed in a crystal sarcophagus, her nakedness provokes a male astronaut's comment, 'I've been in space for six months and she looks perfect to me', but perfection is only skin deep. Once resuscitated, the perfect woman turns out to be 'totally dangerous', possessing men's minds and draining their vital fluids in an obvious metaphor for sexual attraction and intercourse. She is an irresistible force driven by an insatiable lust for men's energy. She is a threat to all but, more specifically, her intemperance challenges the traditional organisation of British patriarchy indicated not least by the name of the spaceship she destroys, the 'Churchill'. Colin Wilson's novel *The Space Vampires*, on which the film is based, was written in the mid-1970s and there is a clear allusion to the upheavals of the sexual revolution of that period. Significantly it is London, the epicentre of permissiveness, that is decimated by the mass eruption of desire which follows the Space Vampires' arrival. *Lifeforce*, however, is less a Festival of Light fable than a blasphemous parable of Christianity's propensity towards spiritual vampirism. The film offers us a monstrous female Christ figure, discovered with two other thieves of life in the configuration of the crucifixion, praised for her perfection and resurrected to preside over London's apocalyptic destruction. She embodies a 'force that can destroy worlds if not contained' and, we are told, her kind have visited Earth before. Unusually for a vampire, she immediately takes up residence in St Paul's Cathedral, surrounded by crucifixes, and proceeds to take the souls of Londoners and channel them heavenwards to re-energise her desiccated angels. Beautiful and sexualised, yet nameless and life-denying, *Lifeforce*'s 'Space Girl' is the alien women cycle's ultimate representation of female monstrosity. Her form is the embodiment of male fantasy, but her own desire is to control men and use them for her own ends. Like her space sisters she is the Otherness against which the male world of British sf is defined: a passionate, carnal, destabilising presence in opposition to the emotionally cool scientific, military and political establishments which so closely delineate the films' masculinist notions of nationhood.

Bibliography

Aldiss, Brian (1975) *Science Fiction Art*, London: New English Library.

Bansak, Bernice (1996) 'From housemaid to space babe: women in space', *Midnight Marquee* 51: 23–32.

Biskind, Peter (1983) *Seeing is Believing: How Hollywood Taught Us to Stop Worrying and Love the Fifties*, London: Pluto.

Brown, Paul J. (1995) *All You Need is Blood: The Films of Norman J Warren*, Upton, Cambridgeshire: Midnight Media.

Harbottle, Philip and Holland, Steve (1992) *Vultures of the Void: A History of British Science Fiction Publishing 1946–1956*, San Bernardino: Borgo Press.

Harrison, Harry (1977) *Great Balls of Fire: A History of Sex in Science Fiction Illustration*, London: Pierrot.

Hill, John (1986) *Sex, Class and Realism: British Cinema 1956–1963*, London: British Film Institute.

Jancovich, Mark (1996) *Rational Fears: American Horror in the 1950s*, Manchester: Manchester University Press.

Johnson, Tom and Del Vecchio, Deborah (1996) *Hammer Films: An Exhaustive Filmography*, Jefferson, NC: McFarland and Co.

Jones, Glynn (1968) 'Island of the Planet', *Zeta* 5 and 6.

Keller, Evelyn F. (1985) *Reflections on Gender and Science*, New Haven, CT: Yale University Press.

Krutnik, Frank (1991) *In a Lonely Street: Film Noir, Genre, Masculinity*, London: Routledge.

Leman, Joy (1991) 'Wise scientists and female androids: class and gender in sci-fi', in John Corner (ed.) *Popular Television in Britain*, London: British Film Institute.

Merrick, Helen (1997) 'The readers feminism doesn't see: feminist fans, critics and science fiction', in Deborah Cartmell, I.Q. Hunter, Heidi Kaye and Imelda Whelehan (eds) *Trash Aesthetics: Popular Culture and its Audience*, London: Pluto.

Nicholls, Peter (1979) *The Encyclopedia of Science Fiction*, London: Granada.

Payton, Barbara (1963) *I am not Ashamed*, Los Angeles: Holloway House.

Pearson, Jacqueline (1990) 'Where no man has gone before: sexual politics and women's science fiction', in Philip John Davies (ed.) *Science Fiction, Social Conflict and War*, Manchester: Manchester University Press.

Rigby, Jonathan (1995) '*Stolen Face*', *Hammer Horror* 5: 34–7.

Sayre, Nora (1982) *Running Time: Films of the Cold War*, New York: The Dial Press.

Schelde, Per (1993) *Androids, Humanoids and Other Science Fiction Monsters: Science and Soul in Science Fiction Films*, New York: New York University Press.

Singer, James (1989) 'Glamour girls from outer space', *Filmfax* 17: 50–7.

Smith, Don G. (1996) 'From helpmate to monster: the evolution of women in sci-fi/horror movies', *Midnight Marquee* 51: 54–60.

Sobchack, Vivian (1985) 'The virginity of astronauts: sex and the science fiction film', in George Slusser and Eric S. Rabkin (eds) *Shadows of the Magic Lamp: Fantasy and Science Fiction in Film*, Carbondale and Edwardsville: Southern Illinois University Press.

Svehla, Gary and Svehla, Susan (eds) (1996) *Bitches, Bimbos and Virgins: Women in the Horror Film*, Baltimore, MD: Midnight Marquee Press.

Svehla, Susan (1996) 'Queen bitches of the universe', in Svehla and Svehla (eds) *Bitches*.

Thomas, Deborah (1992) 'How Hollywood deals with the deviant male', in Ian Cameron (ed.) *The Movie Book of Film Noir*, London: Studio Vista.

Warner, Jr, Harry (1969) *All Our Yesterdays: An Informal History of SF Fandom in the Forties*, Chicago: Advent.

Warren, Bill (1982/86) *Keep Watching the Skies!: American Science Fiction Movies of the Fifties*, 2 vols, London: McFarland.

Wells, Paul (1993) 'The invisible man: shrinking masculinity in the 1950s science fiction B movie', in Pat Kirkham and Janet Thumim (eds) *You Tarzan: Masculinity, Movies and Men*, London: Lawrence and Wishart.

5 'A stiff upper lip and a trembling lower one'

John Wyndham on screen

Andy Sawyer

What little there is written about John Wyndham (John Wyndham Parkes Lucas Beynon Harris, 1903–1969) tends to damn him with faint praise as the exponent of the 'cosy catastrophe' and a writer of science fiction for people who did not read science fiction (Aldiss and Wingrove 1986: 253). That the latter part at least of this statement is true, there is no doubt, but it applies more generally to the film adaptations of his work. *Village of the Damned* (1960), *The Day of the Triffids* (1963) and *Children of the Damned* (1963) – the last effectively a remake of *Village* – were filmed during his lifetime. *Quest for Love* (1971) appeared shortly after his death.[1]

Wyndham was for many years the most widely read science fiction writer in the UK. After a career selling sf stories to the American pulps under various permutations of his name, he returned to science fiction after the Second World War as 'John Wyndham' and achieved major success with *The Day of the Triffids* (1951), and succeeding novels which soon found mass-market publication by Penguin. *Triffids* was followed by *The Kraken Wakes* (1953), *The Chrysalids* (1955), *The Midwich Cuckoos* (1957), *The Outward Urge* (1959), *Trouble With Lichen* (1960), and *Chocky* (1968). Several collections of short stories were also published, and *Web* appeared posthumously in 1979. Science fiction fans appreciated Wyndham, but he was also successfully marketed as a mainstream writer, whose novels were more clearly science fiction than, say, Neville Shute's *On the Beach* (1957), but which could likewise be read by an audience unfamiliar with or even actively hostile to the genre. 'A modified form of what is unhappily known as "science fiction"' was how the publishers described Wyndham's writing, presumably in an attempt to persuade readers that these sober paperbacks with their aura of 'serious literature' for the middlebrow middle class of postwar Britain had nothing to do with lurid American magazines. That distancing, as much as his subject-matter, might well have been the reason for the lack of close attention given to Wyndham by British critics. Film, television and radio adaptations widened his audience, and his books regularly appeared on reading-lists and syllabuses in British schools. The word 'triffid' – the name given to the shambling carnivorous plants of his 1951 novel – became a jokey epithet for 'large, strange-looking plant'. Nevertheless, there has been a sense that Wyndham was a token science fiction writer for the mass audience, and that his 'cosy catastrophes' were designed to soothe the anxieties of British readers in the 1950s, who had survived a World War only to become embroiled in a Cold War in which it was increasingly clear that they were not major players. In *The Day of the Triffids*, where England is devastated by the carnivorous plants which discover a new ecological niche in a world where the vast majority of humanity is blinded, Wyndham is 'striving for the restoration of order – as much to the way it was before as is possible' (Scarborough 1982: 220). Brian Aldiss, meanwhile, describes *Triffids* and *The Kraken Wakes* as 'totally devoid of ideas' (Aldiss and Wingrove 1986: 254).

While Owen Webster, as early as 1959, perceptively argued the case that whatever else Wyndham was, with his slick unpretentious style and 'single-visioned' characters, he was certainly 'a novelist of ideas pertinent to our times' (Webster 1975: 41), the article in which he made this point was not published until 1975, and then in a small-circulation Australian fanzine *SF Commentary*. It was not until 1992 that Rowland Wymer's 'How "safe" is John Wyndham?', published in *Foundation* 55, offered a significant reappraisal of an author in whom 'a completely consistent and bleakly Darwinian view of life' (Wymer 1992: 26) underlies his fiction. These ideas are not completely incompatible with the concept of the 'cosy catastrophe' – it can be argued that competent bourgeois Mandarins who triumph over catastrophe to reinsert the values of England and the Empire are as 'bleakly Darwinian' as any other example of bleak Darwinians – but there is a significant difference between the idea of bland reassurance and the skilful anatomy with which Wyndham lays bare the abyss beneath the comfortable lives of his audience. As Webster concludes, in each of Wyndham's four novels from *Triffids* to *Cuckoos* 'there is a remnant of the fittest who survive with a stiff upper lip and a trembling lower one' (Webster 1975: 58). It is the trembling lower lip which is of more significant interest.

There is also, however, a significant difference between cinematic adaptation of an author's work and that work itself. Three of Wyndham's works, *The Midwich Cuckoos*, *The Day of the Triffids*, and the short story 'Random Quest', became British sf films, and the ways in which they manipulate Wyndham's original texts – as well as how they differ as commentary on contemporary English anxieties – illuminate the degree to which Wyndham has been interpreted and misinterpreted. Yet another perceptive remark of Owen Webster's – made, remember, before the first movie adaptation of a Wyndham story – was that his novels 'conform to the formula of the horror film: "innocent" people are beset by a Monster or a Thing from Outer Space and have to set about destroying it before it destroys them. The difference with John Wyndham is a distinct reluctance to destroy the Thing in the end' (Webster 1975: 41). *Village* recognises this 'difference' and accepts it, building the relationship of Zellaby with the Children as part of the plot. As the adult who becomes the Children's mentor and sees that there can be no compromise between 'cuckoo' and host, Zellaby's position is dramatically ambiguous and essentially tragic. *The Day of the Triffids*, however, sees only the horror formula and creates unintentional comedy, adding more scenes with heroic males protecting their women against shambling monsters but excising Wyndham's bleaker sociology. *Quest for Love* uses romance rather than horror, but again forsakes the ideas in Wyndham's original for a rather turgid love story, although the updating of the essentially 1950s Wyndham to a visually 1960s setting is not without amusement. The science fictional elements which create the story are in the end played for laughs, on the assumption that an audience cannot visualise 'scientist' without adding 'eccentric'.

Wolf Rilla's *Village of the Damned*, apart from some trimming of minor characters and slight amendments to the plot for dramatic reasons, remains faithful to *The Midwich Cuckoos*. The village of Midwich is subject to an alien intrusion: for some hours it is cut off from the rest of England. A hemispherical field around it causes all within it to fall into a deep sleep. No explanation is given (in the book, a photograph taken from high altitude shows 'a pale oval outline…not unlike the inverted bowl of a spoon' (Wyndham 1957: 36); in the film, we lack even this hint), but it is clear that the cause is not natural. It is even clearer when several months later all the female population of the village of childbearing age become pregnant. The children they give birth to are golden-haired, with eyes which (at least in American prints of the film) on occasion mysteriously glow. That they are not 'human' is suggested not only by their origin but by the fact that they communicate telepathically and can enforce their will on the village adults.

The film's first few scenes emphasise the idyllic rural location of a village for which the word 'sleepy' seems to have been invented, and almost instantly makes the expression literal (Wyndham's own text plays on Midwich's 'sleep' through history). George Sanders's languid dialogue as he collapses and the exchange between him and Barbara Winters as they awake borders on the comatose, even taking into account the fact that the characters they play have actually *been* in a deep sleep. Sanders and Winters as the Zellabys – he a cerebral Professor, she his glamorous younger wife – contrast with the properly respectful country bobbies on bikes and the faintly comic, faintly threatening, stupid working-class characters. Fortunately, once the relationship between the characters is established the acting improves. The unexplained 'time out' is covered up by the authorities, and the first sign of the impending events is Anthea Zellaby's purchase of large quantities of pickles in the village shop. Her announcement of her pregnancy to Gordon is delightfully comic, satirising his engagement in plant cross-breeding ('We have apparently succeeded in crossing a Zellaby Gordonius with a Zellaby Antheum. Just what the results will be, we shan't know for some time yet'), but it also ironically foreshadows the fact that cross-breeding between human and alien is precisely what has happened. It is immediately followed by a shot of a desolate young woman being told that she is pregnant despite her husband being away at sea for a year. Hints at attempts to induce miscarriages given in the novel are removed in the film, but it is none the less clear that the mysterious pregnancies are threatening. The women are unable to explain their conditions; the men glower impotently, cuckolded by something they cannot identify.

Anthea's attacks of doubt and fear during her pregnancy are soon dispelled after the birth, although it soon becomes clear that the Children have powers of coercion over their human hosts. Wyndham builds gradually to this, with mothers who have moved from Midwich during their pregnancy being 'compelled' to return after the births and several scenes where babies 'punish' adults after accidental or deliberate assaults. Rilla conflates these latter incidents into a horrific scene where Anthea plunges her hand into boiling water after giving her baby, David, milk that is too hot. As the Children grow, their powers increase. Gordon shows that what one of them learns, they all learn, by means of a simple experiment in teaching his son to open a puzzle box. The Children move together in groups, outcast from the other village children; their strange, precise, cold way of talking and their blond hair and staring eyes causes nervousness in adults. When dressed in dark clothes, they have the eerie look of photographic negatives, which the black-and-white film only emphasises. An advisory committee on which Gordon Zellaby sits discusses what to do with the Children, who it turns out are not the only group world-wide. Zellaby argues for time to study them, which is granted, but adverse circumstances are looming. We have learned that some of the village children have died in mysterious circumstances. When a motorist nearly runs down one of the Children they will him to drive himself into a wall. After an inquest brings a verdict of 'accidental death' the dead man's brother goes after the Children with a shotgun. The Zellabys dissuade him, but too late. As he walks away the Children will him to turn the shotgun on himself and blow his head off.

The stakes are increased when it is discovered that the Russians have shelled a village in which similar Children were born, and the men of Midwich, angered by the second death, march upon the school in which the Children are now living. Carrying burning torches, their resemblance to something out of a bad Dracula movie is only underscored by the ludicrous martial music, but more horror ensues when the ringleader is forced to torch himself. The most horrific scene in the book – in which the obtuse Chief Constable attempts to investigate this incident by the use of threat and bluster and is instilled with utter primal fear – doesn't actually happen in the film but something similar happens to Anthea's military brother Alan, who is told, 'You must be taught to leave us alone', and put into a debilitating state of shock. Following this, David, who has become the main spokesman for the Children, orders his father to get them away. Zellaby, by then the only adult the Children trust at all and whose lessons the Children enjoy, agrees, but he comes to the next lesson with dynamite in his briefcase. The mental shield he puts up – a simple image of a brick wall – is only sufficient to withstand the combined assault of the Children for a few minutes, but it is enough.

Several commentators on Wyndham have noticed the coming generation gap of the 1960s in *The Midwich Cuckoos* (Greenland 1983: 2–3; Wymer 1992:

28). Wyndham's title, of course, as he makes explicit, refers to the bird which lays its eggs in other birds' nests and he shows that behind this Middle England idyll is a nature 'ruthless, hideous, and cruel beyond belief.… There is no conception more fallacious than the sense of cosiness implied by "Mother Nature"' (Wyndham 1957: 112–13). The film's change of title avoids this imagery, although something of Zellaby's analysis that there can be no compromise between the invading Children and their host-society remains. The change, though, does prompt one to ask exactly who are the 'Damned' of Midwich? Is it the Children, demonically elvish invaders from somewhere out in space – or, for all we know, some other dimension entirely – or are we to pay closer attention to the punishment of the adults in the film? From the incident with the hot milk to the villagers' ringleader burning under the Children's pitiless gaze, it is the adults who suffer under the new generation they have brought into the world. The women fuss over the Children – we see the young David tell his mother that 'I can do that myself' as she is clucking nervously about him – while the men ignore them, sloping off to the pub to drink in sullen silence as their 'offspring' are being born. Even Gordon Zellaby, in Sanders's performance the epitome of civilised English upper-middle-class values, is forced by the logic of his position to betray the trust of creatures for whom he is the last possibility of survival. He murders, if not his *own* son, then his wife's, and he can only do this by self-immolation. Other children, who are not part of the charmed elite, are ignored or forced to obey. Roles are reversed, and even what might be uneasy attempts to bridge the gap seem like sociopathic learned responses. When David gives his final cold ultimatum to Zellaby – a scene he introduces by announcing imperiously to his mother, 'I want to see my father' – he nevertheless brings the scene to a close by saying, 'Good night, father'. Golden, attractive, well-spoken (there are no rural accents among them) and isolated from their parents, the Midwich Children are the 'pretty things…the start of the coming race' of whom David Bowie was to sing in the 1970s. They are the children we never wanted to grow up to become, but may well have (see figure 12).

Children of the Damned, directed by Anton M. Leader was *Village* remade, taking the essential idea of the 'alien children' but incorporating it into a thriller involving UNESCO agents. Brought together to be studied, six Children become part of the personal conflicts between two agents, Llewellyn and Neville, and the mysterious thought-amplifying device the Children build becomes the focus of international conflict. Are they a threat, or could the international community work with them? Although the final decision is to call off the military forces surrounding the church in which the Children have taken sanctuary, an accident causes the firepower to be unleashed and the Church explodes in a ball of flame.

The basic situation and the ending recall the earlier film, but although *Children* is obviously indebted to Wyndham it contains few of his ideas apart from the chilling inexplicability of the Children themselves and the undercurrent of Cold War tension. That the Children are multinational and the military

Figure 12 'The start of the coming race': the alien *Children of the Damned* (1963).
Source: Courtesy of the British Cinema and Television Research Group archive

directly involved certainly increase this latter element. The children themselves are, like the Midwich Children, separate from the society into which they are born, but the fact that they share thoughts makes their implications for international espionage both attractive and dangerous to the nations' diplomats. Critics are divided as to which is the most effective film: some call it 'more interesting than the original film' (Hardy 1991: 220); others say that 'the theme is less satisfactorily handled than in the Rilla film' (Brosnan 1978: 149). *Children* is certainly one of the better 'adaptations' of a Wyndham story, but whatever the qualities of the film it is a spin-off, suggested by rather than derived from a Wyndham original and as such direct comparisons are problematic. Wyndham's abandoned sequel, *Midwich Main*, started apparently at the suggestion of MGM, seems, though, to head towards the plot of *Children*. The hero – the narrator of *The Midwich Cuckoos* – is enlisted by a government 'Department' sixteen years later to investigate reports of other aliens or human-alien hybrids and identifies a multinational group of children. Wyndham seems uneasy with the espionage-thriller genre, possibly because its wider stage lacks the highly focused tension which makes his style otherwise so effective.

H.G. Wells believed that one scientific marvel per story was sufficient. The strength of *The Day of the Triffids* is that it has two: the loss of sight by the greater part of humanity following a meteor shower, and the extrapolation of the idea of the carnivorous plant. The wholescale blinding is itself a dramatic device, but the story that followed might have been a genuine cosy catastrophe as the few remaining sighted people guide the blinded back to a restoration of the social status quo. However, Wyndham's tale foregrounds the triffids, which until the blinding have been a normal, if slightly dangerous, part of the environment, farmed for their oils. Now the triffids are on more equal terms, and can act as predators. Blindness means not merely inability to live our normal lives, but exposure to something actively malevolent out there in the dark. It is to this supernatural fear that the story appeals: hence Webster's discerning of the 'horror film' within the book.

Steve Sekeley's adaptation falls too gratefully upon the horror film that is implied within Wyndham's story. It is the most reviled of Wyndham adaptations, although John Carnell, then editor of *New Worlds*, called it 'an example of how to make a good science fiction film' in his enthusiastic review (June 1963). Hardy (1991: 221) calls it 'overblown, turgid', and although production problems must take some of the blame – the film was apparently only completed a year after the major part of the filming, with the totally unrelated subplot being added by Freddie Francis at the insistence of the film's backers (Brosnan 1978: 150) – the imaginative ironies of Wyndham's novel are almost entirely lost. From the dramatic chords over title and credits and the American voice narrating the introduction to this quintessentially English story, to the men in rubber suits impersonating what seem like walking broccoli plants, the film *looks* like a cheap horror movie (see figure 13). Masen (Howard Keel), the main character, waking up in hospital after an eye operation which has prevented him seeing the meteor shower, becomes an American seaman. Instead of confining itself to the south of England, the action takes in France and Spain and loses the novel's sense of cultural claustrophobia. The plot becomes less one of survival and reconstruction and more a simple journey to the naval base where a British submarine is collecting survivors. The triffids are in some way connected with the meteor shower (the preamble says that they have been bought to Earth by meteorites), but the film loses Wyndham's hints that the meteors may be debris from a satellite weapons system which has gone wrong and that the triffids themselves are the result of a Russian bioengineering project, which lessens the richness and paranoia of the plot. However, behind this rightly denigrated film is another which, if the melodrama and rubber suits had been less in evidence, would have allowed the horror of its theme to expand.

One or two scenes verge on the surreal: the blind Londoners groping through the streets; the strange scene at a railway station where passengers wait calmly for rescue until a train pulls up to disgorge a crowd of screaming travellers; a man stumbling out of the crush holding a teddy-bear in front of him, as if it were guiding his way. Light and vision are constant themes, contrasting with humanity's collective loss of sight. A subplot is added concerning the Goodwins, a husband-and-wife scientist team who take refuge in a lighthouse.

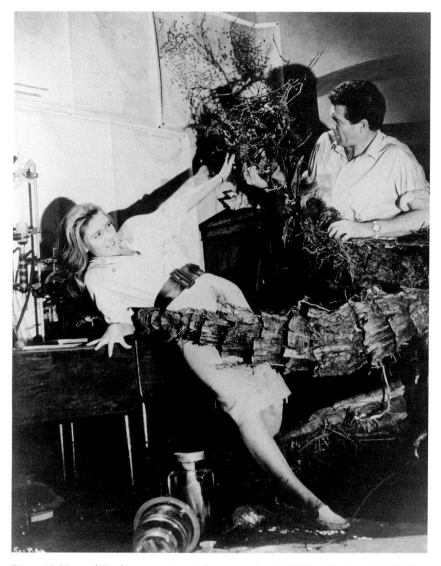

Figure 13 Howard Keel gets to grips with a marauding Triffid in *The Day of the Triffids*
        (1963).
Source: Courtesy of the British Film Institute Stills, Posters and Designs

Although the action there adds nothing to the main plot, the setting is richly
ironic, since a lighthouse is entirely useless in a world in which people cannot
see. The early encounters with the triffids show them looming into vision like
something out of nightmare, more insectoid than plant. The film's one
genuinely unsettling moment is an early episode, not taken from the book, in
which the passengers and crew of an aircraft are in mid-flight. The frightening
calmness of the aircrew – all resolutely stiff-upper-lip in a crisis – emphasises

the nature of the predicament. How, without being able to see the controls, is the pilot going to land the plane? He orders the passengers to fasten their seatbelts and prepare for landing – a charade which can only end one way. Separated from their normal environment, these people are doomed. Yet they behave as if the situation were retrievable, until a child asks the question which is in everyone's mind, 'The pilot – is he blind too?' Then utter panic breaks out. For this scene alone, the film's crudities can almost be forgiven.

Here then we have Wyndham's true thesis: that our social lives function only within the set of communal lies we call 'civilisation', and once they are seen to be illusions our situation is at best precarious. Without the defensive and social strategies enabled by our sense of sight, we have little chance against carnivorous plants better equipped for predation. We cannot, in fact, be unchanged by major paradigm shifts. If we realise that our leaders are 'blind' we are no longer true social animals but an atomised mob. The film's risible ending – the discovery that the triffids are vulnerable to sea-water – is merely the waving of a magic wand. The novel ends with humanity still facing both the triffids and a pressing need to develop new social relations: it is the film's rabbit-out-of-a-hat reassurance which is the true 'cosy catastrophe'. The debate within the book of how best to deal with major disaster – which is Wyndham's way of making his readership face their fear of nuclear war – is stifled. Masen's journey through a devastated England leads him through a number of proto-societies, each reacting in a different way to the disaster, looking to religious fundamentalism, humanitarianism or military dictatorship to provide solutions. Coker, who embodies much of this debate, is in the book a working-class autodidact who realises the impracticality of saving as many blind people as possible until 'rescue' arrives. In the film, Coker is entirely different, an elderly English tourist in France who merely shares the same name. While something of the debate remains when Masen and Susan come across the French community headed by Mme Durant (Nicole Maurey), who represents the 'humanitarian' strand which seeks to look after the blinded, it is sacrificed by the film's inability to engage fully with the ideas implied by the plot.

While Wyndham's narrator Masen, like most of his characters, is something of a flat stereotype, we must beware of reading his English reticence as lack of depth. There are several touching and emotional scenes in the novel as Masen witnesses individual human tragedies in this mass slaughter. Emotion in the film, however, rarely rises above pure pantomime melodrama – Karen Goodwin (Janette Scott) is adept at screaming when triffids appear, but otherwise acts the long-suffering victim of her disillusioned alchoholic husband. Only in the above-mentioned scenes in the tube station and the aircraft do we see real emotional collapse beneath the staid veneer, but the cracks are vivid and the more disturbing for being contrasted with surface stability and calm. The contrast is immediately undercut by Howard Keel's position as foreigner and wanderer (as seaman he is less 'rooted' than Wyndham's char-acter), which marks him as not part of the society he observes, unlike the

Masen of the novel who is observing his own environment crumble about him.

Emotion is the wellspring of Ralph Thomas's *Quest for Love*, in which the short story 'Random Quest' is transformed from a speculative detection story to a weepie which gives the leading players plenty of opportunity to strike wooden poses. At the centre of the plot is the concept of alternative worlds – a lab accident sends physicist Colin Trafford into a parallel 1971 in which time branched off in a different direction in 1938. There has been no Second World War, John F. Kennedy is leader of the League of Nations and Trafford (Tom Bell) is a novelist and playwright deceiving a wife whom he has never seen before – the glamorous Ottalie (Joan Collins) – with a succession of starlets.

The early part of the film, although updating Wyndham's setting by ten years and taking a very different approach to story construction, closely reflects the basic scenario. Bell's dark brooding looks and traces of a working-class accent make him a different Trafford from the one in the short story, but more appropriate to the glamorous decade in which the tale is now set. It is interesting to compare the Zellabys of *Village of the Damned* with the Traffords of *Quest For Love*. Sanders's Zellaby is the old-fashioned male lead, suave, fatherly, in control, while Trafford is the male of the sexual revolution – long-haired, exuding animal sexuality, but unable to understand relationships with women. Barbara Shelley's role gives her more scope than Joan Collins, who hovers uneasily between snapping bitchily and wilting, unable to understand why her husband, who has been a serial adulterer for most of their marriage, is sighing over her as if he has just fallen head-over-heels in love.

Wyndham's basic science fictional premise is the existence of parallel time-tracks, which remains an attractive idea for modern physicists. *Quest for Love* develops this idea up to a point, and then hands over the baton to the romantic element. Trafford's reaction to finding himself on the floor of a London club when he was in a laboratory, dressed in different clothes and being addressed familiarly by perfect strangers, is merely one of bafflement. The clues that this is not his time – the newspapers ('*The News Chronicle* died years ago'), the fact that his friend Tom still possesses the arm he lost in Vietnam, the book in his study titled *Everest the Unconquered* – are dropped neatly into place. Having discovered that he is a version of himself whom he doesn't know among people whose role in his life he doesn't understand, Trafford eventually ends up at his First Night party getting more and more drunk and desperate. Introduced to an 'old school friend' from Stowe, his retort, 'I was at Manchester Grammar myself' is construed as deliberate rude-ness. So it is, but the viewer sees the irony that it is also true.

There is, however, only a limited scope for bewilderment and cross-purposes, and no real attempt is made to explore the differences between the parallel worlds. Culturally (as one might expect) Trafford's alternate 1971 seems closer to the 1930s than the historical 1971, but his anachronistic shaggy locks and slang expressions – he confesses that in his previous setting 'Nobody ever really turned me on' – pass unremarked. There is a desultory attempt to explain what has happened. Wyndham himself glosses over all this by having Ottalie only half-believing Trafford's tentative explanation, but being grateful that he has given up his philandering ways. *Quest for Love* has Trafford meet the 'alternate' of a colleague, Sir Henry Lanstein, who has formulated a theory of the divisibility of time, and persuade him that he is living proof of a theory which, ironically, he had been forced to abandon many years ago. Lanstein lectures to the Traffords, persuading Ottalie that there is some rational explanation to Colin's claim that he is not the 'Colin Trafford' she married, but he comes across as a manic buffoon. The story's science – which as a theory of time is respectable enough today – is undermined by coming from the mouth of a loopy boffin and retires from the plot. The film slips gratefully into its true role as sentimental melodrama: we discover that Ottalie is suffering from a severe and eventually fatal illness.

On her death, Trafford awakens in his original role and spends the rest of the film running around in an increasing frenzy trying to track down the analogue Ottalie before she too dies. Here the film's structure collapses altogether. 'Random Quest' is built upon the fact, established in the first scene, that there is *no* Ottalie Harsholm in Trafford's world, and that the events of the time-slip are part of a story he is telling to the last remaining bearer of the Harsholm name. The film founders upon the need to create the suspense and mystery of the story without sufficiently establishing the conditions necessary for them. The initial scene, long on exposition but short on visual drama, is dropped, which also removes the paradox which powers the story. Wyndham's solution to the mystery of the absent Ottalie is obvious enough, but has some human interest: Dr Harsholm's son managed to impregnate his girl-friend before he died, and a baby who would have been Ottalie Harsholm is born following an emigration to Canada. The film's solution gives us two families living next door, both with month-old children. The 'wrong' baby is rescued from the rubble following an air-raid, and brought up as the orphan of the Harsholm's neighbours. (This is an interesting retreat into conventional morality for a film that emphasises sixties-era free love. The original story, grounded in a period with supposedly more rigid sexual mores, takes illegitimacy as a matter of course.)

It would be trite to suggest that the weaknesses in these films are because the directors 'do not understand science fiction' – an excuse which is constantly offered to explain the embarrassing badness of many sf films. It is more that there is an essential conflict between written science fiction and film when an sf story is adapted for the screen. Although both are visual media, to re-create the 'virtual' visions of many sf novels, a film needs an almost unlimited special effects budget and to go *beyond* state-of-the-art. The heart of much written sf is not a vision of alien spaces or future technology, but a didactic discursive impulse. Science fiction is not at root a matter of bigger and better special effects. It is ideas-driven, transmitting knowledge and speculation. Few film-makers can get away with the 'infodumps' that even skilled novelists find difficult to insert into their work without resorting to cliché. Hence the serious dramatic problems which arise when the films need to insert explanations of the triffids' origin or the theory which allows time to branch into parallel streams.

All in all, the most successful adaptation of Wyndham's work is *Village of the Damned*, which captures the understated atmosphere of his work. Wyndham – or at least the post-war Wyndham – was never a writer of 'sci-fi', but inserted the marvellous and strange for specific effect. *Village* is driven by plot and character rather than by the designer's art. While the British print of the film lacks the striking glowing eyes which are its best-known legacy to cultural history, it is a tribute to the direction and acting that it nevertheless remains powerful and unsettling. The Children's eeriness comes simply from their expressionless voices and carefully constructed blonde wigs which draw attention to slightly bulging foreheads and large eyes. The film works as science fiction, as cognitive estrangement, *because* of the very mundaneness of the invasive force. The horror of the triffids is that they are not at first a major threat, a subtle horror the film overlooks in favour of its pulp values. Like many aspects of our everyday lives – the drugs which cure our diseases, the chemicals which increase our crop yields, the cars which takes us to work and back – the triffids are beneficial until the environment in which they thrive changes in their favour. This is a genuine science fiction argument and precisely the one which is dropped by the film. The unnerving element of *Quest For Love* is the possibility that the choices we make may only be provisional: in some other 'world' we may be living the results of different decisions. Again, this is glossed over.

The horror of the Children is that, though at first sight ordinary human children, their existence implies that the universe is more crowded with menace than we can imagine. But more than this, *Village of the Damned* underlines science fiction's strength as a literature of change. A number of the anxieties unsettling the British public of the 1960s can be discerned in *Village*: fear of the Cold War, of insidious invasion, of totalitarianism (the Children have no individuality), and of a new generation which may not share the values of the old. Both *Triffids* and *Village* centre upon the literalisation of such unconscious terrors. Wyndham's reading public remembered a war in which the very survival not only of 'nations' but of national populations was at stake. His novels ask what would happen to middle-class morality if the survival not only of the nation but of the species itself were endangered. Only *Village* articulates the ultimate question that Wyndham asks: how humanely should a society treat those who are working for its overthrow? Given that Wyndham – and many of his readers – had been fighting against the Nazis, it was a particularly uncomfortable question. The bleakness of Wyndham's answer is perhaps the reason why it was so difficult to translate into popular cinematic form.

Note

1 A third remake of *Village of the Damned*, directed by John Carpenter, was released in 1995. A purely Hollywood production, it draws heavily upon the original story, but in terms of names, characters and settings it is far from the English village of Midwich. *The Day of the Triffids* (1981) and *Chocky* (1984–86) have also been televised by the BBC.

Bibliography

Aldiss, Brian and Wingrove, David (1986) *Trillion Year Spree*, London: Gollancz.

Brosnan, John (1978) *Future Tense: the Cinema of Science Fiction*, London: Macdonald and Jane's.

Greenland, Colin (1983) *The Entropy Exhibition*, London: Routledge.

Hardy, Phil (ed.) (1991) *Aurum Film Encyclopedia: Science Fiction*, 2nd edn, London: Aurum.

Kagarlitsky, Julius (1991) 'John Wyndham', in Noelle Watson and Paul E. Scellinger (eds) *Twentieth Century Science Fiction Writers*, 3rd edn, Chicago: St James Press.

Loban, Lelia (1994) 'If looks could kill', *Scarlet Street* 14: 64–72.

Scarborough, John (1982) 'John Wyndham', in E.F. Bleiler (ed.) *Science Fiction Writers*, New York: Charles Scribner's Sons.

Shipman, David (1984) *A Pictorial History of Science Fiction Films*, Twickenham: Hamlyn.

Webster, Owen (1975) 'John Wyndham as novelist of ideas', *SF Commentary* 44/45: 39–58.

Wingrove, David (ed.) (1985) *Science Fiction Film Sourcebook*, London: Longman.

Wymer, Rowland (1992) 'How "safe" is John Wyndham?', *Foundation* 55: 25–36.

Wyndham, John (1951) *The Day of the Triffids*, London: Michael Joseph.

—— (1957) *The Midwich Cuckoos*, London: Michael Joseph.

—— (1961) 'Random Quest', in *Consider Her Ways and Others*, London: Michael Joseph.

6 Trashing London

The British colossal creature film and fantasies of mass destruction

Ian Conrich

Large parts of London sustained heavy damage in the Blitz of the Second World War. The German air raids of 1940–1 were an unprecedented assault on the capital city, but by the late 1950s the population appeared to be facing a new threat. In a trio of British exploitation films London was shown being destroyed by colossal creatures: *Behemoth the Sea Monster* (1959), a Palaeosaurus; *Gorgo* (1961), mother and baby amphibious beasts, with Megalosaurus resemblance; and *Konga* (1960), a serum-induced giant ape. While parts of the capital were being rebuilt, mock replicas were playfully demolished by film-makers, and in a perverse orgy of destruction their creatures crushed the many famous landmarks that had survived the war.

These British monster movies may be read as allegories of atomic age fears, but they also appear to be articulating tensions created by a crisis in hegemony. As spectacular shows of urban decimation these 'trashing London' productions reveal traces of the disaster film and a return to wartime images.

Origins

Throughout the 1950s America was besieged by colossal creatures: New York was attacked by a rhedosaurus in *The Beast from 20,000 Fathoms* (1953), San Francisco by a giant octopus in *It Came from beneath the Sea* (1955). In Japan, Tokyo became an arena for titanic battles with a variety of fantastic beasts, in the Godzilla films that began with *Gojira* [*Godzilla: King of the Monsters*] (1954), *Mosura* [*Mothra*] (1961) and the series of giant turtle Gamera films that began with *Daikaiju Gamera* [*Gamera the Invincible*] (1965) (see Napier 1996; Noriega 1996). Such was the popular success of these productions that local authorities placed themselves on a waiting list for the honour of having their buildings or monuments modelled for film destruction. In contrast, British film companies made a late and brief attempt at producing colossal creature movies. Prior to the late 1950s Britain had been threatened sporadically: in the silent American film *The Lost World* (1925) a brontosaurus had rampaged through London, while in Hammer's *The Quatermass Experiment* (1955), the capital was menaced by a continually growing space monster that was eventually electrocuted at

Westminster Abbey. This situation was to change with the British work of Eugène Lourié.

The much-travelled Lourié was born in Russia in 1905. He later fled to Turkey and then in 1921 settled in Paris, where he worked as an assistant director and then production designer on classic French films such as *La Grande Illusion* (1937) and *La Règle du Jeu* (1939), before emigrating to Hollywood, where he worked on *This Land is Mine* (1943) and *Limelight* (1952). His directorial debut was *The Beast from 20,000 Fathoms* (1953), which was made the year after the most celebrated colossal creature film, *King Kong* (1933), had been re-released. *The Beast from 20,000 Fathoms* was the first of the postwar colossal creature movies and inspired both *Gojira* and a series of American imitations. Lourié then worked in France and Sweden and came back to America in 1958 to direct the giant robot film *The Colossus of New York* before briefly returning again to Europe.

Working in London he wrote *Behemoth*, which he co-directed with Douglas Hickox, and directed *Gorgo*, for which he co-wrote the story with Daniel Hyatt. Links can be easily discerned to his earlier directorial work. Lourié had been required hurriedly to rewrite the script for *Behemoth* within tight story guidelines provided by the film's producers. They had wanted a reproduction of the profitable *The Beast from 20,000 Fathoms*, a film that Lourié has since described as 'an albatross around my own neck' (Lourié 1985: 241). In 1960 he maintained that he enjoyed doing 'monster' films 'much more than I would enjoy doing doubtful "sex dramas" or pseudo-psychological stories. It is challenging and interesting to conceive and direct fantastic science-fiction films, big visual adventures' (Lourié 1960: 14). But in 1978 he wrote, 'I stopped directing after *Gorgo* in 1961. No one was interested in what I wanted to direct; they all wanted more of the same comic-strip monsters....I was tired of the formula' (Lourié 1978: 53). As he said in his memoirs, he was essentially 'plagiarizing' himself (Lourié 1985: 242). In *The Beast from 20,000 Fathoms*, a dinosaur, frozen in the Arctic, is thawed by atomic testing. It heads for New York, its prehistoric breeding ground, and is destroyed at Coney Island amusement park by a radioactive-loaded harpoon. Similarly, *Behemoth* becomes radioactive as a result of atomic pollution in the sea. The prehistoric beast appears near Port Looe on the Cornwall coast, before heading for London and the freshwater rivers that are essential to its life cycle. Ever increasing in size, it is finally killed in the Thames by a radioactive-loaded torpedo.

Gorgo was produced by the King Brothers, Frank and Maurice, who had approached Lourié for a story similar to *The Beast from 20,000 Fathoms*. He wrote it with a strong mother–baby creature relationship and a non-tragic end. In *Gorgo* the creatures are released from their sub-oceanic cavern by a volcanic eruption off the coast of an Irish island. The baby Gorgo is captured and taken to London where it is exhibited at Battersea Pleasure Gardens before being rescued by its parent. Lourié said (1985: 240) that this more sympathetic story kept a promise he had made to his six-year-old daughter, who had been upset by the death of the creature in *The Beast from 20,000*

Fathoms; she had cried, 'You are bad, Daddy, bad. You killed the nice beast.' This was never referred to in the film's publicity, but instead much was made of the King Brother's affection for their mother. They had reportedly received maternal encouragement to produce the film and it became a 'demonstration' of their love (see figure 14).

These films were made in a period in which a fascination with outer space had contributed to an explosion in the production of fantastic narratives. Space, however, was not the only frontier from which film-makers drew inspiration for their visions of the unknown. Oceans also offered uncharted regions and hidden depths from which colossal creatures could emerge. 'From the untamed seas it came to terrorise the world', declared a 'teaser ad' for *Gorgo*, while the film's mythology was enhanced with a story of precious Viking artefacts on the sea bed: 'They searched for Viking gold and discovered a living terror' ran another ad-line.

Konga, in comparison, is just one of many fantasies of an unexplored darkest Africa. There exists a tradition of western fiction drawn to this supposedly exotic continent, stretching from the Tarzan novels of Edgar Rice Burroughs and H. Rider Haggard's *King Solomon's Mines* (1885), to the giant wasp movie *The Monster from Green Hell* (1957) (see Torgovnick 1991; Root 1996). Konga is a chimp who had rescued Dr Decker, a renowned botanist, when his plane had crashed in remotest Uganda. The chimp had led Decker to the nearest

Figure 14 Worse than the Blitz: mother to the rescue in *Gorgo* (1961).
Source: Courtesy of the British Cinema and Television Research Group archive

village and consequently accompanied Decker when he returned to Britain. A rare carnivorous plant, which contains a growth serum, is also brought back. Decker tests this on Konga to prove a supposed evolutionary link between plant and animal life, but the chimp, who is constantly growing and is now the size of a huge ape, is used by the evil botanist to murder rivals and anyone who interferes. Finally, it strides towards central London, forcing an astonished policeman to utter the immortal lines, 'Fantastic! There's a huge monster gorilla that's constantly growing to outlandish proportions loose on the streets. He's moving to the Embankment area.'

Behemoth, Gorgo and Konga are creatures that emerge from isolated or foreign regions and then journey to a heavily populated metropolis, which they attack. The small Cornish and Irish fishing communities at the start of *Behemoth* and *Gorgo* are not dissimilar to the remote coastal and island communities threatened in a number of British science-fiction films, for instance in Terence Fisher's *Island of Terror* (1966) and *Night of the Big Heat* (1967). *Doomwatch* (1972), in particular, bears a resemblance to *Behemoth*, with both films concerned with contaminated fish and the horrific effects created by the ecological threats posed to local Cornish fishermen. As locations, these close-knit communities, with their customs and regional language (in *Gorgo* the villagers speak Gaelic to exclude the strangers), functioned as rustic, hermetic and distant places in the fantasies of the many British film companies based in cosmopolitan London.

Concept and exploitation

The poster campaigns for *Behemoth*, *Gorgo* and *Konga* are very similar and follow the conventions determined by a sub-genre of colossal creature movies. Across a series of narrative images there exists a circulation of issues: size and proportion, urban chaos and panic, and the dismantling of civilisation.

Dominating the posters is the image of the creature and the film's title. Behemoth, Gorgo and Konga, like previous destructive colossi King Kong and Japan's Gojira are firmly established as focal to the narrative. The title's lettering appears in relation to the creature's physical immensity and its size is reinforced with such references as 'King' or by an awe-inspired epithet: the US title for *Behemoth the Sea Monster*, was *The Giant Behemoth*. Gorgo and Behemoth also carry mythical and biblical associations, signifying primordial might and indomitability. A great marsh land beast, Behemoth, is described in the Hebrew Book of Job (xl. 15–24): 'What strength he has in his loins, what power in the muscles of his belly! His tail sways like a cedar; the sinews of his thighs are close-knit. His bones are tubes of bronze, his limbs like rods of iron.' Gorgo is of Greek origin. The Gorgons of Greek classical mythology were three hideous sisters, two of whom were the immortal daughters of sea gods. Capable of turning their victims to stone, they had serpents for hair, eyes that flamed and brazen claws. Philologists also indicate that the name Gorgon once 'denoted a terrible roaring or bellowing' (*Encyclopedia of World Mythology*

1983: 142). This is not dissimilar to the film-makers' creation. Critics described Gorgo as having 'electric eyes' (Quentin Crewe, *Daily Mail*, 26 October 1961), 'manicured paws' (David Lewin, *Daily Express*, 27 October 1961) and 'a roar like 100 ravening lions unleashed simultaneously at Smithfield meat market' (Alexander Walker, *Evening Standard*, 26 October 1961).

For the establishment of spectacle the dimensions of the colossus are essential and some films, such as *Attack of the 50ft Woman* (1958), emphasise them in the title. The promotions for *Behemoth*, *Gorgo* and *Konga* exploit dimensions in the ad-lines, in the publicity suggestions and in the artwork. The posters for *Behemoth* declare: 'BEHEMOTH – 200 FEET LONG AND AS TALL AS BIG BEN!' For *Gorgo*, the pressbook's 'Exploitips' include the stencilling of huge footprints on pavements leading to the cinema, 'if local bye-laws permit'; cut-outs of the footprint displayed in shoe shop windows, accompanied by the tie-up 'We fit any foot…even Gorgo's…and this is the *Big* one!'; and ads in the personal columns of local papers for a baby Gorgo missed by its mother 'when last seen, GORGO was knocking the top off the Tower of London'.

The graphic layout of the various posters for all three British films repeats a common design of the colossal creature towering over a city being destroyed. As with the posters for the *The Beast from 20,000 Fathoms*, *Tarantula* (1955) and *The Amazing Colossal Man* (1957), buildings are shown crumbling, vehicles crushed and crowds rushing terrified to the fore. Elements of the classic promotional strategies for *King Kong* were repeated in the publicity for *Behemoth* and, appropriately enough, *Konga*. Certain artwork for *King Kong* shows the great ape atop the Empire State Building, holding a helpless woman in his paw, whilst being attacked by aircraft. The poster for *Konga* shows London buses, British bobbies and such significant London landmarks as Big Ben, the Houses of Parliament and St Paul's Cathedral. Jet planes fly around the beast, who, like King Kong, clutches a woman in his paw. (The clutched woman existed only in the publicity. It is Dr Decker (Michael Gough) who is clutched by the giant ape at the climax of *Konga*.) *Behemoth*'s promotions also show Big Ben, the Houses of Parliament, Tower Bridge and a crushed London bus. Attacking this beast are jet planes, a helicopter and a tank. Here the film's location has been exploited for a potential local and foreign audience. The marketing of these British films is partly based on the familiarity of the threatened city, with well-known London sights newly exhibited in a space of chaos and conflict.

Gigantism and spectacle

Colossal creature films emerged as a phenomenon of the television age. In the 1950s, the audience for television grew remarkably, whilst cinema audiences decreased. As Thomas Doherty (1988: 24) writes, television 'forever ended the cultural hegemony of the movies'. Western audiences also began to spend more of their leisure and recreation time on sport and activities centred around the suburban home. Film attempted to retain its audience by doing 'what television could not do in the matter of spectacle (form)' or doing 'what television could not do in the matter of controversial images or narrative (content)' (Doherty 1988: 25–6). The film industry supported new productions with gimmicks and developed projection, image and sound processes to magnify exhibition. Cinerama, introduced in 1952, increased the size of the screen projection threefold and employed multiphonic sound; CinemaScope, which first appeared theatrically in 1953, expanded the width to height ratio of the image; while the 3-D process, successfully marketed in 1953, simulated an effect of increased image depth. Promotional practices promised new techniques such as Glamorama, Thrillerama, Psychorama, Hyptovision and Hypnovista. William Castle, the foremost American promoter of film gimmicks, presented Emergo (the appearance of a model skeleton over the heads of the film audience), Percepto (vibrating theatre seats that gave the audience a mild tingling sensation), and Illusion-O (a viewing apparatus that allowed ghosts to appear and disappear through red and blue filters).

Colossal creature films, with their gimmick of showing cities being crushed, offered wondrous and provocative low-budget narratives centred on size and spectacle. Their outrageous fantasy and imagination also appealed to the youth audience that had begun to constitute film's dominant market. The publicity for *Konga* claimed that it had been filmed with a revolutionary process called SpectaMation, which created 'fantastic never-before-seen shots'. The British pressbook had the reader believe that this was:

> an entirely new form of trick photography, performed by 'tricks' inside the camera. In *Konga* the new technique makes a normal gorilla grow into a gigantic monster over 100 feet tall! It was invented by executive producer Herman Cohen who spent months of research and experiments with the world's leading technicians.

In fact, Konga grew to a giant gorilla through a combination of unimpressive dissolves, in which the image of a chimpanzee was blown up, and the laughable use of a performer in a gorilla costume contrasted against scaled models (see figure 15).

The use of shrunken replicas of cities was the standard method for the foregrounding of size, with copies of famous buildings and monuments constructed and then crushed for a variety of effects. London's landmarks are known internationally and a sense of spectacle is established when they are shown to be as tall as, or smaller than, the attacking creature. When *Behemoth*, *Gorgo* and *Konga* were made, Big Ben (320 feet high) was among Britain's tallest buildings and perhaps the best known of London's perpendicular structures; it is destroyed by Gorgo, while Konga only poses alongside.[1] These colossal creatures are the most unwanted of London's foreign tourists and as they visit London's sights, distinguished buildings of cultural and historical importance are left in ruins. Westminster Bridge is destroyed by Behemoth, while the destruction of Tower Bridge by Gorgo leaves a watching reporter

Figure 15 'Fantastic! There's a huge monster gorilla that's constantly growing to
outlandish proportions loose on the streets.' Michael Gough and friend in
Konga (1960).
Source: Courtesy of the British Film Institute Stills, Posters and Designs

stunned – 'One of London's oldest landmarks smashed like matchwood!' The
ease with which these buildings are crumpled emphasises the enormity of the
creatures' threat and the powerlessness of the metropolis, with its extensive
and comprehensive destruction occupying considerable screen time. A reporter
in *Gorgo* suggests that, 'Words can't describe it. There's been nothing like it.
Not even the worst of the Blitz.'

A little over a quarter of *Gorgo*'s seventy-seven minutes is devoted to the
demolishing of London, with a seemingly endless number of buildings
smashed and toppled. The action is spectacular and excessive. As Forest Pyle
writes (1993: 15), excess necessarily invokes spectacle: 'One makes a spectacle
of oneself by being "too much".' These films are more than just spectacular
and are, crucially, composed of elements of showmanship. The effects often
appear crude, but they are part of a parade of images of gigantism and excess
that have been exploited for entertainment purposes. The promotion for
Behemoth promised a number of awesome sights: 'SEE The monstrous marine
beast surging up from the Thames near Tower Bridge!' and 'SEE The
Woolwich Ferry destroyed by The Behemoth – 200ft. of flaming terror!'
Similarly, *Gorgo*'s publicity exclaimed, '*See* ships capsize and buildings crumble
as the new terror rises from the sea.'

The films' commercial appeal as a series of attractions is echoed in *Gorgo*'s self-reflexive story. The captured baby Gorgo is first paraded through the West End, London's tourist and entertainment centre. Tied to the back of a truck, which follows a travelling musical band, it is transported south along Regent Street, the site of many of London's most notable stores, to Piccadilly Circus with its ostentatious neon advertisements. Baby Gorgo is then installed at a permanent pleasure garden, in a specially constructed cage, as part of Dorkin's Circus. Featured alongside the garden's funfair amusements and big dipper ride, baby Gorgo becomes the principal attraction, exhibited daily in a packed arena – entrance charge five shillings (twenty-five pence) with ice-cream and peanuts on sale. Reminiscent of King Kong, the creature is promoted as 'The Eighth Wonder of the World' and as the 'Most shattering discovery of the twentieth century'. The baby beast is promoted and exploited across London: 'See Gorgo' posters feature on the sides of buses, while in Piccadilly Circus 'Gorgo' flashes in lights above adverts for Schweppes and Coca-Cola.

The real attraction, however, is the mother Gorgo, which at 250 feet tall dwarfs her sixty-five feet tall baby. As in a monster tag-match, the much bigger beast arrives only for the film's climax and, as in *Behemoth* and *Konga*, increasing the size of the colossal creature creates new levels of excess to prevent the spectacle from becoming sterile.

Crisis and conflict

By the late 1950s Britain was declining in world importance and was a weak-ened imperialist power. A defining moment was the Suez affair of 1956, when Britain appeared impotent in its conflict with Egypt. There followed what has been described as a crisis in hegemony. Bennett and Woollacott, in their study of the James Bond novels and films, argue that the Bond films both articulated and disguised the ideological tensions at this period of crisis, operating 'to shift and stabilise subject identities at a time when existing ideological constructions had been placed in doubt and jeopardy' (1987: 280). Like the Bond stories, the British colossal creature films were imaginary attempts to negotiate ideologies and fictionally reaffirm Britain's international status. In *Behemoth*, *Gorgo* and *Konga*, London is prestigiously elected over other great metropolises for the colossal creatures' demonstrations of strength. Characters constantly remind the viewer of London's continuing world importance: in *Behemoth*, an Irish scientist describes London as 'a great city', while a televi-sion reporter talks excitedly about the 'streets of modern London'. The capital is shown to be central to new science: *Behemoth* opens at a London confer-ence on atomic research, an international gathering attended by an array of top scientists. This theme of Britain's centrality to world affairs is most evident in the scenes of the media and war. In the three films multiple methods of communication spread dramatic reports of metropolitan chaos, in which British events lead world news. In *Gorgo*, the BBC keeps the world informed about the capture of the beast. Radio reporters, remote telecast units and television news crews all follow the big story: in *Gorgo* emphasis is placed on the interest shown by the international press, for whom special arrangements are organised.

British politics is depicted as immensely important, with the decisions and actions of the government of world concern. One reporter in *Gorgo* announces that 'Downing Street is in constant communication with other world capitals.' NATO is alerted in both *Gorgo* and *Behemoth* but it is the deployment of the British forces – the army, the Royal Navy and the Royal Air Force – that dominates the climactic moments of conflict. These images of Britain at war are demonstrations of national strength. The enormity of the battle is suggested through shots of aircraft carriers, battleships and submarines and the firing of missiles, depth charges and torpedoes; of tanks, soldiers and bazookas, flamethrowers and guns; and of jet planes, radar tracking stations and war rooms dominated by large maps of Britain. As Patrick Luciano writes (1987: 72), 'the sight of the massive military hardware marching against the invaders is a rallying point'. *Behemoth* and *Konga* are initially unstoppable, but the sea monster is eventually defeated by a newly developed British radioactive torpedo, while the giant ape is killed by a barrage of machinegun and rifle fire. The Godzilla films had reportedly given 'a positive role to the controversial Japanese armed forces…[who were] allowed to use their most modern weapons against Godzilla, in the name of protecting Japan' (*Independent on Sunday*, 31 July 1994: 12). Perhaps this could also be said of *Behemoth* and *Konga*. From the 1950s Britain appeared to lack potency and global credibility, but in these films, when British forces are faced by a mighty enemy, there is reassurance not only that their traditional weapons are still effective, but that they are also able to make formidable use of modern weaponry in defending the nation. In *Gorgo*, mother and baby beasts are not destroyed, but British forces are still exalted, with triumphant music accompanying shots of aircraft and tanks being mobilised.

Panic

Throughout this conflict, the threat posed to urban civilisation is both of the present and suggestive of the past. On the one hand, the British colossal creature films can be read as metaphorical representations of a fear of modern warfare and the atomic threat. On the other, like so many other British science fiction films, they look back to the wartime terror of the Blitz.

America exploded its first hydrogen bomb in November 1952; the Soviet Union exploded its first the following year. Many of the colossal creature films of the 1950s referenced atomic developments within storylines that exploited contemporary insecurity and panic. In *Behemoth* we learn quickly that there have to date been 143 nuclear explosions worldwide, and that as a result of 'radioactive conglomerates' in polluted waters, a biological chain reaction can occur which leads to the creation of a glowing, radioactive dinosaur. These images of the unfamiliar and the unexpected emerged when there was uncertainty and alarm as to the effects of the tremendous power of new warfare.

London, like other world cities, had prepared contingency measures and evacuation procedures for a possible nuclear attack. Warning sirens, shelters, sandbags, public announcements, the civil defence and the emergency services are all featured in the British creature films, but these could equally be seen as recalling events of the Second World War. Chon A. Noriega has written that the Godzilla films exhibit a 'compulsion to repeat a traumatic event in symbolic narrative' (Noriega 1996: 61). Similarly, the British films recycle the audio and visual signifiers of the trauma of the Blitz.

When a Whitehall official in *Behemoth* is asked to start evacuating London, he replies, 'Why we didn't even do that at the height of the Blitz. Yet despite the films' 'panic narratives', they retain a sense of stability and order. Britain under threat is still protected by the powers of an immutable state. Regardless of the period's crisis of hegemony, the Britain of the films depends on and trusts authority. As Andrew Tudor writes, 'We can do nothing but rely on the state, in the form of military, scientific and governmental elites. Only they have the recourse to the technical knowledge and coercive resources necessary for our defence' (Tudor 1987: 220).

Yet it is displays of panic that dominate the films. Terrified crowds rush and stumble; there is even, in *Gorgo*, the standard shot of a little girl's doll being trampled underfoot. Under the title 'PANIC IN THE STREETS', the British press-book for *Behemoth* claims that the 'scenes showing the panic-stricken mobs fleeing in terror…are the most realistic ever seen on the cinema screen'. Relevant here are the exploitation tips in the British pressbooks for the three films, which aimed at stimulating 'unBritish' panic. To publicise *Gorgo*, it is suggested that the local area is adorned with streamers and stickers stating 'RUN FOR YOUR LIVES − GORGO IS COMING!'; the stickers are to be 'fixed to shop windows, on fencing, on cleaning and laundry packages'. For *Behemoth*, promoters are advised to tour the community in a van, making loudspeaker announcements: 'YOUR ATTENTION PLEASE − YOUR ATTENTION PLEASE − YOU HAVE BEEN WARNED, BRITAIN IS IN PERIL, "BEHEMOTH, THE SEA MONSTER" IS HEADING THIS WAY.' Pressbooks for all three films suggested that mock news-papers be distributed on the streets warning of an impending disaster. For *Behemoth* an emergency edition of a fictitious *Graphic Gazette* was to be placed 'outside newspaper shops, on news-sellers stands and with "newsboys" standing at streetcorners', while for *Gorgo* the fictitious *Daily Globe* contained 'eye-witness accounts of Gorgo's terrible path of destruction', supported by newsbills announcing 'Panic as Gorgo approaches'. These were just part of the films' construction of panic arenas: displays of urban chaos performed and exploited for the purpose of entertainment.

Acknowledgements

I would like to thank Sarah Davy, Roy Smith and James Chapman for their invaluable comments and suggestions.

Note

1 In 1964, the Post Office Tower was completed. At 620 feet, it remained until 1980 Britain's tallest building. It is climbed by a giant female ape in the British colossal creature movie *Queen Kong* (1976). An extremely rare film, it was made for some $700, 000 as an attempted parody of the 1976 remake of *King Kong*, which cost $32 million. In *Queen Kong*, a colossal ape is discovered on a tropical island near Brighton and brought to the capital, where it is displayed at the London Palladium. Unfortunately, it is freed by a 'deputation of the nation's women, marching for liberation and equality' and begins demolishing London. The film has never been shown due to a successful court injunction from the producers of both versions of *King Kong*, RKO and Dino de Laurentiis.

Bibliography

Bennett, Tony and Woollacott, Janet (1987) *Bond and Beyond: The Political Career of a Popular Hero*, London: Macmillan.

Doherty, Thomas (1988) *Teenagers and Teenpics: The Juvenilization of American Movies in the 1950s*, London: Unwin Hyman.

Lourié, Gene [Eugène] (1960) 'A background to horror', *Films and Filming* 6, 5: 14.

—— (1978) (untitled), *Film Comment* 14, 3: 51–4.

—— (1985) *My Work in Films*, San Diego: Harcourt, Brace Jovanovich.

Luciano, Patrick (1987) *Them or Us: Archetypal Interpretations of Fifties Alien Invasion Films*, Bloomington: Indiana University Press.

Napier, Susan J. (1996) 'Panic sites: the Japanese imagination of disaster from *Godzilla* to *Akira*', in J. W. Treat (ed.) *Contemporary Japan and Popular Culture*, Surrey: Curzon Press.

Noriega, Chon A. (1996) 'Godzilla and the Japanese imagination: when *Them!* is U.S.', in Mick Broderick (ed.) *Hibakusha Cinema: Hirsohima, Nagasaki and the Nuclear Image in Japanese Film*, London: Kegan Paul.

Pyle, Forest (1993) 'One bad movie too many: Sam Shepherd's visions of excess', *The Velvet Light Trap* 32: 13–22.

Root, Deborah (1996) *Cannibal Culture: Art, Appropriation and the Commodification of Difference*, Oxford: Westview.

Torgovnick, Marianna (1991) *Gone Primitive: Savage Intellects, Modern Lives*, Chicago: University of Chicago Press.

Tudor, Andrew (1987) *Monsters and Mad Scientists: A Cultural History of the Horror Movie*, Oxford: Blackwell.

7   *The Day the Earth Caught Fire*

I. Q. Hunter

Marvellous, isn't it? You never know what's going to hit you next these days. Get across the street safely, there's a bloody jet falling on you – if you don't die of cancer from smoking thirty a day. That's peacetime, that is – without the bleeding Bomb.

80,000 Suspects (1963)

Probably, we will never be able to determine the psychic havoc of the concentration camps and the atom bomb upon the unconscious mind of almost everyone alive in these years.

(Mailer 1961: 282)

In 1954, two years after Britain exploded its first atomic bomb, the director Val Guest wrote a screen treatment about American and Russian nuclear tests throwing the Earth off its axis and sending it on a collision course with the sun. He had been inspired by 'all these people writing to *The Times* and saying how all these atomic tests were changing the atmosphere and the weather, and other people were saying: "What absolute rubbish!" but I suddenly thought: "What if these tests did do that? What could happen?"' (Brosnan 1978: 145). His scenario was unusually serious and 'adult' for a British science fiction film. Whereas most British sf films of the time were about rampaging monsters, like *Gorgo* (1961) and *Konga* (1960), or local incursions of hostile aliens, *The Day the Earth Caught Fire* (1961) combined the disaster epic with romantic melodrama and the social problem film. The absence of monsters, alien blobs and other clichés of the contemporary sf-horror genre made it a hard project to sell. Although Guest had a proven track record in the genre, having prompted the British sf boom with *The Quatermass Experiment* (1955), *The Day the Earth Caught Fire* was rejected by several companies before Michael Balcon and British Lion agreed to back it in 1961, with Guest putting up part of the finance with the profits from his Cliff Richard film *Expresso Bongo* (1959). As Guest recalled:

I got the idea eight years before I made it. It wasn't that I didn't want to do it, but in every one of those years I made a film that was successful and someone would say to me, 'What do you want to do next?' When I told them about *The Day the Earth Caught Fire*, they'd say, 'You must be mad, who wants to know about bombs and things? No, no, get on with the things you know how to do.' And I did that for eight years! But in the eighth year, I thought, 'I'm going to make this, sink or swim.'

(Jezard 1995b: 12)

Guest completed the screenplay with Wolf Mankowitz, his writing partner on *Expresso Bongo*, who appears to have contributed the dialogue and details of the journalistic milieu (Warren 1986: 618). The result, critically acclaimed at the time, remains one of the finest British science fiction films and a minor classic of the genre. Although seemingly little known outside Britain despite its initial success in America (Warren 1986: 614), *The Day the Earth Caught Fire* has kept its reputation: a recent, albeit wholly unscientific, poll of cinephiles classed it among the top 100 British films (*Classic Television* June/July 1998: 10).

The story is told in flashback through the eyes of Peter Stenning (Edward Judd), a journalist at the *Daily Express*, who is a stereotypical semi-alcoholic reporter: his marriage has failed, his talents are going to waste, and he cares only for his young son, who lives with Stenning's estranged wife and her new lover. Reports start to arrive in Fleet Street of bizarre weather all over the world: blizzards in New York, floods in the Sahara, tornados in Russia. Britain experiences first heat, then fog and finally drought. Stenning and the *Express*'s science correspondent, Bill Maguire (Leo McKern), discover the truth hidden by the official explanations: simultaneous nuclear tests by America and Russia have tilted the Earth's axis and diverted its orbit towards the sun. Stenning is passed this information by Jeannie (Janet Munro), a telephone operator at the Meteorological Office with whom he is having an affair. Jeannie is arrested as a traitor, but she is later released and found work at the *Express*. As the Earth swelters, emergency measures are declared, water is rationed and people are evacuated from the cities. Panic ensues around the world, and in Chelsea beatniks run riot, looting and overturning cars. Finally all nations unite in a desperate plan to explode four giant bombs to restore the Earth's orbit. On the day of detonation Stenning dictates a last story on the future of mankind. The *Express* prepares two front page pulls bearing the headlines 'World Doomed' and 'World Saved', but the sound of bells ringing in St Paul's as Stenning walks through a deserted London suggest that the attempt has succeeded and that the Earth will survive.

Guest, who had been a freelance journalist and British editor of *The Hollywood Reporter*, aimed at a *cinema verité* style of realism in his genre films. His approach was influenced by Elia Kazan's *Panic in the Streets* (1950): 'It made a lasting impression on me. It had such immediacy and was so stark that you felt you were really in it' (Jezard 1995a: 13). *The Quatermass Experiment*, he said, was done 'almost factually, as a newsreel or reportage. No science fiction film had been done like that before' (Jezard 1995b: 9). Even his fantastical romp, *When Dinosaurs Ruled the Earth* (1970), was touted as a prehistoric documentary.

While the grey flatness of style of most cheap science fiction films tended in any case to give them a look of impoverished 'realism' – extravagant art direction and special effects were reserved for big-budget American productions such as *The Time Machine* (1960) – Guest sought a more hard-edged, documentary quality by the use of location shooting, quirky characterisations and sympathetic attention to the details of everyday life. The location shooting of London in *The Day the Earth Caught Fire*, in black and white widescreen Dyaliscope, is as vivid as that of Manchester in Guest's *noir*ish crime film, *Hell is a City* (1960), and of Bath in his later 'panic narrative', *80,000 Suspects* (1963). Filming took place across the capital: in Battersea Park, where fog machines created the mists that sweep down the Thames; in Fleet Street, where the police allowed Guest to film for three minutes at a time before the traffic was let through again; and in Trafalgar Square, where the actors mingled with demonstrators at a real anti-nuclear rally (Brosnan 1978: 146). Cameras were invited into the foyer of the *Daily Express* building and into some of its offices and corridors, but most of the interiors were shot in a replica of the editorial rooms built at Shepperton Studios. For authenticity the Editor in the film was played by Arthur Christiansen, who had edited the *Express* till 1958.

To compensate for the low budget of £300,000, stock footage of flood, drought and other natural disasters often stood in for newly created special effects. Les Bowie, who directed the effects, had suggested changes to the screenplay in pre-production that would make the remaining illusions simpler and cheaper to achieve. His work was not always very successful. The mists on the Thames, for example, which required not only fog machines on location but the use of travelling mattes, were especially disappointing, as Bowie himself admitted: 'the result had fringing around it and looked awful so I wanted to do it again but they said no, they couldn't afford the money' (Brosnan 1976: 77). More impressive are the panoramic matte paintings of London stricken and depopulated by the heat. (To indicate the rising temperature some prints were tinted a sickly yellow in the opening and closing scenes.) They produce an estranging and eerily beautiful effect of disturbed normality, rather as if the city were in the aftermath of a nuclear strike. And indeed throughout the film the heat works powerfully as a metaphor of nuclear radiation.

By 1961 nuclear tests were a hackneyed premise of science fiction. Radioactivity had already set loose all manner of seabeasts, giant bugs and other denizens of the exploitation movie. London itself suffered the attentions of such lumbering, oversized metaphors in three 'colossal creature' films – *The Giant Behemoth* (1959), *Gorgo* and *Konga* – which both evoke images of the Blitz and anticipate the devastation of nuclear war (see Conrich, this volume). However, at the end of the 1950s several, more prestigious, American films imagined nuclear fallout without resorting to the exotic allegories of the creature feature. Such films as *On the Beach* (1960) and *The World, the Flesh and the Devil* (1959) were serious, even pretentious, message movies, which aimed at topical social significance, and which aspired to reach an international mainstream audience. The decisive influence on Guest was Stanley Kramer's pompous, leaden but impeccably high-minded *On the Beach*, whose success confirmed that there was a market for big-budget serious science fiction. Guest borrowed Kramer's conceit of the Earth silenced by an apocalypse that was all whimper and no bang, but took a more imaginative and oblique approach (see figure 16). As usual in British sf the focus is on the response of a small community (in this case the *Daily Express*) to 'alien' threats to the British way of life. With the exception of some friendly bobbies, Guest does not show the response of the military and scientific establishments, and keeps politicians, scientists and soldiers firmly off screen. He concentrates instead on journalists, who professionally exploit disaster rather than seek to avert it, and for whom the end of the world is the biggest scoop of all time. This sideways, journalistic perspective lends his film an irreverence and lively cynicism which prevents it from merely celebrating science and the military. Although the drama is unspectacular and often talky, the talk is fortunately that of a fast-moving newspaper film. Instead of the inert pseudo-scientific exchanges of many sf movies, the screenplay consists of sardonic banter delivered in quick-fire overlapping dialogue whose realism drew praise from many reviewers. 'I have never seen a more authentic picture of newsmen at work,' the *Evening Standard* declared (23 November 1961). Even Stenning's portentous voiceover in the final scene makes sense as literally overheated tabloid purple prose. As in *Invasion* (1966) and *The Night of the Big Heat* (1967) the relative lack of action sequences and special effects directs attention not only to the tensions between ordinary people but also to the deeper concern of British sf films at the time: a general, subtly communicated unease about contemporary social tensions, Britain's loss of power, and the psychological impact of what would be called 'Bomb Culture' (Nuttall 1970).

The premise of *The Day the Earth Caught Fire* was certainly topical and politically charged. The first British H-bomb tests had been held at Christmas Island in 1957, and nuclear tests by all countries reached a peak in 1958 with 100 in one year, double the number in 1957. A moratorium was agreed in 1959 but the USA and Russia renewed tests two years later. The film was released in November 1961 at the height of the Campaign for Nuclear Disarmament and only two months after some of the anti-Bomb Committee of 100, including Bertrand Russell, had been arrested (Minnion and Bolsover 1983: 42–55). Consequently many reviewers, especially in the trade press, saw the film as provocative and even advocating disarmament: 'Powder and shot for the Aldermaston marchers,' *Kine Weekly* remarked (16 November 1961); '[it] will cause all classes, and women in particular, furiously to think. In short, the film does the work of a whole army of anti-bomb squatters.' The left-wing press, however, was scathing about its exploitation of contemporary fears and

> its glorification of the popular press. With human kind threatened with extinction, the *Daily Express* manages to keep the Dunkirk spirit intact. A journalistic version of the stiff upper lip is very much in evidence.

Figure 16 A quiet apocalypse': Edward Judd and Janet Munro in *The Day the Earth Caught Fire* (1962).
Source: Courtesy of the British Cinema and Television Research Group archive

What really counts – we are given to understand – is to perpetuate the values personified in the *Daily Express* as we know it.

(*Tribune* 8 December 1961)

The film-makers naturally claimed balance: 'We are not pro-nuclear or anti-nuclear in the film. We are presenting the facts so that the audience can make up its own mind' (*KineWeekly* 25 May 1961: 16).

In fact the film's mild subversiveness lies not so much in its commitment to disarmament, which is ambiguous at best, as in its questioning of 'the Dunkirk spirit' and its cynicism towards the governing class as a whole. There are echoes here of Guest's *Quatermass II* (1957), based on Nigel Kneale's TV serial, in which the establishment is taken over by alien invaders, and progress, represented by Quatermass, is hampered by meddling bureaucrats and unimaginative military minds. In *The Day the Earth Caught Fire* the government and its scientists are not actively malevolent so much as cautious, patronising, ineffectual and self-serving. While the British Establishment waffles and stalls, it is left to the Russians – the totalitarian enemy – eventually to confirm the truth of Stenning's story. The film thus shares with Ealing, the Boultings and the *Carry On* films an hostility both to old-fashioned bureaucracy and to the new paternalism of the Welfare State. Its sympathies are with the individual conscience and the claims of tight little communities like the *Daily Express*, with its newsroom values of professionalism and devotion to a good story. (*Tribune* was right of course to mistrust the film's propaganda for the *Express*, which the newspaper repaid with several weeks of favourable copy (*KineWeekly* 8 February 1962: 22). The *Express* was itself part of the Establishment, being owned by the patriarchal Canadian Beaverbrook, 'the Old Man', and, among other things, was not remotely sympathetic to nuclear disarmament).

The film's cosy anarchism is given a contemporary edge by Stenning, whom the *Monthly Film Bulletin* described as an 'Angry Young Man of Fleet Street' (December 1961: 164). Although brought back into line by the end of the film, he spits out some impressively misanthropic Jimmy Porter-isms along the way: 'Now they want to read about the filthy, self-destructive, self-hating nuclear force humanity carries around rotting in its belly....The human race has been poisoning itself for years with a great big smile on its face!' Stenning's treatment of Jeannie shows the ethics of the press clashing with those of the paternalist state – indeed the *Monthly Film Bulletin* (December 1961: 164) saw the film as an exposé of journalistic practice. Stenning betrays Jeannie in the public good – or rather to secure an exclusive – when she passes secret information to him, but it is the government which seems more dangerous to national security. Jeannie is culpable largely for her naiveté about the Establishment – 'The people at the top are cleverer than we are,' she tells Stenning, 'they know what they're doing.' The film's politics are those of the pub-philosopher who distrusts 'Them' on principle, and appropriately enough much of the action takes place in Harry's Bar, a Fleet Street drinking-hole where Maguire is the resident cynic and voice of the less deceived common man.

Whereas 1950s sf films often mingled fear of the bomb with anticommunism, it is striking that by the end of the decade nuclear disaster was blamed more frequently on science, accident and human frailty than on the Russians. In *The World, the Flesh and the Devil, On the Beach* and even in low-budget American features like *Teenage Caveman* (1958), the cause of armageddon is either unclear or, as later in *Dr Strangelove* (1964), the inevitable outcome of the madness of modern life. Scientists and politicians of all countries are equally at fault in letting science take over. In fact British sf films generally are far more inward looking than American ones and far less paranoid about the Russians. As Marcia Landy says, they 'focus on broad social instability, the false promises of science, and cold war threats, much like their American counterparts [but] do not seem so virulently anti-Communist' (Landy 1991: 395). This is certainly true of *The Day the Earth Caught Fire*, which is unconcerned with the rights and wrongs of the Cold War, but which, like so much British sf, from Wyndham to the 1998 TV serial *Invasion: Earth*, looks backwards instead to the Second World War (see Pirie 1973: 30–3). The experience of the war, and particularly that of the Blitz, is taken as archetypal of Britain's 'unshaken spirit' and sturdy civilian resistance to national danger (Taylor 1975:

612). It was one of those 'moments of supreme crisis', the response to which Orwell found characteristic of the English, when 'the whole nation can suddenly draw together and act upon a species of instinct, really a code of conduct which is understood by almost everyone, though never formulated' (Orwell 1970: 77; on the creation of the myth of the Blitz and literary responses to it, see Hewison 1979: 27–52). Crucially, however, the film asks whether the sustaining myths of British – specifically English – strength of character embodied in the 'spirits' of the Blitz and Dunkirk are capable of surviving Britain's contemporary losses of influence and power.

The allusions to the Blitz are less obvious in *The Day the Earth Caught Fire* than in Britain's first 'atomic film', the Boultings' *Seven Days to Noon* (1950), in which 'familiar, almost nostalgic, images and experiences from the last war are the fabric of the film' (Guy 1999). *The Day the Earth Caught Fire* subtly reworks numerous memories of London under siege: the enemy is unseen; rationing leads to a black market for water; fires break out across the city (some of the newsreel footage seems to be of wartime firefighting); families are evacuated to the country. References to the Blitz pepper the dialogue: 'Like the old Blitz days, isn't it?' Stenning is asked at one point; while a newspaper headline about city-wide fires reads 'Blitz Rescue Goes On All Night'. Even Christiansen, bluff and bullying but with a heart of gold, echoes Churchill's role as wartime leader and propagandist: 'Keep the tone of the paper reasonably optimistic,' he tells his staff as the Earth spins towards its doom: 'The paper goes on forever'. The film's concern is how far the well-rehearsed wartime values of consensus, *sang froid* and the communal spirit are still relevant to Britain post-War and post-Suez. This theme is well summed up in the film's novelisation:

> The doorman sat up: 'I'm all right,' he insisted with a wry grin. He licked his lips: 'Tastes like tea…two lumps for me, miss.' Maguire thought to himself how typical it all was. It was like that wartime Cockney flying-bomb ebullience. Blitz bravado, smiles in the shelters, rationing ribaldry, jokes about Jerry. Anything to deflate the enemy. But this time, he thought soberly, who, or what, is the enemy? Maybe, this time, the enemy's within?
>
> (Wells 1961: 114)

The enemy to fear now is neither the straightforward evil of the Nazis, nor some communist fifth column, as in the Boultings' *High Treason* (1952), nor even an irradiated dinosaur. Rather, as Landy says about *Seven Days to Noon*, the enemy is modern life itself (Landy 1991: 405). The wartime spirit, and the ideas of national character that it reinforced, may no longer effectively perform its ideological work as, among other things, 'a powerful solvent of class antagonism' (Taylor 1975: 612). It may even turn out to be a self-deluding myth of British moral superiority (like the myth of the French Resistance in postwar France).

This is the theme of *It Happened Here* (1966), Kevin Brownlow and Simon Rollo's brilliant counter-historical fable – rather like *Daleks – Invasion Earth 2150 AD* (1966) —about Britain occupied by the Nazis. The British find that they adapt quite well to life under fascism: the ways of the Establishment mesh smoothly with those of the new order; numerous Britons collaborate with the enemy, not so much from political conviction as in order to help get the nation back on its feet; and the proverbial British genius for buckling down and seeing it through works to the Nazis' advantage. The British much prefer normalising the occupation to making a fuss about it and the collective stiff upper lip becomes an excuse for blinkered complacency. *It Happened Here* acknowledges the reality of the wartime spirit (many Britons do resist and become partisans), but questions how widely it was shared at the time and how far it could have withstood the trauma of colonisation. Occupation by Nazis, like alien invasion, nuclear war and the Earth catching fire, is the extreme case which tests to destruction the ideologies of the British character. *The War Game* (1965), Peter Watkins's docu-drama about Britain after a nuclear strike, offers the most bleak prognosis of the relevance of British myths and ideologies: when the bomb falls, civilians panic, the government turns fascist and society falls apart. *The Day the Earth Caught Fire* is more optimistic, for it predicts that Britain would hold out against panic and religious frenzy longer than most other nations, but it too suggests that the ideologies of consensus and national unity are waning because of new social tensions and uncertainties – generational conflict, the selfishness of consumerism, racial divisions, the stress of living always in the shadow of the bomb.

Britain in the film discovers that it is on the margin of events and that the power to change things has passed abroad. The theme was echoed in much sf of the period. As John Griffiths remarks:

> The way in which British writers [at this time] concentrate on the survival of the individual or the small group through or after a disaster suggests surely an underlying recognition, at whatever level of consciousness, that Britain is no longer in a position to determine whether or not such disasters shall take place, or whether or not Britain will survive as a recognisable entity.
>
> (Griffiths 1980: 92)

A sense of this is given by British sf films in the late fifties and early sixties (Hutchings 1993: 42). In the 1950s films like *Spaceways* (1953) and *The Quatermass Experiment* could imagine Britain pursuing its interests into space, but by the start of the 1960s, after Suez had undermined Britain's international prestige, few sf films pretended that Britain would participate in the expansive adventures of the space race and the New Frontier. Such pretensions were a topic fit only for satires like *Mouse on the Moon* and *Heaven's Above!* (both 1963). In *The Day the Earth Caught Fire* not only is Britain at the mercy of the two greater world powers but even its weather is no longer its own. At first the heat is like an Indian summer and the fog is merely an unusually bad pea-souper, but as the heat increases, the holiday atmosphere turns into tropical malaise and British cool and reserve reach melting point. (It is as if the Empire had exported its weather as some bizarre return of the repressed or in revenge for colonialisation.) As a woman in Harry's Bar exclaims to her rowdy male companions: 'All this heat is making you behave like foreigners!' Rather as in *Invasion*, *Night of the Big Heat* and even *Passport to Pimlico* (1949), whose famous opening shot transforms London into a subtropical paradise, it is when the nation hots up that things start to go haywire and Britishness itself starts to crack.

The romantic subplot warms along with the nation (at times it is even counterpointed to global events: for example, the lovers' first kiss is followed by a cut to footage of raging storms). The love scenes are frank, erotic and nuanced, with surprising small details such as Stenning toying with Jeannie's discarded underwear, and their sexual realism compares favourably with that of the 'kitchen sink' films.[1] In some ways *The Day the Earth Caught Fire* might even be seen as more progressive. Jeannie, for example, is a self-possessed modern woman who is more than a match for Stenning's angry young stud. She is stronger and more sexually aware than the hapless, misogynistically portrayed women in the New Wave films, of whom a surprising number fall into one of two grim stereotypes: older women who need sex and younger women who need abortions. Jeannie, for all her political naiveté, remains in control till the final scenes, at first rebuffing Stenning when he is crude and over-eager, though later needing him to rescue her from the rioting beatniks. While sympathising with the lovers, the film nevertheless worries about the unleashing of all this eroticism upon a nation already weakened by changing moralities (Stenning's family, for example, was broken up not only by drink but also by his wife's treacherous adultery). It is nervous about the sort of unbridled, unBritish emotion which finds its ultimate expression in the beat-niks' orgiastic panic and loss of control. This turn to extremism affects Stenning too, for he attacks one of the beatniks who is molesting Jeannie and sends him tumbling down a liftshaft. The dangers of undoing repression are handled more openly in *80,000 Suspects*, in which a drunken adulterous woman contracts smallpox and goes on the run with her lover. Like Caroon in *The Quatermass Experiment*, she creates panic in the streets, but rather than her smallpox it is her errant, uncontrolled and contagious sexuality which draws the film's censure and which seems more dangerous to the city's health. Both *80,000 Suspects* and *The Day the Earth Caught Fire* emphasise the importance of obligation, professional commitment, paternalism and the family, not least because such values are threatened by postwar social changes. The films' watchword therefore is self-restraint. As Durgnat comments (1970: 133), '[*The Day the Earth Caught Fire*] is untypical of Guest in putting the authorities in the dock, but the director's stress on individual responsibility still turns it into the spiritual antithesis of *The War Game*: whatever the threat, discipline and self-discipline will prevail.' Stenning, who learns from Jeannie self-control and ethical responsibility, becomes the film's moral centre. He is that stock character, the man saved by the love of a good woman. As Maguire sardonically remarks, 'Beautiful thing to see a woman reform a man. It only took the world to catch fire to do it.'

The film thus affirms even as it gently ironises the importance of optimism and keeping one's head. In the end London can take it and the nation mostly holds together, though this sometimes comes across as rote docility as much as stout common sense. For example, the Prime Minister's broadcast, a sharp parody of wartime appeals to calm and the stiff upper lip, includes a line worthy of Peter Cook's Harold Macmillan impersonation in *Beyond the Fringe*. Don't worry, he tells listeners: 'In Britain the weather is something we are used to coping with.' Unable to do much else the British can rest assured that they, like mad dogs, know how to put up with a bit of sun. As Hutchings notes, even 'the journalist-hero can do nothing except report the planet's rapid decline. Britain is once again powerless' (Hutchings 1993: 52). Most of the people, being used not only to peculiar weather but also to queuing, rationing, inefficiency, not complaining and making do, wait patiently for the authorities to set the world to rights. This kind of stiff-upper-lippery is lampooned in harsher tones by two later British sf films: *The Bed Sitting Room* (1969), Spike Milligan's aburdist satire about Britain keeping its end up in the aftermath of nuclear war; and *When the Wind Blows* (1986), in which an elderly couple potter around, make cups of tea and recall the cameraderie of the Second World War as they succumb to radiation poisoning: the Blitz spirit as stunned passivity. As Stenning remarks, in bafflement as much as admiration: 'Funny how when the chopper falls everyone just accepts it.'

Although Stenning is angry about the Establishment, it is the young who finally rebel, 'kicking it up a bit' in Chelsea to the sound of a jazz band, and using up the precious reserves of water for 'a real cool clean finish'. The *Daily Worker* (25 November 1961) was dismayed that 'the only long sequence showing how the "people" behave depicts youngsters rioting and looting in an orgy of depravity' (see figure 17). This rather misses the ideological point of the riot scenes, even if they do seem tacked on to provide excitement just when the permutations of the main plot have been exhausted. On the one hand, these scenes serve to divert attention from the causes of the disaster to its unruly effects, and from underlying social tensions to the antics of teenage hoodlums; but on the other hand, the young are not simply demonised, like the Teddy Boys who riot at the end of *Flame in the Streets* (1961). Alienated by the tired, repressive dangerous values of the older generation, they riot from terrified hopelessness as much as unscrupulous panic. Their rebellion, at once therefore feckless and excusable, is a sign, first, that consensus is over and, second, that the national self-image is frayed and unravelling. The rioters might therefore be compared with the consensus-thwarting youngsters who appear in other British science fiction films from the 1960s onwards: the alien children of *Village of the Damned* (1960) and *Children of the Damned* (1963), who hold adult authority in cold contempt; the juvenile delinquents of *The Damned* (1961), whose random thuggery pales next to the scientific sadism of the British state; and the roaming gangs of *A Clockwork Orange* (1971) and *Memoirs of a Survivor* (1981). These alien and alienated children represent a 'social problem' that would be unresponsive to liberal cure and authoritarian threats. So it is with the rioters in *The Day the Earth Caught Fire*, with whom the film sympathises insofar as they have nothing to live for, but whom it condemns for not finding within themselves the existential strength of character to hold out against despair. As Stenning points out, the disaster has come as a relief to many people because it exempts them from the stresses of living and from the terrors of the Cold War: 'A lot of people don't want to live,' he says. 'It's all too difficult. They're tired, puzzled and frightened. They'd rather it was all over than have to go on worrying and being frightened and losing a bit more hope every day, So they want it all to finish.' But, more interestingly, this hints at a deeper-rooted death wish in the culture of the period, which the disaster has brought to the surface and which became a defining theme of sf in the 1960s.

One sees it, for example, in *Quatermass and the Pit*, Nigel Kneale's superb 1958 TV serial, which Hammer filmed in 1967. It too ends with scenes of rioting which reflect suppressed tensions within postwar Britain, but here the riots

Figure 17   Flame in the streets: youth runs riot at the end of *The Day the Earth Caught Fire* (1962).
Source: Courtesy of the British Cinema and Television Research Group archive

are due to a race memory of alien intervention and erupt across the country in bouts of atavistic bloodletting whose purpose is to purify the human species. Kneale links the bloodshed to recent history, from the Holocaust to the race riots in Notting Hill in 1958, but his mystical pessimism puts off any more nuanced understanding of its historical causes. Violence is simply 'the Martian within us', an alien bad seed we must hope to outgrow (Kneale 1960: 188). In the novelisation of *The Day the Earth Caught Fire* Stenning compares the beatniks' 'party' to a race riot, as well as to the irrational, 'unBritish' brutality of the Ku Klux Klan:

> The world was on the brink of a precipice over which, within a few paltry hours, it might hurtle to its doom. These kids were not part of an exciting carnival. This was a defiant orgy, sinister in its undertones. Pete wished he could stop thinking of race riots. He wished, above all, that he did not have the thought of the Ku Klux Klan nagging at his tired, depressed brain; but this seemed to possess many of the elements of what he had ever read about that vicious, terrifying cult…This was a primitive outburst, inspired by fear, hysteria, and bravado, which could end in tragedy.
>
> (Wells 1961: 144)

As in *Quatermass and the Pit* the underlying fear is that postwar social changes, whether represented by the liberated young or by phenomena like race riots, will spark off 'primitive' urges hitherto damped down by consensual ideologies and the repressions of the British character. In *The Day the Earth Caught Fire* the young, with their liking for 'foreign' jazz, their alienation from wartime values and their consumerist contempt for the ethos of rationing, turn out to be the nation's weak point. If the crisis comes it is they who will be the first to give in. But because the riot seems an isolated outbreak of despair the film can stay fairly optimistic about both Britain's resilience and the world's chances of survival. As Robert Murphy comments, referring to Guest's films as a whole: 'Guest's protagonists, even when threatened by various unpleasant forms of extinction, seem to retain their belief in a benign universe where most people are basically decent and friendly' (Murphy 1992: 57).

Such optimism becomes unusual in sf films; Kneale's pessimism, which anticipated the genre's hardlined dystopianism in the 1960s, was both more pervasive and culturally respectable at the time. It is there a few years earlier in William Golding's *Lord of the Flies* (1954), filmed by Peter Brook in 1963, which takes for granted that boys would revert to savagery, territorialism and primitive magic if they were given the chance; and in his prehistorical novel, *The Inheritors* (1955), which depicts the extinction of the peaceful Neanderthals at the hands of Homo Sapiens, whose instinctive enthusiasm is for genocidal violence. It is there too in J.G. Ballard's early disaster novels, *The Drowned World* (1962) and *The Drought* (1964), which seem rather to embrace apocalypse than to fear it. Such Olympian bleakness finds its most unnerving expression in Stanley Kubrick's *Dr Strangelove* (1964), and in *2001: A Space Odyssey* (1968) (whose plot echoes that of *Quatermass and the Pit*). *Dr Strangelove* ends with the world blown up as Vera Lynn sings 'We'll meet again' – again an sf film refers back to the war so as to negate the relevance of its myths and values – while in *2001* mankind is nothing more than a weapon-wielding ape and the puppet of invisible alien masters.

The final shot of *The Day the Earth Caught Fire* is more sentimental, affirmative and audience-pleasing. Panning up to the spire of St Paul's, that icon of wartime resistance, it harks back to Britain's survival of earlier threats to national integrity. The bells ringing over the final credits, and Stenning's sermon-like, scrupulously apolitical voiceover ('what a pleasant thing it is for eyes to see the sun…'), add a vaguely religious note which reinforces the modest utopianism to which the film aspires.[2] The end of the film is therefore inconclusive, but it is not so much an open ending – as in *The Birds* (1963) – as one that is teasingly ajar: we do not see the world survive but it is safe to assume that it does (its survival is unambiguous in the novelisation). Détente, both political and personal, is gently hinted at. The Cold War has been inadvertently, perhaps miraculously, thawed out, and all nations are united as the countdown to detonation begins – the countdown is intoned in various languages over picture postcard shots of the Taj Mahal, the Vatican and so forth. Stenning has earned his moral revival, and defeated alcoholism, by his commitment to the ethos of the *Express* and by his love for Jeannie and his son. Personal differences are set aside too because, as Stenning and his wife agree, 'It all seems pretty ridiculous now, doesn't it?' It fell to later sf films, and especially to the horror genre, to explore the darker consequences of the collapse of wartime values and the corrosive effects of the 'psychic havoc' of the bomb.

Notes

1 The film was even sexier in European prints. The scene of Janet Munro washing her hair was filmed twice: once with her topless, for countries that had lenient censors, and once covered with a towel, for countries like Britain that had more restrictive ones (Jezard 1995b: 12–13).

2 The religious interpretation is explicit, and reminiscent of the pieties of 1950s American sf, in the novelisation of the film, which makes more of the heat being a Biblical punishment like the Flood, and in which Stenning finds himself at the end 'thinking of God quite naturally' (Wells 1961: 158). Unsurprisingly perhaps, religiosity seems an obligation in films about the end being nigh, not only in *On the Beach* but in the more recent *Deep Impact* (1998) and *Armageddon* (1998). To some extent the film's morality coincides with the Biblical sternness of later disaster films like *The Poseidon Adventure* (1972) and *The Towering Inferno* (1974): the good live and prosper, the bad drown, sizzle or tumble to their deaths down liftshafts.

Bibliography

Brosnan, John (1976) *Movie Magic: the Story of Special Effects in the Cinema*, London: Sphere.

—— (1978) *Future Tense: The Cinema of Science Fiction*, London: Macdonald and Jane's.

Durgnat, Raymond (1970) *A Mirror for England: British Movies from Austerity to Affluence*, London: Faber and Faber.

Griffiths, John (1980) *Three Tomorrows: American, British and Soviet Science Fiction*, London: Macmillan.

Guy, Stephen (1999) ' "Someone presses a button and it's goodbye Sally": *Seven Days to Noon* (1950) and the threat of the atomic bomb', in Alan Burton, Tim O'Sullivan and Paul Wells (eds) *The Family Way: The Boulting Brothers and British Film Culture*, Trowbridge: Flicks Books.

Hewison, Robert (1979) *Under Siege: Literary Life in London 1939–45*, London: Quartet.

Hutchings, Peter (1993) *Hammer and Beyond: The British Horror Film*, Manchester: Manchester University Press.

Jezard, Adam (1995a) '*Hell is a City*', *Hammer Horror* 5: 12–15.

—— (1995b) 'Reel life', *Hammer Horror* 7: 8–13.

Kneale, Nigel (1960) *Quatermass and the Pit*, Harmondsworth: Penguin.

Landy, Marcia (1991) *British Genres: Cinema and Society 1930–1960* Princeton, NJ: Princeton University Press.

Mailer, Norman (1961) 'The white negro' in *Advertisements for Myself*, London: Andre Deutsch.

Minnion, John and Bolsover, Philip (eds) (1983) *The CND Story*, London: Allison and Busby.

Murphy, Robert (1992) *Sixties British Cinema*, London: British Film Institute.

Nuttall, Jeff (1970) *Bomb Culture*, London: Paladin.

Orwell, George (1970) 'The lion and the unicorn', in Sonia Orwell and Ian Angus (eds) *The Collected Essays, Journalism and Letters of George Orwell: Volume II: My Country Right or Left 1940–1943*, Harmondsworth, Penguin.

Pirie, David (1973) *A Heritage of Horror: The English Gothic Cinema 1946–1972*, London: Gordon Fraser.

Taylor, A.J.P. (1975) *English History 1914–1945*, Harmondsworth: Penguin.

Warren, Bill (1986) *Keep Watching the Skies!: American Science Fiction Movies of the Fifties, Volume II: 1958–1962*, Jefferson, NC: McFarland.

Wells, Barry (1961) *The Day the Earth Caught Fire*, London: New English Library.

8 Adapting telefantasy

The *Doctor Who and the Daleks* films

John R. Cook

'Small screen invader': British sf tv versus British sf cinema

Why is British TV science fiction on the whole so much more remembered and loved than British science fiction cinema? Throughout its history, television has frequently been labelled 'the ephemeral medium' and it is only very recently that British broadcasters have developed anything remotely like a policy of preserving old material. Yet ask any thirty- or forty-something to list their favourite British screen sf of the postwar decades and the chances are high that it will be TV's *Quatermass* serials, *Thunderbirds* and *Blake's Seven* which will be named, not *Village of the Damned* (1960), *Invasion* (1966) or *Moon Zero Two* (1969).

Why is this? One explanation lies in simple nostalgia. Because TV intrudes so decisively into personal domestic space, its programmes are often able to achieve a greater degree of intimacy with their audience than the more communal, one-off spectacle of cinema viewing. In addition, as part of the domestic furniture of our existence, TV is inextricably bound up with the progress through time of our own lives. Old shows have the power momentarily to evoke flickering memories of long-gone eras of private history, underlining TV's unrivalled capacity for intimacy. Now, we chuckle fondly to each other as we reminisce how, as children, we used to hide behind the sofa whenever a Dalek appeared on the TV screen but what the child knew and the adults forget is that because of the very presence of TV in the home, the monster really had got right inside our living-rooms. And it was terrifying.

The capacity of science fiction creators to use television in this way not only to invade our homes but our whole sensibilities has to be contrasted with the very different attitudes which governed British cinema in the postwar era. As Julian Petley has argued, the dominant aesthetic was realism and, particularly in the immediate aftermath of the war, there was a strong movement 'among certain sections of the film industry and the critical fraternity' to create 'a distinctively British "quality film"' based around notions of emotional restraint and dramatic understatement which left little place for what Petley has tellingly labelled 'British cinema's repressed underlife' (Petley

1986: 109, 117). For him, there is a 'lost continent' of imaginative film which film critics of the postwar era, because of their general adherence to a 'quality' cinema of realism, consistently rubbished. Yet as Charles Barr has also pointed out, at the same time 'that cinema was disparaging its grasp of the fictional' during this period, television 'was rapidly developing its own strong forms of popular fiction' (Barr 1986: 215).

Certainly, a glance at the history of British science fiction films of the postwar years reveals the extent of the debt owed to that rival alien invader, television. With no substantial British sf tradition to draw upon (in contrast to the USA, with its rich store of comic-books and pulp novels), what is significant about British sf films, from Hammer onwards, was how many derived their inspiration and their sources from television, beginning life as dramas made for BBC TV.

The reason why television in those years offered such fruitful ground for a genre generally despised elsewhere in British culture was largely because it was then such a new and untried medium. As Nigel Kneale, author of the celebrated *Quatermass* TV serials (1953, 1955, 1958) as well as the BBC play, *The Creature* (1955) (all of which were later remade as feature films), notes in an interview elsewhere in this volume, nobody working in television during that period really knew what the medium was or could do. The rules of what constituted 'good' television drama were still being written and consequently, for a talented writer like Kneale, if one was lucky or astute enough to find a gap in the schedules which could be skilfully wrested away from the programme controllers, there was a chance to experiment with the medium in order 'to do something different'. This sense of freedom was in turn allied to the BBC's position as a monopoly public broadcaster in the early fifties. Having no commercial competitor (ITV was not launched until 1955) nor, in contrast to British cinema, any great need to develop product that might sell in international markets, there was, for a time, considerable space at the BBC for Kneale and others to create fantasy adventures which addressed themselves exclusively to British culture of the period and to the particular fears and concerns of the native audience.

What early pioneers like Kneale discovered in the process, through the success of *Quatermass* and its various sequels and derivatives, was TV's capacity for an intimate terror. The crabbed conditions of early British television – the small flickering screen in the darkened living-room, plus the primitive technical necessities of production which tended to favour the claustrophobic close-up – meant that it was comparatively easy to reach into the home and manipulate the feelings and fears of an attentive audience.

The two films based on the BBC's popular 1960s successor to *Quatermass*, *Doctor Who* – *Doctor Who and the Daleks* (1965) and *Daleks – Invasion Earth 2150 AD* (1966), both directed by Gordon Flemyng – provide a vivid illustration of the differences between what was possible in sf on British TV during this period compared to the general juvenilisation, exploitation and critical marginalisation of sf in British cinema. Yet in order for these differences to be properly understood, one must first of all consider the history of *Doctor Who* as a TV show, particularly the Doctor's genesis at the hands of his own unique 'Time Lord': the former Head of BBC TV Drama, Sydney Newman.

'The TV time machine': origins of the Doctor

An indispensable pioneer in many areas of British television drama, the late Sydney Newman effectively invented *Doctor Who*, laying out the parameters of the show in a two-page memo which he drafted for Donald Wilson, Head of TV Serials, in 1963, during the first months of his highly successful five-year tenure as Head of BBC TV's drama output. In the course of a lengthy personal interview with Newman in 1990, the veteran producer and executive recalled for me the original inspiration behind what was to become a celebrated thirty-year television franchise.[1] Most importantly for the subsequent films, his comments reveal that if British sf cinema of the period was not averse to raiding the TV schedules in its search for a popular hit, neither, too, were TV executives like Newman afraid to borrow liberally from the most interesting movies of the day.

It was, Newman explained, his admiration for George Pal's 1960 Hollywood adaptation of H.G.Wells's classic science fiction novel, *The Time Machine*, which provided him with the most immediate inspiration for *Doctor Who*. Newman had always been a big fan of science fiction and fascinated by its imaginative possibilities; an interest which had led him, between 1959 and 1961, to produce three successful series of a children's sf TV drama, titled *Pathfinders…*, in his previous capacity as Supervisor of Drama Production with the independent television company, ABC. If this fact again underscores how, particularly in British culture, science fiction tended to be collapsed with the 'juvenile', at the same time Newman's personal commitment to the genre would ensure that, once, installed as Head of Drama at the BBC, he would make every effort to push sf forward as one means of attracting popular audiences back to BBC Drama whilst it struggled to win the ratings war over its new commercial competitor, ITV. Accordingly, Newman was instrumental in developing such 'adult' science fiction series as the fondly remembered *Out of the Unknown* for BBC-2 (1965–71): a play strand in which short science fiction stories were dramatised for TV. It would be the much more mundane, earth-bound problem of how to keep Saturday night tea-time audiences watching BBC-1 which would lead him, however, towards *Doctor Who*.

The problem was that between 5.15 pm on Saturday evenings when the popular sports programme *Grandstand* ended and 5.45 pm when the equally popular teenage music show, *Juke Box Jury* began, there was a huge ratings dip as BBC-1 screened children's serial drama which consisted of adaptations of classic novels. Newman's brief from the programme controllers was to come up with a 'sexier' serial idea for a younger audience which would help build ratings as well as keep viewers tuned for *Juke Box Jury*. It was in this way that Newman, after considering various ideas, reached for science fiction as one 'catch-all' genre which might appeal to children and also bridge the gap between sports fans and the teenage pop music audience.

As Newman freely admitted in interview, having remembered Pal's film from several years before, he 'stole the idea of a time machine from H.G.Wells'. He also 'borrowed' the idea of an obsessed Edwardian-style inventor: an eccentric 'Doctor' figure who was 'a bizarre person'; a crotchety frock-coated old man who, via his machine, could fly backwards and forwards in time and space and 'land in the future or the past'. Newman, too, wanted the show to have an educational flavour for its young audience, in keeping with the BBC's ideals of public service. Ironically in the light of the serial's later development, he particularly stipulated that the show have 'no bug-eyed monsters' since he regarded this as 'the cheapest form of science fiction'. Instead, *Doctor Who* was to weave its adventures out of known scientific fact and it would also try to offer dramatised lessons from history. As Newman recalled in 1990:

> [*Doctor Who*] was defined as educational. If it went into outer space, it was never to transcend the scientific. It would teach kids about weightlessness, for example. It would also dramatise history. We would actually see Rome burning as Nero fiddled and so on. Its history lessons would be dramatic.

Just like the Doctor's invention, we the audience, in other words, would get to experience history at first hand through our own personal technological wonder: the TV set. In this way, Newman was recognising and exploiting the inherent quality of TV itself to be a kind of time machine, with the capacity to transcend time, offering up images from a variety of different periods and places.

Since we ourselves would be armchair travellers through time and space, accompanying the Doctor on his various adventures, Newman needed to make sure there were representative figures within the drama with whom audiences could identify. Accordingly and in keeping with the wide range of viewers the programme was trying to capture, the Doctor's first travelling companions were designated as three contemporary characters from 1963: two adults, one male, one female, and a teenager, the Doctor's 15-year-old 'granddaughter', Susan (played by Carol Anne Ford). Echoing the show's original educational intention, it was eventually decided that the adults, Ian and Barbara (William Russell and Jacqueline Hill), would be young schoolteachers who become intrigued by the mysterious behaviour of Susan at school and decide to visit her home in the very first transmitted episode, 'An Unearthly Child' (transmission date (tx.) BBC TV 23.11.63), only to discover she resides in a junkyard with her 'Grandfather': an irascible old man called the Doctor (played by William Hartnell). Not only that but Susan and the Doctor are revealed to be alien time travellers from an advanced civilisation – 'wanderers in the fourth dimension' – who, exiled from their home planet, now use their TARDIS (Time and Relative Dimensions in Space – a spaceship disguised as a police box which is actually bigger on the inside than it appears on the outside) in order to move through time and space. Having discovered the travellers' secret, Ian and Barbara find themselves reluctant passengers on the TARDIS as the Doctor realises he cannot let Susan leave with them. Frustratedly activating the TARDIS's controls, he inadvertently propels his companions into a series of adventures, set either in different periods of history or on different planets.

As *Doctor Who* progressed, Newman's original conception of the show as a series of dramatised history lessons gradually came to be superseded by a greater emphasis on science fiction, once it became clear these stories were actually more popular with audiences. In many ways, 'The Mutants', the second story of the first season, set the seal for what would follow. Written by Terry Nation, it is a seven-part tale (tx. BBC TV 21.12.63–1.2.64) which unfolds in the distant future on a 'dead planet', called Skaro, on which the Doctor and his companions land. It quickly becomes evident that some horrendous 'Neutronic' war between advanced civilisations has wiped out nearly all living things on the planet, leaving only scattered groups of survivors. On discovering a magnificent metallic city gleaming in the distance, the Doctor's curiosity gets the better of him and the old man knowingly tricks his companions into investigating by telling them a false story that the TARDIS's fluid link needs more mercury to get them off the planet. There, in the city, the travellers come face to face with what are to become the Doctor's arch-enemies, the Daleks: horribly mutated creatures which have encased themselves completely in dome-shaped metal structures as protection from the radiation outside and which, in so doing, have turned themselves into the absolute personification of cold, machine-like evil; their complete disregard for other life-forms chillingly summed up by their famous, metallic war cry: 'Ex – term – in – ate!!'

To the surprise of even the production team, this first appearance of the Daleks became a phenomenon, changing the whole course of *Doctor Who*. Something about these metal monsters clicked with the general public at the time. The Daleks helped *Doctor Who*'s ratings jump from an initial six million for the first story to around nine million for 'The Mutants', soon making the serial a national tea-time institution (Howe *et al.* 1992: 25). Inevitably, other Dalek stories followed in the next season (1964–5), beginning with 'The Dalek Invasion of Earth' in which the Daleks invade London in the year 2164 and later, 'The Chase' where the Doctor and his companions have to flee a group of time-travelling Dalek executioners, hell-bent on revenge for previous defeats. By this time, *Doctor Who* was at the height of its popularity, the second Daleks story having increased ratings by a third as many viewers again; for the first time, propelling the show into the weekly top ten chart of most-watched programmes (Howe *et al.* 1992: 43).

Despite being precisely the 'bug-eyed monsters' he had wished to avoid, the Daleks ensured the success of Newman's original commissioning goal for *Doctor Who*: the programme fulfilled its basic brief of attracting 8- to 14-year-olds to BBC-1 but at the same time, by not 'talking down' to its audience, it did not alienate elder siblings and parents while they waited for the later programmes. The large ratings indicated that adults were indeed tuning in, attracted by the imaginative quality of the themes and ideas which the show explored, as well as its clever use of the old-fashioned stand-by of the 'cliff-hanger' at the end of every episode. In marked contrast with the general marginalisation of British films of the period, Sydney Newman and his colleagues had shown that via television and programmes like *Doctor Who*, science fiction could cross over into the mainstream.

Decade of the Daleks

The wave of 'Dalekmania' which swept the country in 1964 did not go unnoticed by Milton Subotsky, a New York film producer based in England, who, along with fellow American Max J. Rosenberg, ran the production company Amicus, then a commercial rival to Hammer. In partnership with film financier, Joe Vegoda, Subotsky approached the BBC with the suggestion of producing a low-budget British film that would capitalise on the Daleks' success (on the making of the *Doctor Who* films, see Anonymous 1982: 26–30; Hollis 1984: 20–34; Miller and Gatiss 1996: 62–3). By December 1964, Subotsky and Vegoda had negotiated with the corporation and the Daleks' creator, Terry Nation (who owned part copyright), a deal whereby Vegoda's company, Aaru, would co-finance a film based on Nation's scripts for the first Dalek story. Also agreed was an option for making a second Dalek film should the first prove successful. In addition to co-producing the film with Rosenberg (while Vegoda took on the role of executive producer), Subotsky himself quickly adapted Nation's seven-part script into a ninety-minute screenplay, ready for the start of shooting at Shepperton Studios on 8 March 1965, under the direction of Gordon Flemyng.

 While the resulting *Doctor Who and the Daleks* film is essentially a remake of Nation's 'The Mutants', some of the key revisions and abridgements which Subotsky made to the original provide crucial clues as to his intentions for the film, as well as his perceptions of where its audience might lie. Together these offer a telling illustration of some of the widespread assumptions about what was deemed commercially possible for British science fiction in the cinema during this period as opposed to on television. If the BBC and Sydney Newman saw the *Doctor Who* concept as a means of fulfilling a public service remit by 'reaching across' to as wide a cross-section of the audience as possible, in the cinema, Subotsky perceived his best hopes lay in refashioning it into a vehicle specially 'niche-marketed' for children.

 In this way, *Doctor Who and the Daleks* irons out much of the adult content that might be thought 'troublesome' for children. A good example is how the character of the Doctor himself is reconceptualised. In the TV serial, he is an alien and accordingly, somewhat of a distant and detached figure. As portrayed by William Hartnell, he is an irritable old man, brilliant intellectually as well as deeply humane, yet not averse to taking out his frustrations on his companions, such as in 'The Mutants', where he wilfully deceives the others, endangering their lives through his curiosity to explore the Dalek city.

In the cinema version, such character depth and 'adult' complexity are gone. One of Subotsky's first decisions was that an international star name must play the Doctor. Accordingly, a heavily made up Peter Cushing was cast as the old man since Cushing was an actor whose many roles in Hammer horror films had made him instantly recognisable in America (see figure 18). In the two films, Cushing portrays 'Doctor Who' (this is how the role is billed in the credits) as the very epitome of the kindly, if eccentric, grandfather – a figure who, far from being 'alien' and intimidating, actively invites identification from the child audience. This is well illustrated in the very first scene of *Doctor Who and the Daleks* in which we discover Doctor Who at home on Earth with Barbara and Susan. Far from residing in a junkyard, this Doctor lives in a comfortable town house in London and when we first meet him, he is seen reading in his lounge beside Susan and Barbara, dressed in a velvet smoking jacket. Yet what is he reading? He puts the material down with a sigh of 'Most exciting!', as we discover it is none other than the *Eagle* comic featuring the popular science fiction hero Dan Dare. It is a clever joke with which to begin the film. It tips us off that in the next ninety minutes we, the audience, are in for a science fiction adventure of truly comic-book proportions. It also wittily suggests that for a true vision of the shape of things to come, the brightest minds turn to the pages of science fiction since the future is always going to be far more astounding than anything present-day science fact can predict. At the same time, the reading of the *Eagle* comic sets up instant identification between Doctor Who and the world of the child: not only is he a lovable grandfather but he is immersed in the same fantasy world as the child. He dreams about the future with the same sense of fresh-eyed curiosity and wonder.

Right from the start, Subotsky's version of *Doctor Who* makes a direct equation between science fiction and the 'magical' world of the child's imagination. This is in turn reinforced by the way the film version recasts the initial exposition scenes detailing how the old man and his companions begin their adventures in time and space. Interestingly, Subotsky draws upon the same source material as that which originally inspired Sydney Newman to conceive the TV programme: *The Time Machine*. Thus in the film version, Doctor Who is not an alien but very much human: a 'brilliant science professor', according to the unseen voice in the film's original trailer, who has invented a time machine which can whisk his companions off to strange new worlds and 'unimagined thrills' (*Dalekmania* 1995).[2] With his smoking jacket, silk cravat and frock coat for outdoors, he represents, like Hartnell in the TV version, the popular stereotype of the wise but eccentric inventor – an Edwardian fantasy figure straight out of H.G. Wells. When he pits himself against the machine-like Daleks, his is the old romantic image of the 'good scientist': the quirky, enquiring, free spirit committed to science as a means of individual emancipation and progress, versus the more modernist image of science gone wrong in the form of the coldly rational, dehumanising Daleks. In short: 'good' science as old-fashioned magic versus 'bad' science as new-fangled terror.

The film's most explicit link between the 'magical' qualities of Doctor

Figure 18 The Doctor (Peter Cushing) and his companions manhandle a pepperpot
Nazi in *Doctor Who and the Daleks*.
Source: Courtesy of the British Film Institute Stills, Posters and Designs

Who and childhood is made through the figure of the Doctor's granddaughter,
Susan. In marked contrast to the unearthly teenager of the TV serial, she is
recast as a child (played by Roberta Tovey) and portrayed as very much a human
granddaughter. Her function is clearly to provide a convenient point of identification for the target child audience. She is shown to be the brightest of
Doctor Who's companions in terms of her understanding of science and consequently, hers is a special, privileged relationship with the old man. Both she
and Doctor Who have the same innate curiosity to explore the Dalek planet
when they land and in this way, the old man's deceitfulness in the TV version
is recast by Subotsky as kindly collusion with Susan's questing spirit: a shared
sense of adventure in terms of a special bond between grandparent and grand-
child; one with which every young audience member is invited to identify.

Likewise, Subotsky reinvents the two adult companions who accompany
Doctor Who and Susan on their adventures – in particular, getting rid of any
uncommercial associations with education and the authority of schoolteachers. In *Doctor Who and the Daleks*, Barbara (Jennie Linden) is reimagined
as glamorous 'big sister' to Susan while Ian becomes her boyfriend who
happens to call at Doctor Who's house just as her grandfather is putting the
finishing touches to the TARDIS. As played by the popular performer, Roy
Castle, Ian's function in the film is to provide comic relief, as well as some

male action heroics, and his many prat-falls in the movie (whilst largely irritating to adults) are designed to make children laugh. It is Ian, for example, who unintentionally whisks the others off to adventure on the Dalek world after Barbara greets him in the TARDIS with a big hug and he accidently falls over on to the time machine's controls – once again, in contrast to the TV serial, absolving the Doctor of all blame. A year later, in *Daleks – Invasion Earth 2150 AD*, Subotsky and the director Gordon Flemyng adopted the same formula yet with some new characters – retaining the casting of Doctor Who and Susan but putting another popular face, Bernard Cribbins, in the role of Tom Campbell; a policeman who finds himself a reluctant stowaway on the TARDIS after he mistakes the time machine for an ordinary police box. His comic facial expressions and slapstick routines provide the light relief, while Jill Curzon as Louise, Doctor Who's 'niece', provides the glamour.

In this fashion, what was first conceived as a semi-educational, science fiction TV programme appealing to children and adults alike was reworked by Subotsky and Flemyng into two commercial movies explicitly aimed at Dalek-crazed schoolchildren. All of the changes to the original Doctor Who concept were made with this intention in mind. As Roberta Tovey (the actress who played Susan in both films) has summed these up, the changes were all to give the movies a 'much warmer atmosphere' and to make them 'much more family-orientated' (*Dalekmania* 1995). According to Gordon Flemyng, that was 'most emphatically' the market they were targeting, yet as he also points out, the producers quite consciously aimed for a 'U' certificate (universal for all) because 'most children went to see these ['U'] films without adults [and] they could shout and scream and cheer and do what they liked' (Howe *et al.* 1992: 130).

The movies were deliberately released during the school holidays: *Doctor Who and the Daleks* was premiered in London on 24 June 1965, while *Daleks – Invasion Earth 2150 AD* was premiered on 22 July 1966 before going on general release from 5 August 1966. As children's movies, both films do indeed try to endear themselves to their young audience by being 'warm-hearted' and 'magical' – *Doctor Who and the Daleks* in particular reinventing the neutron-blasted 'dead planet' of the TV serial into a kind of magic kingdom for a wondrous child to explore, with no apparent sense of irony. The only major aspect which has not been softened for the cinema is the actual presentation of the Daleks themselves. Though Subotsky and Rosenberg spent £4,500 in constructing bigger Daleks for Technicolor (quite a fortune in 1965), these are essentially the same creatures as on TV. Their ruthless menace has to remain intact as, after all, they were the principal motivation for producing the two Doctor Who movies in the first place. Even the very titles emphasise this – the original poster for *Doctor Who and the Daleks* foregrounding the word 'Daleks' in large block letters compared to the much smaller legend 'Doctor Who', whilst in *Daleks – Invasion Earth 2150 AD* the words 'Doctor Who' are not even mentioned at all.

War babies

What was it, therefore, that made the Daleks such popular icons in the mid-1960s? Undoubtedly, one reason was that, compared to the usual science fiction monsters of the time, they looked plausible: they were emphatically not 'men in rubber suits'. They were wholly non-humanoid in shape and therefore 'alien'. In large part, this believability was due to the efforts of the original designer of the TV version, Raymond Cusick, who, working from a brief by Terry Nation, that the Daleks should 'have no human features' and be 'legless, moving on a round base', decided the actors operating the Daleks should be completely enclosed in a dome-shaped metal casing that would appear to glide smoothly across the set. The Daleks were conceived by Nation and Cusick like 'Georgian State Dancers who performed dances in which their feet were hidden beneath long, flowing skirts' – elegant yet at the same time, 'hideous, machine-like creatures' (Howe *et al.* 1992: 124).

If the Daleks glided along like Dodgem cars at a fairground, they were also emphatically envisioned as horrible end-products of the machine age. Compared to the dream of science as the progress of humanity embodied by the Doctor, they represent the corresponding nightmare vision of science as the road to utter dehumanisation. In *Doctor Who and the Daleks*, these two competing visions are well illustrated by the difference between the Daleks and their enemies, the Thals. Borrowing heavily from images of the gentle, surface-dwelling Eloi versus the hideous subterranean Morlocks in *The Time Machine*, the Thals are represented as essentially peace-loving and agrarian. They are tribal wanderers who live in the open air, roaming the planet and farming it only for the food they need. Everyone is accorded the status of an individual and all are in complete harmony with nature. By contrast, in the Daleks, we find creatures that have utterly estranged themselves from the natural world to such an extent that they can no longer survive anywhere other than in special cities constructed entirely of metal. Moreover, they progress through collective, ant-like colonies, in which there are clear lines of structure and hierarchy – a wholly 'rational' order – but where any sense of individuality or emotion has been completely expunged. Theirs is the nightmare of urban dehumanisation in a mass society. Not only that but as the plot of the film unfolds, they (and we the audience) come to realise that far from their original purpose of using the city as a means of shelter from the effects of fall-out after a 'neutronic' war, the Daleks have mutated so horribly they now can no longer survive without radiation. Locked up in their cities, cut off from nature and immersed in a 'Cold War' with the Thals, the Daleks have become creatures of the nuclear age. To all intents and purposes, for audiences of the sixties, they are a lot like us.

If this may be one reason why the Daleks achieved such iconic status in the decade of the 'white heat' of technology, at the same time, it does not explain why thousands of fans actually *loved* them (on fan responses to *Doctor Who*, see Jenkins and Tulloch 1995). On one level, the Daleks may be the apotheosis of sixties Cold War fears but on another, clearly, there was something endearing, kitsch and even cute about them. This dual personality is well illustrated by Sydney Newman's recollections of the BBC Weekly Programme Review meetings he used to have to attend as Head of Drama, during the original TV run of 'The Mutants' story. There, voices were raised amongst departmental heads that the Daleks were perhaps too frightening. Newman well remembered the response of Huw Wheldon, the overall Programme Controller who was chairing the meeting: 'Nonsense,' he roared, 'I've got two little kids and they put waste paper baskets on their heads and run around yelling "Exterminate, exterminate!" (Howe *et al.* 1992: 27).

The Daleks were so successful not so much because they could be frightening but because they were so easily imitable to an extent that children came to identify with them. In terms of the two films, revealing insights into this come from the testimony of actor Barrie Ingham who played the Thal leader, Alydon, in *Doctor Who and the Daleks*. He remembers how there was 'this feeling amongst kids at the time not to be too beastly to the Daleks because they kind of can't help it'. The reason, he suggests, is because 'they were kind of like kids' (*Dalekmania* 1995). In short, just like children surrounded by a world of adults, the Daleks, beseiged on all sides by humanoids in their world, represented some kind of 'Other' to which children could relate. Protected in their shells and able to zap anyone who got in their way without consequence to themselves, the Daleks, in that sense, embodied a kind of wish-fulfilment for children. As Ingham sums the idea up: 'If I had an arrow around me as a kid and had known I could have zapped people as well, I would have felt great. That was the great thing about them to kids' (*Dalekmania* 1995).

Just like children in the exuberance of play, the Daleks really could not 'help it' if they did things of which 'responsible' human adults often did not approve. Besides, they were only machines. It was for this reason that on the *Doctor Who and the Daleks* film, Ingham remembers how 'a lot of very serious' discussion went on among the production team when it came to hurting the real creatures inside the machine structures. This resulted in a conscious decision that as Ingham puts it, 'we mustn't really hurt the kids – the creatures – inside the Dalek' (*Dalekmania* 1995). Instead, it is noticeable how, throughout both the Doctor Who films, the Daleks are never physically destroyed by their human foes but always 'exterminate' themselves. When, in climactic scenes, humans battle an army of Daleks, they invariably disable them by blinding their vision and pushing them round so that the Daleks come to point and fire at each other. In that sense, as with the old joke about how do you fool a Dalek (A.: Show it some stairs), it is actually rather easy to destroy them: a fact which only adds to their endearing appeal, especially to the 'vulnerable' young. Moreover, as Hammer expert Marcus Hearn has recounted, a special-effects creature for inside the Dalek was actually built for the first *Doctor Who* film but in the end not used because Subotsky disliked the violence and gore of his rival, Hammer Films. As Hearn puts it, everything in *Doctor Who and the Daleks* 'had to inhabit the same fairy tale land that Subotsky adored' (*Dalekmania*

1995) – a giant adventure playground for children where the Daleks became not so much the stuff of nightmares but simply that day's play opponent in a land of utter make-believe.

All of this was quite a long way from Terry Nation's conception in the original TV version of the machine-like Daleks as 'the ultimate Nazis' (Howe *et al.* 1992: 31). Interestingly, however, both films retain the sense, tangible in Nation's TV plots, of offering a partisan perspective on Britain's experience in the Second World War. Thus in *Doctor Who and the Daleks*, the inhumane collectivity of the Dalek 'reich' is pitted against the brave, plucky Thals who may not have the cold efficiency nor military might of their ruthless opponents but who more than make up for it in their willingness to stand up against all odds in defence of their freedom. There are also echoes of the Holocaust. The Daleks' war cry is 'exterminate, exterminate' while the Thals, at first, resemble the Jews: an innocent 'wandering tribe' who are tricked into entering the metal city on the pretext of receiving food, only to be slaughtered *en masse* by the Daleks.

Betrayed by the Daleks' 'racist' distrust of those who are different, it is at this point that the Thals are forced to move from 'jaw, jaw' to 'war, war'. As peace-lovers, however, they are extremely reluctant to take up arms and crucially, it is only through the intervention of Doctor Who that they are persuaded to resist. Camped out in the petrified jungle, the Thal leaders and the human time travellers debate whether to fight. The Thals protest they are a peaceful people and see no reason to kill others, to which Doctor Who retorts: 'Even when you know they would kill you?' The Thals reply: 'The last [neutronic] war destroyed almost everything on this planet....We do not want another.'

This replays the appeasement debate of the 1930s: the Great War as 'the war to end all wars' versus the Churchillian Doctor urging a fight for freedom against the Nazi-like tyranny of the Daleks. Like the TV version before it, the film leaves us in no doubt who is right: Doctor Who urges his companion, Ian, to pretend to lead a Thal woman away to the Daleks. Suddenly, this 'moral outrage' sparks something in the Thals – the woman's male companion pulls her away and punches Ian violently on the nose. Doctor Who looks triumphant: 'You see, you will fight for something,' he says. The political and moral argument has been settled. Male aggression is justified in some circumstances – for example, when one's own private 'territory' is 'invaded'. Hence the Thals will fight. As one reviewer of the film from the right-wing *Daily Telegraph* put it (21 June 1965): 'Very immoral, the way [the Doctor] overcomes his allies' tendency to pacifism and we are left with the idea that might is right, which will perhaps upset those in ivory towers but hardly ruffle practical parents.'

Doctor Who and the Daleks's ideological message was crystal clear to adult viewers of the time. The Churchillian ethos of morally justifiable aggression was what was being taught to the children of 'practical parents'. In common with many of the British science fiction films looked at in this volume, the

Daleks films recycle simple heroic myths of the Second World War. The important point, however, is that this takes place against the much less morally certain backdrop of Cold War nuclear politics, with its overhanging threat of global annihilation. It was one not lost on the reviewer of the left-wing *Daily Worker* who saw *Doctor Who and the Daleks* as 'a rather blimpish and militaristic' film 'in which pacifists were persuaded to become war-like citizens' (*Dalekmania* 1995).

Produced at a time when memories of the Cuban missile crisis were still fresh and the Campaign for Unilateral Nuclear Disarmament (CND) at its height, *Doctor Who and the Daleks*'s discourse on the 'impracticalities' of pacifism marks it out as a Cold War text. As with the original TV version, the film recognises, in its awareness of the radiation-scarred Dalek planet, the sheer horror of nuclear devastation but at the same time, its clear message is that freedom from tyranny is a price worth paying, even at the cost of utter annihilation. Britain's experience in the Second World War, projected forward into the nuclear age, becomes the ideological touchstone – in particular, the Churchillian romance of the plucky underdogs at their best only when called to fight; confronting impossible odds for the ultimate 'rightness' of a cherished democratic principle. The film contemplates the scenarios that might attend the onset of a Third World War, yet it can only conceptualise these according to national myths surrounding Britain's experience in the Second.

The most overt illustration comes in the second Dalek film, *Daleks – Invasion Earth 2150* AD which was based on Terry Nation's TV scripts for 'The Dalek Invasion of Earth' (tx. BBC-1 21.11–26.12.64). As *Films and Filming* (September 1966) pointed out of the movie version's futuristic moniker: 'if this is what London will look like in 2150 AD, I can only say it looks very old-fashioned.' When the Daleks invade, it is a bombed-out, rubble-strewn London which they move through; one that seems explicitly designed to evoke memories of the Blitz. Their human subjects are all decked out in twentieth-century dress, while the 'Resistance' movement of freedom fighters which Doctor Who and his companions join is to be found deep within the bowels of that archetypal Blitz icon: the London Underground. On one level, the film plays out through the Daleks, its 'ultimate Nazis', what might have happened had Britain been invaded by a totalitarian power in the Second World War: presenting images of the Daleks enslaving the population and turning them into dehumanised, mindless drones (called Robomen). Yet the Daleks are also creatures of the radiation age and at the end of the second film, the full futuristic horror of their plot is revealed when it emerges their plan is to explode a nuclear device at the Earth's core in order to use the resulting magnetic imbalance to pilot it to their own planet and occupy it.

Hence, as with *Doctor Who and the Daleks*, Second World War images of heroic British resistance are pitted against the possibility of imminent nuclear apocalypse. *Daleks – Invasion Earth 2150 AD* invites its audience to contemplate the threat of invasion and enslavement from a hostile 'nuclear power', asking how would the British people cope? Would they unite together and resist heroically, rediscovering the spirit of the Blitz, or would society completely break down and descend into moral anarchy? Again, the film can only answer these questions with reference back to the experience of the Second World War. The second Daleks feature has a grimmer, more 'realistic' feel. The post-invasion Britain explored by Doctor Who is a land consisting of great acts of selfless heroism but also one of fear and collaboration with the enemy. Just like the experience of Occupied Europe in the Second World War, there are those willing to betray 'the Resistance', as well as black-marketeers and war profiteers such as the mysterious rain-coated figure, Brockley (played powerfully by Philip Madoc) who is prepared to collaborate with the Daleks, handing over Doctor Who to the invaders for his own personal gain as the film reaches its climax.

Despite this generally more intense air, not to mention its bigger budget and more ubiquitous and spectacular action scenes, the second Daleks film did not do as well in box-office profits as the first. The mid-sixties 'Dalekmania' which had propelled the production of the feature films was gradually winding down and as a result, Subotsky and Rosenberg's plans to make a third Dalek movie, based on 'The Chase', fell through.

Back to the future

Flash forward in the 'TV Time Machine' to exactly thirty years later and the appearance of a new *Doctor Who* feature-length movie in 1996, starring Paul McGann as the Doctor. Yet in contrast to the earlier Subotsky films, this was not a movie designed for the cinema but one actually made for television – the processes of production having altered so fundamentally in the previous three decades that the 'cinematisation' of television drama had now become almost *de rigeur*.

Moreover, far from being produced as a British film by London-based American entrepreneurs for a market of indigenous schoolchildren, the new *Doctor Who* movie was made by British personnel yet working in conjunction with an American (Hollywood-based) production company, Universal and with an explicitly American target audience in mind. Not only that but in contrast to the critical marginalisation of science fiction in British cinema of the sixties, which had tended to lead to the juvenilisation of the genre and its reduction to the level of commercial exploitation, science fiction had grown up thoroughly in the previous thirty years. Effects-laden sf was now a serious industry money-spinner and a genre enjoyed by adults as well as children across a new global market.

The new *Doctor Who* film was designed to reach that affluent under-45 adult audience – for example, featuring as Doctor not an elderly grandfather kind to children but a young, energetic British lead who not only engages in strenuous physical heroics but also, at one point, even shares a chaste kiss with his new American assistant, Grace. The old differences between the commer-cial simplicities deemed necessary for *Doctor Who* on film versus the greater story complexities afforded by the public service context of the show on TV had also all eroded. Now the interests of 'public service' and commerce had become inextricably intertwined. This new *Doctor Who* film had been made for US and subsequent world-wide distribution with the explicit co-operation of the BBC's 'commercial arm', BBC Enterprises, which had long recognised the unique selling power of the *Doctor Who* concept (not to mention the possibilities of memorabilia and merchandising) in terms of the large international army of fans that had remained fiercely loyal to the 'franchise', even after the final demise of the BBC TV programme in 1989.

Hence although the 1996 TV movie did not do as well with the crucial American TV market as had been hoped (plans for an American TV series have, at the time of writing, been shelved), at the same time there could be no doubt things had come full circle for Doctor Who since the days of Milton Subotsky's simple visions of a Dalek fairy-tale world for holidaying schoolchildren.[3] Now, there was a new 'alien' world for the inveterate time traveller to explore – a strange new world in which everything seemed to have been turned completely upside down. An 'unearthly child' indeed.

Notes

1 The interview with Sydney Newman was conducted and recorded by the author on 28 February 1990 in north London. Unless otherwise stated in the text, all quotations attributed to Newman are taken from this interview.
2 This and all subsequent references in the text attributed to *Dalekmania* are to the 1995 UK video release *Dalekmania* directed by Kevin Barnes for Lumiere Video. This highly useful documentary on the making of the two sixties *Doctor Who* films contains interviews with many of the cast members and production crew, as well as the complete original trailers for both movies.
3 Despite the lacklustre reception for the 1996 *Doctor Who* movie, newspaper reports from the 1998 Cannes Film Festival suggest plans may be afoot by the BBC to make another *Doctor Who* film – this time featuring the Daleks. There may be life in Subotsky's old dream yet.

Bibliography

Anonymous (1982) 'Doctor Who in the movies', *Doctor Who Monthly* November: 26–30.
Barr, Charles (1986) 'Broadcasting and cinema: screens within screens', in Barr (ed.) *All our Yesterdays*, London: British Film Institute.
Hollis, Richard (1984) 'The Dalek movies', *Doctor Who Monthly* January: 20–34.
Howe, D.J., Stammers, M., and Walker, Stephen James (1992) *Doctor Who: The Sixties*, London: Virgin.
Jenkins, Henry and Tulloch, John (1995) *Science Fiction Audiences: Watching Doctor Who and Star Trek*, London: Routledge.
Miller, David and Gatiss, Mark (1996) *They Came from Outer Space: Alien Encounters in the Movies*, London: Visual Imagination.
Petley, Julian (1986) 'The lost continent', in Barr, *All our Yesterdays*.

9 'A bit of the old ultra-violence'

A Clockwork Orange

James Chapman

'Nothing dates quite so rapidly as our ideas of what the future might be like,' remarks film critic Philip French (French 1990: 87). The main problem for science fiction in the cinema has always been that visions of the future which might seem prescient for their time can quickly become dated, anachronistic and absurd. Given the perishability of the genre, therefore, perhaps the most remarkable thing about Stanley Kubrick's film *A Clockwork Orange* (1971) is that it still seems so fresh some thirty years later. The film's early-1970s apocalyptic vision of a near-future Britain where law and order have collapsed and an authoritarian right-wing government resorts to brainwashing as a method of social control remains a powerful and often disturbing picture of a society in a state of moral and political decay. Indeed, there are some voices on the left which might argue that the film's prophecy was fulfilled by the events between 1979 and 1997: a Tory government in power for a whole generation, presiding over an increasingly divided society in which violent crime has become more and more commonplace. This is not to say that *A Clockwork Orange* should be interpreted as a prophetic allegory of Thatcherism, though clearly some of its themes and ideas did continue to have relevance during the Thatcher years. What can be said, however, is that *A Clockwork Orange* belongs to that particular brand of futurist science fiction which remains close enough to the present that it can legitimately be described as a realist text rather than a fantasy. There are no ray-guns or space-flights in *A Clockwork Orange*, nor even any elaborate special effects. The differences between this and its director's previous film, *2001: A Space Odyssey* (1968), with its technological fantasy and elaborate sci-fi hardware, could not be more pronounced.

A Clockwork Orange was based on the novel by the English author, Anthony Burgess, first published in 1962. The film, which for the most part follows the novel quite closely, tells the story of Alex DeLarge (Malcolm McDowell). It is set in the near future ('Just as soon as you could imagine it, but not too far ahead – it's just not today, that's all,' explains Alex in the opening voice-over). At the beginning of the film the teenage Alex is the leader of a gang of 'droogs', Dim, Pete and Georgie, who spend their evenings hanging around the Korova Milkbar. Stimulated by their intake of 'milk-plus' (drugs), they get their fun by indulging their appetite for 'a bit of the old ultra-violence'. Alex's gang kicks to death a tramp and then takes on and beats the rival gang of Billyboy in a gang-fight in a derelict opera house. Stealing a car, Alex and his gang drive around causing mayhem until they arrive at a remote house in the country. Alex tricks his way inside by pretending to have been involved in an accident. Once inside the house, Alex and his companions embark on an orgy of violence, severely beating the owner Mr Alexander (Patrick Magee) and forcing him to watch as they gang-rape his wife (Adrienne Corri). The next day, while his parents are out, Alex is visited by a social worker; later he enjoys sex with two girls he has picked up. Meeting up with his droogs again, Alex slashes Dim (Warren Clarke) across the hand to assert his authority after Dim has made fun of Alex's fondness for Beethoven (whom he refers to as 'Ludwig Van'). The gang embark on another night of senseless violence, this time raiding a luxury health farm where Alex kills the owner, the Cat Lady (Miriam Karlin) by bludgeoning her to death with her collection of erotic *objects d'art*. However, the police arrive, and, although his droogs escape, Alex is captured and sentenced to prison for fourteen years for murder.

Two years into his prison term, Alex is approached by the Minister of the Interior (Anthony Sharp), who persuades him to volunteer for the government's new experimental programme of aversion therapy, known as the 'Ludovico Technique', to cure him of his violent tendencies. The treatment is no less than a form of brainwashing in which Alex is pumped full of drugs and forced to watch a succession of pornographic and violent images, to the accompaniment of Beethoven's Ninth Symphony, which he can no longer listen to without suffering nausea. After two weeks Alex is released back into society, but upon returning home he finds that his parents have taken in a lodger who has replaced him in their affections. Homeless, he encounters two of his former droogs, Dim and Georgie, who are now policemen and who beat him savagely and leave him for dead in the middle of nowhere. Alex struggles to the nearest house, which happens to be the home of Mr Alexander, now a cripple and a widower, his wife having died after her traumatic ordeal at the hands of Alex's gang. Alex does not recognise his former victim, but Alexander remembers him and takes him in. Alex tells his apparent benefactor all that had happened, including the details of his treatment by the government. It transpires that Alexander, a writer and intellectual, is planning a coup against the government, and he sees in Alex the opportunity to discredit the government while exacting his own personal revenge. He imprisons Alex in the attic and tortures him by playing Beethoven's Ninth Symphony, which Alex can only escape by throwing himself out of the window in a suicide bid. Alex survives the fall, however, and awakening in hospital he is visited by the Minister who tells him that Alexander's conspiracy has been discovered and suppressed. The Minister believes that Alex is cured and wants to show the press and public that the policy of aversion-therapy has been a success. 'I was cured all right,' Alex remarks in voice-over, and the film ends with him lying on his hospital bed, listening contentedly to Beethoven (which no longer induces nausea) whilst fantasising about a life of more sex and violence.

Most commentators agree that, while the film follows the novel quite closely, nevertheless the dominant authorial voice is that of Stanley Kubrick rather than Anthony Burgess. It is placed in the context of Kubrick's *oeuvre*, comparable in both thematic and stylistic terms to his other films. To quote, for example, Philip Strick: 'That it *is* his [Kubrick's] tale…is obvious from the parallels in structure, emphasis and technique with all Kubrick's other dramas, from *Day of the Fight* in which arenas and split personalities find an uncanny preface, to *Full Metal Jacket* in which, once again, conditioned killers pursue the excesses of a fiercely private war' (Strick 1997: 218). The precision of Kubrick's *mise-en-scène*, the almost clinical formalism that is a characteristic of his work, is evident here, for example in the long tracking shots which open so many scenes and in the set dressings which add so much background detail (paintings, sculptures) that is not always present in the novel. Kubrick's obsession with aspects of film form is exemplified in the early sequence where Alex and his gang set upon a drunken tramp. The location is an urban underpass and the formal composition of the scene is a textbook example of expressionism: the set is lit by one strong light from the back (the entrance to the tunnel) while the foreground and edges of the frame are in almost total darkness. The gang members are silhouetted against the backlight, casting long shadows, their faces in blackness. The hoodlums therefore merge into the darkness of the tunnel, becoming, as in the classic cinema of German Expressionism, part of the environment which they inhabit. The fight between Alex and Billyboy's rival gangs is another sequence where action is staged for aesthetic effect. The location is a derelict opera house and the fight takes place on the stage, filmed in frontal tableau. The stage is lit by shafts of light across its rubbish-strewn floor, where even the debris is arranged in carefully abstract patterns. Many critics have remarked upon the balletic qualities of the gang-fight, and the movement is choreographed with all the precision of a dance routine in a musical. The most kinetic and violent sequences, moreover, are set to music, ranging from Rossini's 'Thieving Magpie' during the joy-ride in the stolen car, to 'Singin' in the Rain', which Alex sings mockingly during the assault on Mr and Mrs Alexander (see figure 19).

Thematically, as well as stylistically, *A Clockwork Orange* bears relation to Kubrick's other work. In particular, it has been seen as the third in a loose trilogy of futurist films which each, albeit in their very different ways, expose the dark underside of technology and progress and reveal a deep disquiet about the future of humanity. Philip French considers that *A Clockwork Orange* joins *Dr Strangelove* (1964) and *2001* 'to complete a trilogy of admonitory fables set in a bleak, dehumanised future' (French 1990: 86). In certain respects, *A Clockwork Orange* is a counterpoint to *2001*. If *2001* can be interpreted as a text of the late 1960s embodying the spirit of the flourishing counter-cultures in breaking away from oppressive social and political forces – most famously and spectacularly illustrated in the climactic 'stargate' sequence which is often

Figure 19 'Viddy well, little brother, viddy well': sex and ultraviolence in *A Clockwork Orange* (1971).
Source: Courtesy of the British Cinema and Television Research Group archive

interpreted as a hallucinogenic 'trip' – then *A Clockwork Orange* is a text of the early 1970s in which social control and authority is re-imposed by the ruling elite. Although the films are very different in that *2001* is a technological fantasy whereas *A Clockwork Orange* is much more a down-to-earth Orwellian nightmare of political repression and social control, there are nevertheless some thematic similarities in so far as both films posit a problematic relationship between humanity and science in the future. And both films also, of course, make extensive use of classical music.

In placing the film in the context of the Kubrick *oeuvre*, however, it is important not to lose sight of the contribution made by Anthony Burgess. Although Burgess was not involved in the production of the film – the screenplay was written by Kubrick himself – the finished film does show his influence as well as its director's. *A Clockwork Orange* was one of five novels which Burgess wrote in the course of 1961–2, his prolific output at this time due to the fact that he had been diagnosed (incorrectly as it turned out) as suffering from an inoperable brain tumour and given only a short time to live. It is perhaps his most personal novel in that it was shaped by events which Burgess had experienced at first hand. He wrote it shortly after returning from six years working abroad as an officer in the Colonial Service in Malaya.

Upon his return to Britain, Burgess was struck by the development of teenage gangs such as the Mods and Rockers, and the sub-cultures of coffee-bars, dress codes and slang vocabularies which they created for themselves. Living in Hove on the south coast, Burgess was able to observe the Bank Holiday gang-fights in seaside resorts such as Brighton. The novel, set roughly ten years in the future, describes a society where gang violence has escalated out of control and the government has resorted to Pavlovian techniques of brain-washing and conditioned response to control the offenders. One of the specific incidents in the novel had an even more personal basis. During the Second World War, when Burgess was stationed in Gibraltar, his first wife was savagely attacked and raped by a gang of four American GI deserters in London. She suffered a miscarriage, and Burgess always attributed her early death to the trauma. It is hard not to read the novel without seeing the character of Mr Alexander (a writer) as Burgess himself and Mrs Alexander as Burgess's wife, Lynne.

For all his personal and tragic experience of violence, however, the target of Burgess's book was not so much the gang culture itself as the notion that violent behaviour could be controlled by brainwashing. Burgess had been disturbed by accounts of new behaviourist methods of reforming criminals, particularly the work of American psychologist B.F. Skinner, who believed that the experiments conducted by Pavlov in the behaviour modification of animals could be applied to human beings. Burgess believed that this would erode the freedom of people to make moral choices. The freedom of choice, even if it was the choice to commit rape and murder, was, in Burgess's view, essential for humanity. As the literary critic Blake Morrison writes: 'His book, even before Kubrick's film, caught the anti-mechanistic spirit of the culture, or counter-culture, of the sixties, and took its place, somewhat awkwardly, alongside Ken Kesey's *One Flew Over the Cuckoo's Nest*, the works of R.D. Laing, and other books attacking the erosion of individual rights by penal and medical institutions' (Morrison 1996: xxiii).

The novel of *A Clockwork Orange* was published in Britain in May 1962 to generally negative reviews. Many critics complained that it was difficult to read. This was due to the style which Burgess had adopted whereby he used a first-person narration (by Alex) in an invented language which was meant to approximate the language of teenage gangs. 'Nadsat' was a mixture of American-English, colloquial Russian, Slavic gypsy dialect and Cockney rhyming slang. It is the language which Alex and his droogs speak, and the language in which Alex narrates the story. As a result the novel is quite difficult to read, and, indeed, when it was published in an American edition a glossary of 'Nadsat' words was added by the publishers, much to Burgess's disapproval. Furthermore, the American edition omitted the last chapter of the book, which had a profound effect on the story in terms of both structure and content. The British edition had twenty-one chapters structured in three sections of seven chapters each (each of the seven sections beginning with the rhetorical question 'What's it going to be then, eh?'). In the final chapter Alex has been released from hospital and is hanging around the Korova Milkbar again with a new gang of droogs. However, he now renounces violence, and instead has visions of settling down in domestic bliss with a wife and baby. It is symbolic that this occurs in the twenty-first chapter in so far as twenty-one is the age at which children traditionally reach adulthood. And, as the last chapter also begins with the question 'What's it going to be then, eh?', it is clear that Alex has made the conscious choice between right and wrong. But by dropping the last chapter, the American edition not only lacked the structural and numerical unity of the British edition, but it also ended on a much more downbeat and pessimistic note with Alex still in hospital and his future uncertain. 'My book was Kennedyan and accepted the notion of moral progress,' Burgess later remarked. 'What was really wanted was a Nixonian book with no shred of moral optimism in it' (quoted in Morrison 1996: xvii).

The novel aroused interest from Paramount Pictures in the late 1960s, and a script was prepared by Michael Cooper and Terry Southern, but in the event it was Kubrick who was to make the film, in Britain, backed by Warner Bros. However, it was the American edition of the book which Kubrick adapted for the film. Whether this was deliberate on Kubrick's part, or whether he was unaware of the difference between the two editions, is unclear. The result, however, was that the film omitted the more affirmative ending which Burgess himself preferred. While the original novel suggested that Alex had mended his ways, the film ends with the implicit suggestion that he is still looking forward to a life of sex and violence. In most other respects, however, the film is a faithful adaptation of Burgess's novel, and shows his original intent. The narrative of the film follows that of the novel in all but the smallest details, and the key sequences are transcribed from page to screen with much fidelity. Crucially, the film maintains Alex's first-person narration through the technique of a voice-over by McDowell and the extensive use of subjective camerawork, brilliantly exemplified in the point-of-view shot of Alex's attempted suicide where the camera was dropped down the side of a building to simulate his view as he falls.

The association of the spectator with Alex's point-of-view in the film is nevertheless uncomfortable and at times disturbing. This is particularly so in the scenes of violence, the most unsettling of which is the rape of Mrs Alexander. While the novel also describes the rape from Alex's perspective, a certain barrier is created by the use of the 'Nadsat' language which distances the reader from the full horror of the actions which are being described ('So he did the strong-man on the devotchka, who was still creech creech creeching away in very horrorshow four-in-a-bar, locking her rookers from the back, while I ripped away at this and that and the other, the others going haw haw haw still, and real good horrorshow groodies they were that then exhibited their pink glazzies, O my brothers, while I untrussed and got ready for the plunge' (Burgess 1996: 22).) However, what in a novel is left to the mind's-eye of the reader can be shown graphically through the medium of film. The rape is presented on screen with a degree of explicit and graphic detail that was unprecedented in mainstream cinema. Not only is the terrorised victim shown in full-frontal nudity, but a hand-held camera is used to film the action in close-up. The resulting scene is extremely uncomfortable, implicating the spectator in the rape as a voyeur. Burgess, who had admired *2001* and had hoped that the film of *A Clockwork Orange* would aspire to a similar level of 'visual futurism', felt that the representation of sexual violence was too stark. A Catholic, he privately felt that the film was pornographic, although in public he praised Kubrick for his 'technically brilliant, thoughtful, relevant, poetic, mind-opening' film (quoted in Morrison 1996: xviii). Perhaps surprisingly, given its content, the film was passed uncut by the British censors, a decision which provoked much controversy (Robertson 1993: 143–50).

Kubrick himself argued that the violence perpetrated by Alex in the first part of the film was necessary in dramatic terms as a counterweight to the brainwashing which he then received. In a rare interview he told *Sight and Sound*:

> It was absolutely necessary to give weight to Alex's brutality, otherwise I think there would be a moral confusion with respect to what the government does to him. If he were a lesser villain, then one could say: 'Oh, yes, of course, he should not be given this psychological conditioning; it's all too horrible and he really wasn't all that bad after all.' On the other hand, when you have shown him committing such atrocious acts, and you still realise the immense evil on the part of the government in turning him into something less than human in order to make him good, then I think the essential moral idea of the book is clear. It is necessary for man to have choice to be good or evil, even if he chooses evil. To deprive him of this choice is to make him something less than human – a clockwork orange.
>
> (Strick and Houston 1972: 63)

For Kubrick, then, as for Burgess, the essential theme of the story was the right to free choice. However, this makes it all the more curious that Kubrick should have based the film on the American edition of the novel rather than on the British edition where Alex is shown in the end to have made the choice between good and evil. Furthermore, Kubrick's explanation of the title in this context is also quite interesting in that the film omits to explain it. In the novel, 'A Clockwork Orange' is the title of a manuscript which Mr Alexander is working on and which Alex destroys as he ransacks Alexander's home. The incongruous juxtaposition is noticed by Alex ('That's a fair gloopy title. Who ever heard of a clockwork orange?'). This reference, however, is not included in the film.

Kubrick's justification of the film's violent content notwithstanding, it is that aspect of the film which has dominated critical debate around it. The critical reception at the time was mixed, though, as Charles Barr has shown, most of the serious film critics tended to be favourably inclined towards the film (Barr 1972). However, there was an orchestrated chorus of disapproval from the popular press and from the anti-permissive lobby exemplified by the Festival of Light and the National Viewers and Listeners' Association, with the latter body calling on Robert Carr, the Home Secretary in the Heath government, to ban it. A press campaign was orchestrated against the film, and there were several hysterical though unsubstantiated reports that it had led young people to commit copy-cat acts of violence (Robertson 1993: 146–9). Although *A Clockwork Orange* won acclaim abroad, being nominated for three Oscars (Best Film, Best Director and Best Screenplay) and winning the prize for Best Foreign Film at the 1972 Venice Film Festival, the controversy around the film caused Kubrick, who owns the domestic distribution rights, to withdraw it from distribution in Britain after its initial run. Thus the film has not been shown publicly in Britain since the early 1970s: the National Film Archive has no viewing copy and there has been no video release (though pirated copies do exist). When the Scala Cinema in London showed the film in 1993, the legal action which followed resulted in the cinema being closed down. Kubrick's decision to withdraw the film, which he has never fully explained, is probably the most effective censorship of a completed film ever implemented in Britain.

The current unavailability of *A Clockwork Orange* in Britain (it continues to be shown freely abroad, and has enjoyed extensive runs in Paris) means that for all the controversy around the film relatively few people in Britain have actually seen it. The film's critical reputation is therefore based mostly on judgements passed down by others. Its notoriety is exemplified by the harsh, opinionated verdict of the most widely read of all popular film critics. 'A repulsive film in which intellectuals have found acres of social and political meaning,' opined Leslie Halliwell; 'the average judgement is likely to remain that it is pretentious and nasty rubbish for sick minds who do not mind jazzed-up images and incoherent sound' (Halliwell 1987: 201). The sort of intellectual analysis which the great populist Halliwell held in such disdain would presumably be exemplified by the entry on Kubrick in the *Oxford History of World Cinema*, a rather more academic work than Halliwell's *Film Guide*, which suggests that in *A Clockwork Orange* 'the choreography of violence acts as a grotesque mask for a deep pessimism towards utopian beliefs in the rational management of social tension and conflict' (Usai 1996: 458–9). A similar point was made, though at rather greater length, by the *Monthly Film Bulletin* upon the film's initial release:

> From *Paths of Glory* to *Lolita*, *Dr Strangelove* to *2001*, Stanley Kubrick has shown himself an intrepid explorer of closed universes. The no-exit situations through which he rotates his characters result from so finely dovetailed a relationship between psychological obsession and social mechanism, that it is impossible to determine whether his characters' minds are intended as metaphors for society's prison or their external universe as a magnifying glass held up to the barren confines of the

human soul. Macro- and microcosm become interchangeable in Kubrick's coherent cosmos. A sardonic moralist, he charts the closing – in the name of progress – of the fields of moral choice; and his hermetic worlds breed the heroes they deserve. If *A Clockwork Orange* emerges as his most cynical and disturbing film to date, this is less because – as was already the case in *Dr Strangelove* – the nightmare future which it predicates is a recognisable extension of the present day, than because it so devastatingly and totally reduces its audience to the level of its characters, all of them perfectly adapted to the cynical system which contains them.

(*Monthly Film Bulletin* February 1972: 29)

Thus speaks the voice of the intellectual critic reading acres of social and political meaning into the film. The critic here is a woman (Jan Dawson), and it is significant not only that she attributes all meaning in the film to Kubrick, not Burgess, but also that she seems to side with Alex and finds his violence, even against women, less disturbing than the therapy to which he is then subjected:

If we are shocked by Alex's violation of bourgeois property (women included), it is only on an intellectual level, since Kubrick carefully distances his effects, postponing our physical discomfort for the moment when the 'therapists' screw their clamps on to Alex's eyes; by the time Alex regains consciousness in his hospital bed, Kubrick has us rooting for him to resume his thuggery – the only way left to us or him of saying 'no' to this dehumanised society.

The inverted commas around 'therapists' (the rapists?) implies what their treatment of Alex amounts to.

The debate around the violence of *A Clockwork Orange* has overshadowed all other aspects of the film to such an extent that its place and status in the history of British cinema, and of British science fiction, has been largely overlooked. It is difficult to place *A Clockwork Orange* in a particular cycle or sub-genre, although comparisons to individual films do suggest themselves. *Things to Come* (1936), for example, had posited a future (albeit after a destructive world war) where civilisation had broken down and authority was exercised by gangster warlords. A benevolent form of social control became necessary, implemented through the 'peace gas' of John Cabal (Raymond Massey) and other scientists in the name of humanity. The difference between the 1930s and the 1970s, however, is that whereas the earlier film had affirmed faith in progress and a utopian future, the later film was pessimistic about that future. On the one hand *A Clockwork Orange* shows a society threatened by the violent anarchy of the young, while on the other hand it asserts that in order to control that anarchy (which is itself a form of free expression) through behavioural conditioning will result in repression and the destruction of humanity. The implication of *A Clockwork Orange* seems to be that, either way, the outlook for the future is bleak. Unlike *Things to Come*, where science and mankind are ultimately shown to be in harmony, *A Clockwork Orange* implies that science and humanity are incompatible. It is a dystopian film rather than a utopian one, and in this context the closest comparison is to George Orwell's *Nineteen Eighty-Four* (1949), which also presents a totalitarian, authoritarian Britain of the near future. The similarities between Orwell's 'Thought Police' and the 'Ludovico Technique' are obvious. A comparison could also be made with *Fahrenheit 451* (1966), another film made in Britain by an overseas director (François Truffaut), in which a futurist fascist state asserts its social and political control through burning books. And Nicolas Roeg's *The Man Who Fell To Earth* (1976) shares some thematic similarities in its story of an alien visitor who comes to Earth on a mission to save his own planet but is corrupted by the influence of mankind. Like Alex, Newton (David Bowie) comes to revel in sex and drugs as the ultimate expression of freedom. What these films have in common is that they were all imaginative (if not necessarily entirely successful) works by directors of note who also worked in other genres besides science fiction. In the last analysis, then, *A Clockwork Orange* is not a film which can be located easily in the normal generic profile of British cinema, suggesting that it should instead be placed in an authorial context – a context which allows as much for the voice of Anthony Burgess as of Stanley Kubrick.

Bibliography

Barr, Charles (1972) '*Straw Dogs, A Clockwork Orange* and the critics', *Screen* 13, 2: 17–31.

Burgess, Anthony (1996) *A Clockwork Orange*, London: Penguin.

French, Philip (1990) '*A Clockwork Orange*', *Sight and Sound* Spring: 84–7.

Halliwell, Leslie (1987) *Halliwell's Film Guide*, sixth edn, London: Grafton.

Morrison, Blake (1996) 'Introduction' to Burgess, *A Clockwork Orange*.

Robertson, James C. (1993) *The Hidden Cinema: British Film Censorship in Action 1913–1975*, London: Routledge.

Strick, Philip (1997) '*A Clockwork Orange*', in Laurie Collier Hillstrom (ed.), *International Dictionary of Films and Filmmakers*, third edn, vol. I: Films, London: St James Press.

Strick, Philip and Penelope Houston (1972), 'Interview with Stanley Kubrick', *Sight and Sound* Spring: 62–6.

Usai, Paolo Cerchi (1996) 'Stanley Kubrick', in Geoffrey Nowell-Smith (ed.) *The Oxford History of World Cinema*, Oxford: Oxford University Press.

10 The British post-*Alien* intrusion film

Peter Wright

Although science fiction cinema has often explored the possibility of human–extraterrestrial reproduction, it was not until Ridley Scott's *Alien* (1979) that the theme received the disturbing treatment it invited. Following *Alien*'s release, the British sf film displayed a corresponding interest in making the human body a realm for intimate alien intrusion, for 'reworking...the primal scene, the scene of birth in relation to other forms of copulation and reproduction' (Creed 1993: 17). However, unlike *Alien*, which disturbs gender distinctions by depicting a man penetrated and giving birth, and by envisaging a post-feminist future (Kavanagh 1990: 77), the British sf-horror films *Inseminoid* (1980), *Xtro* (1982), *Lifeforce* (1985) and *Split Second* (1991) all adopt a more conservative, patriarchal view of women and sex.

Unfairly dismissed as a low-budget imitation of *Alien*, Norman J. Warren's *Inseminoid* follows an archaeological team as they occupy a research facility on a remote, inhospitable planet. Whilst investigating unexplored catacombs, Sandy (Judy Geeson) is inseminated by an alien. When she is brought back to base, she is two months pregnant. Growing heavier by the hour and consumed by an unnatural bloodlust, she destroys much of the installation and cannibalises her colleagues. After giving birth to alien twins, she loses her superhuman strength and is killed by Mark (Robin Clarke), who then becomes a victim of her offspring. Only corpses remain to greet the rescue shuttle, which departs with two stowaway alien twins.

Despite *Inseminoid*'s opening exploratory sequence, its labyrinthine base (filmed atmospherically in Chislehurst Caves), and its apparently derivative plotting, all of which recall *Alien*, Warren assures his critics that none of the crew had seen Scott's film (see Brown 1995: 30). What makes this assurance appear dubious is a seemingly imitative meal sequence in which Ricky (David Baxt), feeling unwell after his exposure to alien crystals, foils audience expectations by absenting himself rather than giving birth to a monstrous progeny. Nevertheless, the production schedules for each film do not sustain accusations of plagiarism. When Nick and Gloria Maley wrote *Inseminoid*'s screenplay, *Alien* was being shot on closed sets; when *Inseminoid* went into production, *Alien* had not been released in Britain. Hence, *Inseminoid* is post-

Alien in chronological terms alone, and its differences are more significant than its similarities.

Whereas Scott's alien represents 'a potent expression of male terror at female sexuality and at castrating females in general' (Newton 1990: 85) through its status as a fetish object of the nightmarish archaic mother, Sandy is a direct manifestation of masculine anxiety regarding female reproductive capacity (see Creed 1993: 16–30). Rather than transferring this fear of woman onto the alien other, *Inseminoid* constructs woman-as-other, overturning *Alien's* concluding reassurance of the persistence of conventional female sexuality by locating the source of terror within that sexuality. Like *Demon Seed* (1977), in which Proteus IV, a computer wishing to create a new form of humanity, violates Susan (Julie Christie), *Inseminoid* depends upon scenes of rape and birth for much of its horrific effect. In both films, women are framed as 'Other' by their sexual congress with more conventional iconic others: the machine and the alien. Accordingly, *Inseminoid* follows the 'ideological project' of the horror film, which attempts to 'shore up the symbolic order by constructing the feminine as an "imaginary other" which must be repressed and controlled to secure and protect the social order' (Creed 1990: 140). (See figure 20.)

This construction begins with Sandy's insemination, a sequence which, although explicit, is deliberately de-eroticised for veracity (and to avoid censorship). Rendered both surreal and clinical by Warren's direction and John

Figure 20 Sandy (Judy Geeson) as the monstrous feminine in *Inseminoid* (1980).
Source: Courtesy of the British Cinema and Television Research Group archive

Metcalfe's brittle lighting, the scene transforms Sandy from character to object as it affirms patriarchal power over women. This theme is developed by Warren, who intercuts and thereby equates images of the team's doctor, Karl (Barry Houghton), inoculating Sandy with close-ups of the alien's transparent penis/hypodermic penetrating and ejaculating into her. The hallucinated presence of the doctor during coitus not only suggests Sandy's confusion, but also associates Karl's administration of intravenous contraceptives to the female crew-members with the alien's deposition of its seed. It seems likely, therefore, that Sandy's rape is framed as an act of retribution, visited upon her for her avoidance of natural motherhood. Hence *Inseminoid* attacks the very notion of female sexual freedom whilst suggesting, paradoxically, that contraception is the responsibility of women. Ironically, by adopting this confused standpoint, the film reveals its coherent sexism.

Sandy's insemination is instrumental in marking her as abject Other. After her rape, Sandy is abjected further by her accelerated pregnancy, her destructiveness and her cannibalism. Like David Cronenberg's *The Brood* (1979), *Inseminoid* constructs the mother as an abject human/animal figure and as a personification of the monstrous womb. The viewer's understanding of Sandy's monstrousness is confirmed when she gives birth to non-human twins instantly capable of murder. In its depiction of Sandy's pregnancy, *Inseminoid* signifies the intense male paranoia driving its narrative. In many ways, Sandy's behaviour is an outrageous expression of stereotypical images of pregnant women. Her voracious appetite alludes to the colloquial 'eating for two', and her destruction of the base in preparation for the delivery shows her as 'a home-maker'. More significant are those exaggerations of actual phenomena observable during pregnancy. For example, Sandy's hunger for human flesh is a ghoulish rendering of an expectant mother's increased requirement for amino acids. In Larry Miller's imaginative and misogynistic novelisation, the fear of pregnancy permeating the film is combined with outright disgust. The book is charged with images of revulsion at Sandy's body. In one scene, absent from the film, Gary has sex with Sandy only to discover that 'Her skin had changed. Scaly aberrations had formed. Small open sores were visible....Her body was coated in sweat as was his...but he knew the green droplets forming at her nipples were not sweat' (Miller 1981: 110–11).

Significantly, the images designed to evoke the reader's horror and disable sympathy are all nightmarish forms of the potential effects of pregnancy. Sandy's open sores suggest the skin outbreaks some women experience due to increased oil secretion. The pus-like substance leaking from her nipples recalls colostrum, the pre-milk that may be emitted during sexual stimulation in the later weeks of pregnancy. Similarly, her sweat-stained body indicates an increase in metabolic rate, which rises 20 per cent during normal pregnancy. When Sandy's skin changes hue later in the novel, Miller alludes to the chloasma, the 'mask of pregnancy' that may appear on the forehead, nose and cheeks. Even Sandy's sexual aggressiveness reflects the increased desire experienced by some women when pregnant.

Gary's post-coitus repulsion is contrasted later with Sandy's view of her body:

> Her stomach had become large and round. Her skin was pulled so tightly by the swelling that wide stretch marks ran the length and breadth of her body. Sandy was intrigued by these scars and touched them....Time was growing near. She could feel her breasts filling with fluid. They weighed her down with their gargantuan proportions.
>
> (Miller 1981: 127)

Whereas Gary is revolted by Sandy's body, Sandy is merely 'intrigued' by her physiological changes (although it is interesting that Miller equates stretch marks with deformity and maintains a tone of horror). Whether because of her rape, or of her transformed psyche, Sandy accepts her transformation as natural. In this way, Miller draws a distinction between Sandy's acceptance of her link with the (alien) animal world and the masculine rejection of that link.

In the film, a relentless pace hampers a comparable expression of disgust, yet pregnancy is still shown as a source of horror. Like Miller, Warren and his writers align Sandy with the natural order as she becomes increasingly feral. Associated with images of blood and amniotic fluid, of woman in her reproductive role, Sandy horrifies her colleagues. As Gary (Steven Grives) remarks, rather sourly, he and his colleagues are being 'terrorised by an expectant mother'. Sandy generates this terror like Nola in *The Brood*, whose 'ability to give birth...links her directly to the animal world and to the great cycle of birth, decay and death...[which] reminds man of his mortality and the fragility of the symbolic order' (Creed 1993: 47). In this context, *Inseminoid* becomes an expression of the conflict between the maternal and the patriarchal.

Clearly it can be argued that Sandy overturns patriarchal authority and endangers masculine potency by menacing her colleagues and reducing their capability to function logically as a team. However, her powers are scrupulously limited to avoid distressing the male viewer unnecessarily. Of the six male crew-members, she is permitted to kill only Gary, *Inseminoid*'s least sympathetic character. As Gary once stood upon Sandy's swelling abdomen, his death is framed as an act of retribution and thereby justified and excused. More important is the nature of Gary's death. Weakened by a poisonous atmosphere, he is killed easily in a scene that suggests a woman could never possess sufficient strength to threaten violence to a healthy male. Hence *Inseminoid* both disturbs and reassures its male viewer by presenting the image of an irrational and deadly pregnant woman who, despite augmented strength, is still incapable of overpowering a man.

Rather than overthrowing the patriarchal order, Sandy actually reinstates it. Through her actions, she deconstructs *Inseminoid*'s post-feminist micro-society and allows Mark to emerge triumphant: he is both survivor and mission commander, albeit until the twins avenge their mother. Mark's victory over

Sandy appears to function in the same manner as the climactic sequence of *Alien*. In both films, conventional sexuality is restored. In *Alien* Ripley undresses at the end and displays herself as pleasurable to the audience; similarly, *Inseminoid* asserts the durability of established gender roles, despite the survival of the twins. However, unlike *Alien*, *Inseminoid* retains its power to disturb as Sandy's words to Mark resound long after the final frame: 'You can't get away from me, you know. It doesn't matter what you do. You'll have to come out sometime. There's no other way.…You can't escape me.' The generative mother has spoken, reinforced her eternal presence, and departed to haunt the dreams of men.

With considerable subtlety, Warren emphasises the inescapability of the mother by framing *Inseminoid* with visual and dialogic allusions to her procreative capacity. The opening graphics, a combination of oils shot by Oxford Scientific Films, are suggestively uterine and cervical, indicating that the viewer is entering the realm of the monstrous womb. To emblematise this initiation and the depiction of pregnancy as a source of horror, the titling reveals a microscopic insect resident in the body of a larger organism. At the film's conclusion, the rescue shuttle arrives twenty-eight days after the base's last transmitted message. This duration is immediately suggestive of the menstrual cycle, which continues unchecked both within and beyond the frame of the film, and which will result in the deaths of millions when the twins begin to reproduce. Significantly, the destruction of the facility is described as an 'internal disturbance of some kind', an ironic phrase which encapsulates the film's vision of pregnancy as an irruption of Otherness from within.

Inseminoid's emphasis on abjection and the monstrosity of the womb also informs Harry Bromley Davenport's *Xtro*. As the film opens, a young boy, Tony (Simon Nash) sees his father, Sam (Philip Sayer) abducted by a spacecraft. Three years later Tony, his mother Rachel (Bernice Stegers), and her lover Joe (Danny Brainin) are living in London with their French *au pair* Analise (a pre-Bond Maryam D'Abo). Unbeknown to them, Sam has returned to Earth in extraterrestrial form (see figure 21). When the Xtro-Sam rapes a young woman (Susie Silvery), her body swells grotesquely until Sam is reborn full-grown and apparently human.

Sam's rebirth, clearly influenced by imagery from *The Brood* and *Alien*, is a key sequence. Unlike *The Terminator* (1984) and *Starman* (1984), which depict reborn males as incarnations of 'innocence, sweetness, inexperience, curiosity, and vulnerability…semiotically linked with…[a]…significant patriarchal residue: biological maturity, privileged knowledge and vast power' (Sobchack 1991: 25), *Xtro* negates Sam's child-like qualities by emphasising his 'significant patriarchal residue'. When Sam emerges from the ruined corpse of his surrogate mother, and bites through his own umbilicus, his mature independence is affirmed. Importantly, the incident not only maintains the vision of woman as abject, but also functions to disenfranchise her of her nurturing influence. Born familiar with the rationality and logic of the patriarchal order, Sam is free from fear of castration by the mother, quickly separated and distanced from

"**XTRO**" (18) – NEW REALM ENTERTAINMENTS

Figure 21 The 'post-*Alien*' intruder of *Xtro* (1981).
Source: Courtesy of the British Cinema and Television Research Group archive

the 'tyranny' of the mother's 'unclean' association with the natural world, and physically prepared to re-adopt the role of father. His victim's accelerated pregnancy, bracketed as it is by the rape and death which make her completely 'safe', minimises the indispensable role of the female in the gestation, birth and rearing of the child. Consequently, the sequence represents a patriarchal fantasy in which the symbolic order is preserved unchallenged whilst the contribution made to that order by the nurturing mother is diminished to non-existence.

From this scene, it appears that a genuine contempt for the nurturing role of the mother infects the film. However, *Xtro*'s central project is social criticism; it is a polemic for the patriarchal family order, produced when that order was in jeopardy. To enunciate its argument, *Xtro* is structured as an asymmetric interplanetary custody battle between Sam and Rachel for Tony. Following his rebirth, the film charts Sam's troubled return to the family and his recruitment of Tony, Tony's transformation of Analise into an alien egg-producing cocoon, and the permanent reunion of father and son. In the penultimate moments, Rachel watches Sam, now in alien form, take Tony's half-human, half-Xtro hand, and lead him aboard a spaceship. She then returns home to discover Analise's eggs. As she examines one, a testicular-phallic larva erupts to penetrate her mouth and leave her bleeding on the floor.

Seen in the larger context of the film, Sam's behaviour represents an argument for effective parenting and for the adequate socialisation of the child. Sam's amorality can be attributed, metaphorically, to his lack of a family upbringing. Whilst this may seem unlikely, a corresponding, though more literal lack, is evident in the relationship between Tony, Rachel and Joe. Rachel's actions during Sam's absence have had a negative effect upon Tony, and *Xtro* submits an implicit criticism of her conduct. The film's censure of Rachel depends on her choice of a cynical lover indifferent to Tony's needs. Joe's attempts to engage the child are uncommitted and easily derailed by Tony's idealisation of Sam, which seems to arise from Rachel's failings after Sam disappeared. The opening scene, in which Rachel, Sam and Tony are at their Home Counties cottage, provides evidence for this reading. When Rachel drives away, Tony, who has until this moment been playing happily with his father, follows her car, watching it recede with a forlorn expression. It is probable, therefore, that at this point Tony's attachment to both parents was equal and that his subsequent faith in his father is a consequence of events after the abduction. This aspect of Tony's characterisation forms a criticism of Rachel as a mother who appears to have placed her own happiness before that of her child, something the film presents as unacceptable. As Analise observes, somewhat ironically given her own preoccupations, Tony 'only needs a little time and care', attention neither his mother nor his surrogate father are prepared to give.

Xtro's concern for the negative emotional and psychological influences exerted by negligent mothers is complicated by its anxiety regarding the effect of unprincipled fathers. When Sam's true purposes are revealed in an almost paedophilic vampire sequence, during which Sam injects Tony with his alien essence, the image of Sam as frustrated father is revised into a vision of the father as a disingenuous, avenging Other intent upon reclaiming and transforming his offspring. The viewer's fear for Tony is disarmed by Tony's love for Sam, and by his commitment to Sam's cause, which make his abduction as much an idyllic reunion of two lonely souls as it is indicative of Sam's reassertion of his paternal authority through the re-appropriation of his 'seed'.

However, Sam's actions must be seen in a broader context: they are the corruption of an innocent boy made vulnerable by his devotion to an absent father. The triumph of Sam's paternal power is, therefore, nothing to be celebrated, despite the 'happy ending' it seems to offer. As Sobchack indicates, 'Infancy and childhood have…been popularly represented as the cultural site of such "positive" virtues as innocence, transparency, and a "pure" and wonderful curiosity not yet informed by sexuality (no matter what Freud said)' (Sobchack 1991: 6). Sam perverts this innocence and clouds Tony's transparency by providing him with telekinetic powers that give adult form and force to his child's anger. Interestingly, and in keeping with the film's identification of the ineffective mother as the source of the child's vulnerability to perversion, it is Rachel who initiates the destruction of Tony's 'purity' when she inadvertently allows Tony to observe her having sex with Joe. Nevertheless, Tony's 'education' is largely the responsibility of his father.

Consequently, as in many horror films of the 1980s, from *The Shining* (1980) to *The Stepfather* (1987), *Xtro* demonises the father as the monster in the middle-class family.

Unlike Warren, who denies *Inseminoid* a British ambience for commercial and aesthetic purposes, Davenport locates his film in a very specific milieu: early Thatcherite Britain, a period identified with mass unemployment, civil unrest and financial hardship. With over three million people registered as unemployed (the majority of whom were men because of practices in quantification), the traditional British nuclear family was under threat. Men as husbands and fathers, traditionally represented as the major source of income, were increasingly alienated from traditional gender roles by economic circumstances.

Xtro takes this social and familial alienation and literalises it. Sam, stolen from his family for three years, is incapable of supporting his wife and son; he is denied his status as a provider and authority figure. Upon his return, he seeks to re-establish himself as the head of the household but unfortunately for Sam, his wife's lover stands in his way. He is confronted, therefore, by an unfaithful wife incapable of caring for her son without assistance from the sexually preoccupied Analise. Worst of all, his home and his wife have been invaded by another man. With his paternal authority in jeopardy, Sam elicits a certain amount of understanding from the (male) viewer, despite having murdered three people. This compassion is evoked when the audience accepts Sam as a beleaguered father, anxious over the fate of his son, rather than as a rapacious alien. His rage is that 'of a paternity denied the economic and political benefits of patriarchal power' (Sobchack 1991: 10). Hence, the viewer can empathise, and even sympathise, with Sam's predicament.

Sam's status as a sympathetic figure is enhanced by Joe's open hostility towards him. When Sam first returns home, Rachel introduces him to Joe:

Joe: What are your plans?
Sam: I don't know. I haven't got any work lined up, if that's what you mean.
Joe: Things are pretty tight. It won't be easy.
Sam: I hear you've been busy.
Joe: I've been lucky. You know me Sam: look British, think Yiddish.
            . . .
Joe: Look Sam, what do you want?
Sam: I want to be home.
Joe: This isn't your home anymore. That should be obvious.

With impressive brevity, this exchange emphasises Britain's economic situation, Sam's unemployed, non-status, and the fact that Joe was once Sam's friend, while highlighting Sam's financial powerlessness, Joe's possessiveness, and the nature of Rachel's infidelity: she is having sex with her husband's friend. Thus, rather than structuring *Xtro* as a simple alien-in-the-family scenario, Davenport uses the form to explore paternity through two converging forms of invasion. From Joe's perspective, Sam is the invader; from Sam's point of view, Joe is the intruder. The audience is positioned in a rather ambiguous relationship to these characters, though Joe's cynicism and Sam's apparent ingenuousness frame Joe as the interloper opposed to the reinstatement of the nuclear family. Ironically, in the early stages of Sam's return, it is another man who prevents Sam from re-establishing his paternity: the Other is human. The ensuing battle for paternity is significant for highlighting that patriarchy and the patriarchal order are never under threat in *Xtro*, either from within or without. Even if the eggs laid by Analise become the spearhead of an alien incursion, it seems likely from the evidence of the film that these invaders will impose or adhere to a patriarchal structure of their own.

Caught between an ineffectual mother, her lover and a predatory father, Tony has little chance and less will to preserve either his innocence or his humanity. Unlike Sam, whose alienation derives primarily from his abduction and subsequent failure, or unwillingness, to re-integrate, Tony's estrangement arises from his failure to integrate with a new family order and then from his abduction. This contrary movement from literal to figurative/figurative to literal alienation finds its resolution in the passage of father and son into both a new world and a new physical existence, into an ultimate and irredeemable state of alienation from the human.

Both a critique of deficient female nurture and a celebration of the triumph of an amoral father, *Xtro* is a steadfastly conservative affirmation of the importance of the extant patriarchal order, whose implicit idealisation of the bourgeois family advocates the validity of 'traditional' capitalist, heterosexual and patriarchal values.

Like *Xtro*, Tobe Hooper's *Lifeforce* employs the theme of alien–human reproduction to assert the importance of bourgeois values and patriarchal relations. Co-scripted by *Alien* screenwriter Dan O'Bannon from Colin Wilson's neo-existentialist novel *The Space Vampires* (1976), *Lifeforce* begins with an Anglo-American mission to Halley's Comet. There, the space shuttle *Churchill* locates a vast alien ship in which Colonel Carlsen (Steve Railsback) and his team discover the remains of huge bat-like creatures and three humanoids, one female and two male, held in stasis. Carlsen immediately aborts the mission and returns to Earth with the aliens.

Once the aliens are brought to London, the film's reactionary representation of sexuality, and its underlying sexual conservatism, are made manifest. Freed from her stasis chamber, the strikingly beautiful Space Girl (Mathilda May) rises to suck the lifeforce from her guard with a lingering kiss before she walks naked from the European Space Research Centre. Meanwhile, the guard rises as a shrivelled yet ravenous energy vampire designed and built by *Inseminoid* co-writer and Prosthetics Supervisor Nick Maley (see Nutman 1985: 21–4; Brown 1991: 9–13). The girl's attack on the guard reveals her as a monster, a woman rendered abject by her transgression of the boundary between acceptable female sexuality within the patriarchal order and unrestrained female sexual desire. Importantly, the film emphasises that the girl's appetite for lifeforce is equally an appetite for sex when she makes love to Carlsen. 'You're taking too much!' he screams as she steals a portion of his energy, threatening literally to 'suck him dry' with her vigorous, vampiric lovemaking. Here, and elsewhere, 'lifeforce' is a metaphor for semen.

That the girl's function is to embody liberated sexuality is emphasised by her nudity throughout the film. Whilst May's statuesque body provides unarguable titillation for the male audience, it also foregrounds her confident rejection of worldly (that is, patriarchal, middle-class) values. An unrestrained figure, she threatens the entire patriarchal structure of England by unleashing a form of uncontrollable lasciviousness. She begins transforming the population into energy parasites, which leads to a frenzy of carnality in London's streets where each act of vampirism equates to a form of orgiastic self-gratification. 'Once transformed, the victims need regular infusions of energy,' Dr Fallade (Frank Finlay) explains, or they explode in a burst of pseudo-sexual frustration. Unlike the *Quatermass* films (1955–67), *Lifeforce* shows England threatened not by alien manifestations alone, but by the collapse of English reserve into unbridled debauchery.

Nowhere is the girl's threat to the very fabric of the symbolic order more apparent than in those scenes where she is associated with 'abnormal' sexual practices. After some off-screen lesbianism, the girl instigates on-screen homosexuality. Her reanimated guard embraces another man in a vampiric kiss, identified visually with the earlier erotic exchange between the guard and the girl. More significant, however, are the events at Thurlston Hospital where the girl possesses the administrator, Dr Armstrong (Patrick Stewart). Drugged and strapped down, Armstrong is questioned by Carlsen, who sees the girl's face superimposed continually over Armstrong's. Eventually, her seductiveness is too much for Carlsen and he descends to kiss Armstrong's lips. Heterosexual propriety intrudes when SAS colonel Caine (Peter Firth) and an orderly drag Carlsen back from the brink of sexual transgression. (In the 1986 MGM/UA Home Video extended Widescreen edition, this scene includes an actual kiss between Carlsen and Armstrong (see Willsmer 1995: 48–9).)

With the sf film's usual conservatism, *Lifeforce* shows this weakening of the patriarchal structure not as a liberating phenomenon but as a threat to be opposed. Bourgeois 'normality' must be restored and maintained, no matter what the cost. Although the film's pace and pyrotechnics do not allow for a vision of this normality, the narrative provides sufficient clues for the viewer to perceive its nature. When Fallade reflects on the Space Girl's behaviour – 'That girl was no girl. She's totally alien to this planet and our life form, and totally dangerous' – he draws attention to the western cultural connotations of 'girl': qualities of youth, vigour, innocence and, very probably, virginity. The Space Girl fails to conform to the conventional meaning of 'girl' not least because she does not fulfil bourgeois stereotypes of female sexuality and the expected propriety of 'girlhood'. It is her sexuality rather than her extraterrestrial nature that renders her truly alien and transgressive. The normality advocated by *Lifeforce* requires women to abandon, or suppress, their own sexuality.

This fundamental element of the film is apparent when Carlsen exorcises the Space Girl's psyche from Ellen (Nancy Paul), a nurse at Thurlston Hospital. Carlsen beats, partly strips, and finally kisses Ellen into unconsciousness, while Caine, 'a natural voyeur', watches closely. In this sequence, Ellen is both objectified – she is 'something' requiring 'normalisation' – and subjected to Carlsen's physical assault. She is tamed and passive once her 'unnatural appetites' have been expelled. No longer under the influence of the Space Girl, she is reinstated into the patriarchal order as an 'acceptable' woman: weak, demure, (s)exploitable.

The power required to restore the patriarchal order is symbolised by the phallic leaded iron sword Fallade appropriates from a museum. The weapon once belonged to 'Capt. Leigh John Masters', upon whose name the camera lingers for several seconds. If the viewer reads the name as Legion Masters, the blade becomes an expression of the power of the one (man) over the many, be they vampires or women (the distinction is somewhat blurred in *Lifeforce*). (See figure 22.)

After the male vampires are banished with the sword, Carlsen and Caine confront the girl in St Paul's Cathedral where she is channelling lifeforce

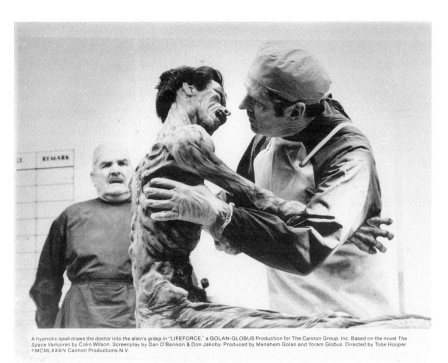

A hypnotic spell draws the doctor into the alien's grasp in "LIFEFORCE," a GOLAN-GLOBUS Production for The Cannon Group, Inc. Based on the novel *The Space Vampires* by Colin Wilson. Screenplay by Dan O'Bannon & Don Jakoby. Produced by Menahem Golan and Yoram Globus. Directed by Tobe Hooper. ©MCMLXXXIV Cannon Productions N.V.

Figure 22 Sucking him dry: sexual transgression in *Lifeforce* (1985).
Source: Courtesy of the British Cinema and Television Research Group archive

energy to her ship. Using Master's sword, Carlsen impales himself to the girl during a final, orgiastic embrace. However, the girl does not die, but ascends to the ship with Carlsen amidst a constellation of captured souls. Thus the film removes two threats to the patriarchal structure: a sexually precocious female and an easily seduced, irrational male who, since his seduction, has lost his 'proper' masculine authority and indifference. Carlsen is obsessed with the girl. Even after sabotaging the Churchill in an attempt to prevent the vampires reaching Earth, he recounts how, 'She killed all my friends and I still didn't want to leave. Leaving her was the hardest thing I ever did.' As he explains, 'I was in love on a level you'd never know.' Metaphorically emasculated, he is doomed to complete alienation through his unconditional desire for a transcendent *femme fatale*. The Space Girl is his ultimate sexual fantasy. 'I took my shape from your mind,' she tells him. 'I became the woman I found there in your deepest thoughts, your deepest...needs.'

Accordingly, *Lifeforce* is structured as a morality tale alerting men to the dangers inherent not only in loving a sexually liberated, self-reliant woman, but in the masturbatory fantasy of being in love with such a 'creature'. The film's statement of male fear of female sexuality concludes as an expression of anxiety towards female reproductive potential. Like Sandy, the Space Girl is a mother figure, a monstrous metaphorical womb when she generates her brood of energy vampires and a literal womb when she mysteriously repopulates her spaceship. In the closing moments of *Lifeforce*, as the ship departs Earth, the empty chambers that originally surrounded the girl's sarcophagus are occupied by what appear to be huge infants. By revealing the Space Girl as a would-be mother, the film identifes her (s)exploitation of Carlsen as an expression of self-interest: the source of female desire is located within her need to reproduce. In this way *Lifeforce* counsels men to beware of sexually predatory women whose promises of love are merely the means to a reproductive end.

Whereas *Lifeforce*, *Xtro* and *Inseminoid* all advocate the maintenance of patriarchal, bourgeois society through the theme of alien intrusion, Tony Maylam's *Split Second* attempts to avoid such conservatism by attributing to its Other a multitude of conflicting signs. However, even Maylam's eclectic creature cannot avoid identification as a mother figure.

Set in 2008, in a London flooded by global warming, *Split Second* documents the hunt for a monstrous serial killer that steals its victims' hearts. Driven by desire for revenge upon the creature that murdered his partner, detective Harley Stone (Rutger Hauer) is assigned to the case. Stone is joined by straight-laced Oxford graduate Dick Durkin (Neil Duncan). An odd couple, they hunt down the beast who by this time has abducted Michelle (Kim Cattrall), Stone's lover and his partner's widow. In an explosive finale (directed by Ian Sharp), the beast is destroyed in the abandoned London Underground.

The derivative nature of the film is confirmed by its assembly of cinematic character-types, dialogue and visual codes. The aptly named hard-man Stone is the traditional rogue cop, a combination of Dirty Harry and Martin Riggs from *Lethal Weapon* (1987). A paranoid, coffee-swilling, chocolate munching, guilt-ridden chain smoker, he is a caricature of a modern cinematic archetype. His laconic and dryly humorous dialogue and specific visual icons mark him as a pastiche of the protagonists who dominate rogue cop/vigilante movies: his boots are Snake Plisskin's from *Escape from New York* (1981); his weaponry recalls Stallone's and Schwarzenegger's; while his shades remind the audience that beneath it all, he is truly cool. To complete the image, Stone lives in a slummy tenement with a Harley Davidson motorcycle in his living room.

Split Second's plot is a similar patchwork affair. In the format of a police procedural, the narrative is punctuated with imagery from slasher movies, from the urban action film (*Predator 2* (1990) is a distinct source), and from *Alien* and *Aliens* (1986). The debt to the *Alien* films is obvious – the extraterrestrial is a 'Big Monster With Teeth' (Hardy 1995: 476), which it is futile to combat with superior firepower. When the mild-mannered Durkin first sees the creature, he is metaphorically emasculated by its primal force and seeks reassurance from phallic firepower: 'We've got to get bigger guns…big fucking guns….Stone, we need some big, big, fucking guns.' Of course, the association of 'fuck' and 'guns' is hardly coincidental, nor is the amusement Durkin's anxiety is likely to arouse in the audience. At this moment, *Split Second* demonstrates best its status as a pastiche of action film conventions.

The ultimate ineffectiveness of Stone's and Durkin's 'big, big, fucking guns' forces Stone to tear out the creature's heart with his bare hands. This act reaffirms masculine power over the other, as might be expected in a film so obsessed with expressions of male potency. The nature of Stone's victory remains obscure, however, since the precise identity of the vanquished creature is not disclosed. A number of theories are offered (monster as mutant, monster as demon, monster as Satan himself) but none is realised fully. Even so, the actions of the beast are clear enough: it appropriates its victims' genetic material and internalises the codes to develop its own form using 'multiple restriction polymorphic DNA sequences'. This process of absorption is a further twist on the theme of conception, in which the male's genetic material is 'absorbed' and 'internalised' by the female. In this sense, the beast is a maternal figure, constantly giving birth to itself. Like most horror films, *Split Second* repudiates that figure.

Yet the film is so unthinkingly derivative and so concerned with its own intertextuality that it is simply not interested in presenting a consistent vision, either of its monster or of its attitude to female sexuality. Like its vicious assailant, *Split Second* 'has the [metaphorical] DNA structure of all its victims'. It appropriates and synthesises, but ultimately falls apart, breaking incoherently into its component signifiers. It is nothing if not a playfully comic postmodern film, constructed as pastiche or 'blank parody' – a parody lacking 'parody's ulterior motive, without the satirical impulse, without laughter, without that latent feeling that there exists something normal compared to which what is being imitated is rather comic' (Jameson 1991: 114). As Hans

Bertens remarks, 'In the age of total eclecticism pastiche is all that remains of a parody that has lost its former function' (Bertens 1995: 162). Rather than parodying the form it imitates, *Split Second* is content to exploit a commercial bricolage of cinematic allusions without reflecting upon their sources. Its humour derives not from comments upon the excesses of the films it mimics, but from its own inherent excesses. *Split Second*, which lacks the coherence of the other films' ideological project, seems to attest to the exhaustion of the post-*Alien* intrusion narrative, at least in the British sf film.

From the energetic exuberance of *Inseminoid* to the weary mimicry of *Split Second*, the British post-*Alien* intrusion film has expressed a remarkably consistent bourgeois and patriarchal attitude towards women and motherhood. Such a political stance is symptomatic of the science fiction film's continuing failure to fulfil its potential because of commercial pressures and patriarchal control over the industry. The economic imperatives of film-making required that each of the films discussed above allowed for the possibility of a sequel. *Inseminoid* has its twins journey towards fresh hunting grounds; Analise's eggs await the unwary; an entire ship of space vampires prepares for the eventuality of *Lifeforce II*; and, in the flooded tunnels of a crumbling London, Something Nasty disturbs the waters of a dark and oily pool.[1] There is, however, some hope to be found for the sf film in the exhausted tone of *Split Second*. Perhaps, now the post-*Alien* narrative has become so tired (a tiredness confirmed by *Alien Resurrection* (1998)), the sf film will fulfil its potential and deliver more radically disorientating and enlightening visions of the future. It is just possible, with more financial support now available to its film industry, that Britain, the birthplace of science fiction, will herald this regeneration.

Acknowledgements

I am extremely grateful for the assistance of Mr Norman J. Warren who answered a multitude of questions regarding the production of *Inseminoid* with wit and courtesy.

Note

1 Although Harry Bromley Davenport directed two *Alien*-derived US follow-ups, *Xtro II: The Second Encounter* (1991) and *Xtro: Watch the Skies* (1995), neither displays a narrative connection to the original.

Bibliography

Bertens, Hans (1995) *The Idea of the Postmodern: A History*, London: Routledge.
Brown, Paul J. (1991) '*Lifeforce*', *Fantasynopsis* 4: 9–13.
—— (1995) *All You Need Is Blood: The Films of Norman J. Warren*, Upton: Midnight Media.
Creed, Barbara (1990) '*Alien* and the monstrous feminine', in Annette Kuhn (ed.) *Alien Zone: Cultural Theory and Contemporary Science Fiction Cinema*, London: Verso.

—— (1993) *The Monstrous Feminine: Film, Feminism and Psychoanalysis*, London: Routledge.

Hardy, Phil (ed.) (1995) *The Aurum Film Encyclopedia: Science Fiction*, London: Aurum Press.

Jameson, Fredric (1991) *Postmodernism, or the Cultural Theory of Late Capitalism*, Durham, NC: Duke University Press.

Kavanagh, James H. (1990) 'Feminism, humanism and science in *Alien*', in Kuhn, *Alien Zone*.

Kuhn, Annette (ed.) (1990) *Alien Zone: Cultural Theory and Contemporary Science Fiction Cinema*, London: Verso.

Miller, Larry (1981) *Inseminoid*, London: New English Library.

Newton, Judith (1990) 'Feminism and anxiety in *Alien*', in Kuhn, *Alien Zone*.

Nutman, Philip (1985) 'Space bats and spirit suckers: the *Lifeforce* makeup FX of Nick Maley', *Fangoria* 47: 21–4.

Sobchack, Vivian (1991) 'Child/alien/father: patriarchal crisis and generic exchange', in Constance Penley *et al.*, *Close Encounters: Film Feminism and Science Fiction*, London: University of Minnesota Press.

Willsmer, Trevor (1995), '*Lifeforce*', *Movie Collector* 2.2: 48–9.

Wilson, Colin (1976) *The Space Vampires*, London: Hart-Davis, MacGibbon Ltd.

11 Dream girls and mechanic panic

Dystopia and its others in *Brazil* and *Nineteen Eighty-Four*

Linda Ruth Williams

In 1983 a short Terry Gilliam film was released as B-feature to *Monty Python's The Meaning of Life*, but *The Crimson Permanent Assurance* could also be seen as the companion text to *Brazil* (1985), Gilliam's next full-scale project. A group of slavishly downtrodden office lackeys (old guard refugees from a world when commerce was more gentlemanly) rise up and mutiny, overthrowing their free-market corporate oppressors, an act so miraculous that it transforms their building into a galleon, which sets sail on the Gilliamesque 'wide accountant-sea'. The complete defeat of the parent company, The Very Big Corporation of America, is next on their list. Opening, as the voice-over puts it, 'in the bleak days of 1983, as England languished in the doldrums of a ruinous monetarist policy', the fantasy of 'reasonably violent' office-pirates successfully trashing their erstwhile employers is hardly subtle. A utopian day-dream of collective action, which, in the time-honoured tradition of using the bosses' ropes to hang them with, turns filing cabinets into cannons, coat-hooks into cutlasses and office minions into vigilante heroes. Unlike other filmic utopias, which focus on personal gain or map out brave new future-worlds, the mission of Gilliam's men is to overthrow corporate dominance. Part-way between an Ealingesque revenge-of-the-little-man and *Battleship Potemkin* (1925). (Gilliam also parodies the Odessa steps sequence in *Brazil*), *The Crimson Permanent Assurance* replaces proletarian sweat with bureaucratic drudgery, but the defeated enemy is still the same: 'A financial district swollen with multinationals, conglomerates, and fat, bloated merchant banks.' Nothing can stop the victorious ship – except the fact that this is utopia (ou-topia – no-place) not Thatcher's Britain, and it happens to be cartoon-flat. The ship drops off the edge of the earth.

Then in 1985 came *Brazil* (one working-title of which was *1984½*), a dark, surrealistically-witty dystopian vision of an unlocatable time in which bureaucracy manipulates people rather than the other way around, and the compliant hero/cog-in-the-wheel (Sam Lowry, played by Jonathan Pryce) is finally punished for his conformist complicity. *Brazil* is quintessentially Gilliamesque, in blurring the distinction between real and dream-states, sane and mad, inside and outside; in its fascination with the machine as body and the body in the machine; and in its obsession with systems. It is uneasily pitched somewhere between past and future, generally identifiable yet also quite specific: the opening text reads '8.49 pm: Somewhere in the twentieth century'.

Quite a different film was the previous year's *Nineteen Eighty-Four*. Directed by Michael Radford, this was the second cinematic reworking of George Orwell's 1949 novel (the first was Michael Anderson's rather dutiful 1956 version). Winston Smith (played by John Hurt) might be Sam Lowry's depressed brother, positioned against a canvas of a totalitarian but visibly mid-twentieth-century Britain (despite its renaming as Airstrip One, the centre of Oceana, now one of the world's three superpowers). Oceana is engaged in an ongoing war with Eurasia, and news reports give constant updates, broadcast incessantly, along with messages from Party leader Big Brother, through the omnipresent two-way telecast screens which are fixed into every room, breaking down the distinction between the public and the private. Propaganda infuses every scene; indeed, it is Winston's job at the Ministry of Truth to rewrite history according to the purposes of the Party, inscribed in Newspeak. Truth is a commodity, manipulable and entirely subject to power. As the film proceeds, and as Winston's distance from these 'truths' becomes more marked, the question of whether the war – and indeed Big Brother – are real, or just a fabrication used to manipulate the populace into compliance, is raised. The ultimate rule-breaking comes when Winston meets the free-spirited Julia. In a society which has outlawed not just private life but the orgasm itself, the pair become erotic dissidents by embarking on a sexual relationship. They are punished for it: arrested, tortured (Winston is taken to the dreaded Room 101 to confront his worst fears), brainwashed into compliance and mutual betrayal, the pair finally submit individual identity and will to the overarching vision of the Party and the world of 'doublethink' (see figure 23).

Brazil's strange future-past is altogether different, although the films have some uncanny similarities. *Nineteen Eighty-Four* fits quite neatly into a long tradition of filmically imaged worlds both better and worse, and *Brazil* too might be read alongside other black-humorous, parodic-postmodern dystopias of the 1980s and 1990s – *Delicatessen* (1990), *Prayer of the Rollerboys* (1991), even *Mad Max* (1979) – although it owes far more to Kafka or Lewis Carroll than to the visual stylistics of the pop video, and is infused with a dark eco-horror which echoes *Blade Runner* (1982) and looks towards *The Fifth Element* (1997). *Brazil* is a vertiginous urban nightmare – it is also very funny.

Bureaucracies are Gilliam's particular *bête noire*, and machines themselves, more than how they are used, become his prime signifiers. Gilliam's 'tech *noir*' is never 'high tech' – the grungy, Heath-Robinsonesque machines which are the externalisation of baroque bureaucracies and psyches are the most striking element of his *mise-en-scène* – think of the devil's machines in *Time Bandits* (1981), the time machines in *Twelve Monkeys* (1996). As Gilliam said with a shrug in a recent interview, 'It just seems that I have this German-Expressionistic-Destructivist-Russian-Constructivist view of the future' (Morgan 1996: 20). *Brazil* is set in an enclosed world when even outdoors feels like indoors, when social stratification is keen, but success is particularly marked both by the pleasures

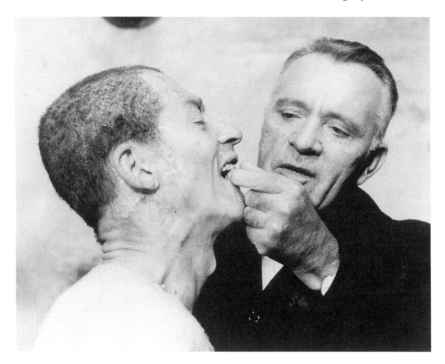

Figure 23 O' Brien (Richard Burton) (right) prepares Winston (John Hurt) for the
worst thing in the world in *Nineteen Eighty-Four* (1984).
Source: Courtesy of the British Film Institute Stills, Posters and Designs

of conspicuous consumption and by the power to manipulate bureaucratic
processes. But all inhabitants seem to be equal prisoners of their disastrous world:
this is not *Metropolis* (1926), the golden palace built on the slavery of workers
doomed to pay for others' excesses which benefits an elite strata. Here there
are no winners.

Like Winston Smith, Sam Lowry is a lowly government pen-pusher, existing
in a Hades of office procedure at the Ministry of Information. If Winston
Smith collapses or subsumes his private, dissenting self into a flat faith in
public 'truths', Sam retains a private self as a space of escape: his 'real' life exists
in his dreams of a blonde damsel in distress, who gives him the chance to be a
hero (the inane 1930s song 'Brazil', which gives the film its title, is about
escape or return to a lost romantic idyll). Retreat into fantasy as interior
dream-state or as mass romance is crucial to the film's sense of darkness. The
images of Hollywood icons which cram the walls of Sam's flat are little glim-
mers of light; his nocturnal heroics set the futile drudgery of daytime into
relief. The sinister surveillance systems which, in *Nineteen Eighty-Four*, bear
out the phrase 'Big Brother is Watching You', are subverted into a bizarre facility
for fantasy-escape in *Brazil*: the 'surveyors' use their telescreens not to look
out for illegalities but to hack into old movies.

However, Sam has connections in higher places. He is persuaded to take up a job at the leaner, meaner department of Information Retrieval, and so is able to trace this dream-girl, whom he has stumbled upon in real life. Jill (Kim Griest) is a suspected terrorist, and after Sam gets involved with her, he is arrested and tortured (by his best friend Jack Lint (Michael Palin), who is only doing his job). The film ends twice: first, in the 'happy' ending preferred by Universal Studios in America (who insisted on a more cheerful, shorter edit for US audiences), with the couple's heroic escape to an idyllic rural location; second, when this is revealed as a false ending, and we cut back to Sam's blank face in the torture chamber. Rural escape is then just Sam's mental act, a hallucination dreamed up to negate the horror of torture.

Brazil is infused with a machine-age panic, the keynote of its dystopianism, reminiscent of Chaplin's famous factory-floor pantomime in *Modern Times* (1936): the motors – actual or procedural – just keep running, sometimes to excess and always regardless of the bodies that are in the way. Flailing around the edges of the process are human beings – worried conformists (like Sam), exuberant vigilantes (like Robert De Niro's Tuttle), real victims (like Buttle's family), frustrated punters passed from desk to desk (like Jill, before she gets into her truck and takes action). Gilliam's machines act like fleshly and extrapolated bureaucratic systems. When Sam's air-conditioning system goes wrong it invades his flat and forces him to retreat into the fridge: the very fabric of the building revolts. He can do nothing without Form 27B/6 which jobsworth Central Services engineer Spoor (Bob Hoskins) demands before he will make Sam's life livable again. The film thus partly investigates the success of the totalitarian personality: how or whether Sam can *become* worker DZ/015 when he finally takes up the job at Information Retrieval. If *Nineteen Eighty-Four* shows the success a brutal system has in slotting its minions into their allotted roles given enough acts of 'persuasion', *Brazil* shows how hard it is to enforce absolute compliance. If its characters conform, it is only with great resistance and difficulty. Even Spoor's procedural arch-perfectionism is not an act of selfless submission, as it might be in *Nineteen Eighty-Four*, but a sadistic strategy: Hoskins's performance is more that of a cowboy builder who's taking you for a ride than a by-the-book drone. The stupidity of a baroque rule-system has become a way of inflicting psychological pain or flaunting petty power-gains.

The grotesque is also more interesting to Gilliam than the normal or the natural. In *Brazil* standardisation breeds weirdness; there are cracks and we get to glimpse what oozes out of them – even the storm-troopers are caught practising Christmas carols in the basement. In one of the film's most impressive performances, Kathryn Pogson plays repressed spinster Shirley as a twitchy, gauche bundle of neurosis, the animated sign of familial and social ill-health. Clearer walking examples of the system's failure to guarantee completely the response of its people are Gilliam's maverick heroes, who can't be bothered with form-filling and cannot be identified by Information Retrieval (these wild men are everywhere – De Niro here is echoed in Robin Williams's fallen yuppie in *The Fisher King* (1991); a darker escapee is Bruce Willis's character in *Twelve Monkeys*, split between two time zones and belonging in neither). But in actual fact it is hard to find *any* images of a fully and successfully mechanised self in *Brazil*, despite the film's obsession with processes of control. One exception might be the audio-typist who works for torturer Lint, cheerfully typing the screams and pleas she's hearing through her headphones, her powers of comprehension bypassed by a skill developed so perfectly that information can come in (through the ears) and go out (onto paper) without ever pausing in her conscience.

A dialogue of difference and similarity animates comparison between *Nineteen Eighty-Four* and *Brazil*, yet the closer they are scrutinised the more different they become. It is hard to find a contemporary review which doesn't mention the Orwellian nature of Gilliam's film, which he himself had tagged 'a post-Orwellian view of a pre-Orwellian world' (Johnson 1993: 204). Philip French called *Brazil* 'pop-Orwell played for laughs' (*Observer* 24 February 1985), whilst Mat Snow saw it as a 'Pythonised' *Nineteen Eighty-Four* (*New Musical Express* 23 February 1985). Keith Nurse wrote that 'if [*Brazil*] is Orwellian in tone, it is also positively Pythonesque in form' (*Daily Telegraph* 22 February 1985), whilst George Perry's *Sunday Times* headline was 'Big Brother and the Python' (*Sunday Times* 27 January 1985). Both films are haunted by the spectre of 1984 as a real year as well as an Orwellian horror. *Nineteen Eighty-Four* is not just *any* 1980s film (it would have been perverse to have released it, say, in 1982 or 1985); it hangs on to the legend not just of its text but of its year. As the closing credits roll at the film's conclusion its claim to authenticity is sealed by the message, 'This film was photographed in and around London during the period April–June 1984, the exact time and setting imagined by the author.' Though it went into production later than *Brazil*, its producers ensured that it would nevertheless appear in its eponymous year. After Gilliam's protracted battle with Universal, his film finally premiered in the US in 1985. Although *Brazil* was backed by American finance and directed by a born-American, it was shot mostly in Britain (except for a couple of scenes shot in France) using a largely British cast and crew; Gilliam had lived and worked in Britain for close to twenty years prior to its release; and it was received as the product and representation of a very British sensibility. That both films work through peculiarly British dystopian visions is crucial to their tone, cult status and relationship to their moment.

But that both films retain traces of *utopianism* is also crucial to the tone of their darkness. It is hard to discuss dystopias without addressing their imaginative Other; utopia is implied by dystopia, in these films and in wider thought. Few theorists address one without reference to the other: study of dystopianism is sometimes understood as a sub-set of the much larger area of utopian studies, which has burgeoned since the 1960s. Indeed, the distinction between the two, the sense that dystopias and utopias are negative and positive definitions of each other, is further blurred by the frequent argument that one man's utopia is another man's dystopia. In her illuminating 1990 survey of utopian thought, Ruth Levitas discusses how both Aldous Huxley's *Brave New World* (1932) and B.F. Skinner's *Walden Two* (1948) 'were received by some as utopias and by others as anti-utopias' (Levitas 1990: 22). '[T]he optimism of utopia and the pessimism of dystopia,' writes Levitas, 'represent opposite sides of the same coin – the hope of what the future could be at best, the fear of what it may be at worst' (Levitas 1990: 139, discussing Kumar 1987). In the films under discussion here, utopian moments are contained within a largely dystopian vision. True, almost every detail of *Nineteen Eighty-Four*'s *mise-en-scène* is discomforting and at times quite hard to watch, and the film's morbid 'message' is viscerally clear. The ending of *Brazil* is one of the bleakest in 1980s cinema. Fredric Jameson argues that 'anti-Utopianism constitutes a far more easily decodable and unambiguous political position' than its utopian Other (Jameson 1988: 76); dystopian images, like Orwell's, are for Jameson a version of utopian socialism rendered in negatives, and *Nineteen Eighty-Four*, film and novel, bears this out. However, I will argue here that at the heart of these bleak visions of totalitarian control lies a singular utopian image, the vision of a woman, the centre of both films' dystopic contradictions. Woman functions in *Brazil* and *Nineteen Eighty-Four* as a spectacle of interruption, an escape from the dark dystopic terrain – a sublime 'pause' which opens up a set of crucial issues about the inextricability of dream and despair in 1980s cinematic culture.

'The other side of now': *Nineteen Eighty-Four* as topical allusion

If in the 1960s 'the question of Utopia' was reinvented (Jameson 1988: 75), the 1970s and 1980s also saw its dystopian Other explored afresh. H. Bruce Franklin begins his survey of 'Visions of the future in science fiction films from 1970 to 1982' with the crashing generalisation, 'By the end of the 1960s, it seemed that we were experiencing the most profound crisis in human history': 'visions of decay and doom had become the normal Anglo-American cinematic view of our possible future' (Franklin 1990: 19). It may also be that by the time Terry Gilliam and Michael Radford came to make *Brazil* and *Nineteen Eighty-Four* respectively in the mid-1980s, dystopianism was not primarily a means of articulating a feared future or of fending off an alternative (socialist) social structure (as was Orwell's original novel), but a shrewd engagement with Britain's present (Gilliam's 'bleak days of 1983').

Fredric Jameson's important 1977 discussion of cultural utopianism, 'Of islands and trenches: neutralisation and the production of utopian discourse' (in Jameson 1988), bears this out. Although Jameson is addressing how utopian thought functions as a critique of the conditions which bring it into being, much of what he has to say is relevant to this analysis. For Jameson, one of the 'distinctive traits' of the utopian text is contemporaneity: an element 'of topical allusion,' he writes, 'is structurally indispensable in the constitution of the Utopian text' (Jameson 1988: 82). Utopias operate dialectically by neutralising the (dystopian) world from which they sprung. This is in keeping with a wider tradition of utopian criticism, but dystopias function in a similar way. Ruth Levitas writes that dystopias have often been read 'as apologetics for the status quo', but she highlights Krishan Kumar's view that dystopianism is 'intimately connected to the utopian impulse itself and...may be deeply critical of the present' (Levitas 1990: 176). *Brazil's* Preliminary Production Notes situated the film in a 'retro-future' which is defined as 'a way of looking at the future through the past, of revealing, so to speak, the other side of now'. If Orwell's novel addressed *his* present, Radford's and Gilliam's films address *theirs*.

Critics have found it hard to discuss *Nineteen Eighty-Four* outside of a debate about adaptation and the film's faithfulness to Orwell's original text. A narrative if not visionary ancestor is also George Lucas's *THX 1138* (1970), featuring a story-line of illicit love dragged straight out of Orwell, but worked through visionary *mise-en-scène* which is Lucas's own, focusing on star-crossed lovers who discover illicit desire in the shadow of a nebulous totalitarian regime. When read in terms of Anthony Burgess's point that *Nineteen Eighty-Four* is not future but past, not dystopian prediction but nihilistic analysis of Orwell's own 1948, the film's timely appearance in 1984 itself seems perhaps irrelevant. Clearly its tone and design evoke the grim postwar austerity of Orwell's anti-communist tract rather than conjuring up any dark scene of future shock – this is a future built from the past.

How, then, do we read the film through Jameson's observation, that 'The ultimate subject matter of Utopian discourse...[is]...its own conditions of possibility as discourse' (Jameson 1988: 101)? Is it necessary to read *Nineteen Eighty-Four* as itself a reading of 1984, not 1948, suspended as it is – in *mise-en-scène*, in its identity as film-of-novel, in its peculiar faithfulness to a postwar vision – between two times, and two different cultural forms? Or – in Krishan Kumar's words – 'How much is 1984 like *Nineteen Eighty-Four*?' (Kumar 1987: 292). Kumar (whose discussion is confined to analysis of Orwell's text and does not touch on Radford's film) is keen to retain the possibility that a novel ostensibly written about or for 1948 still addresses the real 1984 which Orwell did not live to see. For Kumar, its contemporaneity is bound up with its Englishness: '*Nineteen Eighty-Four* is about us,' he writes, 'it is about our own times. That, as Orwell points out, is one reason for the English setting of the novel: to show that it *could* happen here' (Kumar 1987: 295). The film's producer, however, preferred to see *Nineteen Eighty-Four* as a bizarre kind of feelgood film: Sheila Johnston quotes Simon Perry as saying 'Orwell's vision mercifully bears little resemblance to the real state of things in this year of 1984....When you come out of the theatre, it will be a lift to find the world as it actually is' (*Monthly Film Bulletin* December 1984). Some hope. Those who saw the whole of Thatcher's reign as a trial of totalitarianism may be tempted to schematically map film events onto real events (and Kumar's 'here' may even extend to 1997, when I noticed that a security and surveillance company employed by one Liverpool store was calling itself 'Big Brother Inc'). However, this is an extension of critical practice adopted in relation to Orwell's text itself. A whole area of Orwell studies is dominated by analysis of the novel as prophecy not fiction, with critics merrily 'ticking off' what Orwell got right and what he got wrong as history passes.

But given *Nineteen Eighty-Four*'s acute scrutiny of the problem of truth in the form of propaganda, reading its fictional history as an adjunct of real history seems strange. If anything, the film suggests that we can never know the truth of our moment behind the obfuscation of what 'they' would want us to know of it. It does, after all, begin with the lines:

> Who controls the past controls the future
> Who controls the present controls the past.

This is a 'truth' which Radford, and maybe Orwell himself, would have us read across the film and back out to our own awareness of the conditions of our history and readings.

The film adds another layer to this quandary of the real and the fictive, of the fictive as a prophetic allegory of the real. In this it goes one visual stage better than its source-novel. One of its primary assaults on the senses is the incessant telescreen announcements which saturate all levels of the world of *Nineteen Eighty-Four*. Wherever Winston goes there is a telescreen, showing documentary war footage or the still image of Big Brother, accompanied by a flat, triumphal, dogmatic Voice orating the latest Newspeak of the war with Eurasia. The images are often real (the film uses 'found' documentary footage rather in the manner of Oliver Stone in *JFK* (1991) and *Nixon* (1995). *Nineteen Eighty-Four* thus in part takes in a history of real conflict which stands in, visually, for the perpetual war Oceana is fighting. Only three locations offer a brief escape from the Voice and the telescreen, which is obligatory in every room: the countryside visited on an illegal Sunday excursion, the bedroom which Winston and Julia rent for their liaisons, and – most significantly – O'Brien's (Richard Burton's) office. As a high-ranking Party official, O'Brien has the power to turn the Voice off (one of his privileges, he says – even though the telescreen is mouthing *his* truths), so turn it off he does.

But what the Voice speaks is lies; what the images tell us are both lies and truth: 'These are our people', says the announcement as we see soldiers going over the top, planes crashing, blitzed houses, tanks advancing, all apparently 'found' images from the major conflicts of the twentieth century, accompanied by the Voice telling us of Oceana's glorious victories. A vague composite of Nazi rallies, holocaust victims, fleeing refugees, is montaged in sync with an Oceana-specific spoken text. Later in the film, as Winston sinks into ideological scepticism, the same footage is repeated, this time accompanied by Winston's own gloss: 'War is not real,' he says 'or when it is victory is not possible. The war is not meant to be won, it is meant to be continuous.' Finally, in the film's last sequence when Winston has conformed, the same images recur for a third time, with a voice-over which returns to its triumphal mode. What we see and what we hear are then two different things. What we *see* is recognisably 'our' history. The images reach, if not to the war beyond the image, then at least to a history of news and newsreel images we know (or thought we knew) were images of the real. Even in the half-seen flashes of moments of conflict, surrender, defeat and execution which pervade the film on the omnipresent telescreens, the awful roll-call of twentieth-century warfare is all too clear, its malleable truth-value even clearer. But what we *hear* accompanying this is a pastiche of propaganda, a controlling fiction masked as news. We see our history, we hear someone else's fiction. Between real 'found' images and the Voice itself there is a gap which begs the question, if that is not an image of the defeat of Eurasia, which does not exist, what is it? Whose truth? The truth and not the truth: a sepia staccato history of war from the moment it could first be filmed, undermined, resignified, in its juxtaposition with words. The distrust of the visual is pervasive, even when what you see rightly 'belongs to' and speaks of a world outside of the film's fiction.

However, perhaps more important than *Nineteen Eighty-Four*'s deployment of historical footage to signify its Otherness is the way it uses images which are far more familiar – grassy fields, glamorous women, sexual excess – to signify utopian escape, offering a confrontation of difference which Jameson calls the 'utopian event'. I want to turn back to Jameson briefly to explain how this utopic Otherness is displayed rather than told.

The utopian event: spectacle and narrative

For Jameson, utopian texts are important not because of what they *are* but because of what they *do*, functioning as critique (like Thomas More's 'neutralisation' of Tudor England as the negative referent in *Utopia* (1516)) and as a kind of imaginative provocation, encouraging a contemplation both of what is and of what could be. The post-1960s moment is for Jameson not Bruce Franklin's dystopian backlash of decay and doom, but a space of positive reflection and theorising that is the logical follow-up to the action of May 1968, with the 1970s inaugurating 'the maturation of a whole new generation of literary Utopias': 'The transition from the 60s to the 70s was a passage from spontaneous practice to renewed theoretical reflection…after the reawakening of the Utopian impulse of the previous decade' (Jameson 1988: 76–7). For Jameson, cultural texts (and he is particularly interested in Ursula LeGuin's *The Dispossessed* (1974)) can enact that theoretical reflection, but they do so in a very specific way, privileging spectacle and exegesis rather than narrative explanation and dynamism. '[I]t is less revealing', writes Jameson,

> to consider Utopian discourse as a mode of narrative, comparable, say, with novel or epic, than it is to grasp it as an object of mediation, analogous to the riddles or *koan* of the various mystical traditions, or the aporias of classical philosophy, whose function is to provoke a fruitful bewilderment and to jar the mind into some heightened but unconceptualisable consciousness of its own powers, functions, aims, and structural limits.
>
> (Jameson 1988: 87–8)

Utopias thus work by instigating 'a concrete set of mental operations', rather than setting out 'someone's "idea" of a "perfect society"'' (Jameson 1988: 81). The utopian moment is a kind of hesitation or hiatus, a shock or disjunctive interval when narrative action is subordinated in an act of showing.

Throughout 'Of Islands and Trenches' Jameson quotes (and heavily depends upon) Louis Marin's *Utopiques: Jeux d'espaces* (1973). Developing the notion of utopia as a 'break' which neutralises the conditions from which it springs, he writes that, 'the Utopian event itself' is a 'revolutionary *fête* [in which]... historical time was suspended' (Marin quoted in Jameson 1988: 77). A moment outside of history – outside of narrative unfolding? Jameson seems to edge closer to suggesting an almost deistic possibility of the suspension of time. But we might more positively see this as an activation of that etymological rendering of utopia as 'no place'. Utopia in Jameson is a suspension of *this* place which enables something else to be imagined. Thus by definition utopia cannot be ordinarily 'eventful':

> if things can really happen in Utopia, if real disorder, change, transgression, novelty, in brief if history is possible at all, then we begin to doubt whether it can really be a Utopia after all, and its institutions...slowly begin to turn around into their opposite, a more properly dystopian repression of the unique existential experience of individual lives.
>
> (Jameson 1988: 95)

Jameson's balancing act here is subtle. I am reminded of that David Byrne line, 'heaven is a place where nothing ever happens' – and earth is a place where everything does. It is so tempting to read this within a theological framework which would deem earthly action – movement or drive – as the agent, if not of the devil, then of the dystopic, with the stillness and stasis of utopia as a reinvented heavenly, if revolutionary, space. Jameson's moment of *fête* is not empty, however, even if it *is* non-narrative. 'In Utopian discourse,' writes Jameson, 'it is the narrative itself that tends to be effaced by and assimilated to sheer description, as anyone knows who has ever nodded over the more garrulous explanatory passages in the classical Utopias' (Jameson 1988: 95) Utopia is spectacle more than story (or explanation); it is a kind of provocative *showing*. Although he is discussing literary texts, Jameson picks open a form of writing which might be likened to the cinematic spectacle, calling utopian writing a 'timeless maplike extension of the nonplace' (Jameson 1988: 95). There is, of course, a paradox here. With the suspension of history in that 'revolutionary *fête*' goes narrative too, particularly difficult since the texts Jameson is dealing with are utopian *narratives*. As the plethora of utopian titles indicates (William Morris's *News from Nowhere* (1890), Samuel Butler's *Erewhon* (1872), or Tom Moylan's survey of feminist utopias, *Demand the Impossible* (1896)), utopias are essentially impossible, and they address impossibility. This is what I think Jameson means when he writes,

Utopia's deepest subject, and the source of all that is most vibrantly political about it is precisely our inability to conceive it, our incapacity to
produce it as a vision, our failure to project the Other of what is, a failure
that, as with fireworks dissolving back into the night sky, must once again
leave us alone with *this* history.

(Jameson 1988: 101)

Utopian narratives are then not only stories which enact a hesitation in the
history from which they came, but narratives which ask to be read outside of
the time they are formally and historically subject to, as *fête*, event, a literary
form of *showing*. Utopian discourse is profoundly characterised by a tension,
'between description and narrative, between the effort of the text to establish
the co-ordinates of a stable geographical entity, and its other vocation as sheer
movement and restless displacement, as itinerary and exploration and, ultimately, as event' (Jameson 1988: 95). This tension, this crisis between 'events' and
'display', shows the utopian hiatus, in Jameson's literary texts, to be remarkably
like the kind of work in which our *dystopian* films are engaged. Dystopian as
well as utopian texts are provocative rather than representational, important
not because of what they *are* but because of what they *do*. The dystopias under
discussion here are important not because of what they overtly *say* – their
dark 'content', their narrative gloom and enveloping pessimism – but because
of how they provoke the reflection and conceptual stimulus which Jameson
identifies in the utopian. They also contain within them – bear out, as it were,
in miniature – their own utopian moments, which 'suspend' the active sweep
of the film. Though not classic examples of 'action cinema', both films expose
a contradiction in its general aesthetic. For during the 1980s and 1990s the
term 'action' came to mean not dynamic narrative movement but regular
interruptions of the spectacular. Moments of spectacular interruption *are*,
then, the action. 'Action' is thus, paradoxically, not narrative movement but
visual event: shoot-outs, sex scenes, exploding helicopters. Such cinematically
spectacular 'moments' do not necessarily 'provoke fruitful bewilderment', but
there is still something particularly appropriate about Jameson's utopian
argument deployed as a politicised film theory. Both *Brazil* and *Nineteen Eighty-
Four* are dystopian narratives 'interrupted' by utopian spectacles. But these
films' utopian images are arguably far more explicitly 'suspending' than
conventional 'action' could be: they are dystopic visions which contain within
them moments of explicitly utopian hesitation and contemplation – figured
in each film as the spectacle of a woman's body. If we take utopia to mean not
just (literally and etymologically) 'no place' but also as provocative critical
vision, then the dark dreams of *Nineteen Eighty-Four* and *Brazil* must be read
as uncomfortable forms of utopian cinema.

Utopia's female face

Both dystopia and utopia in *Nineteen Eighty-Four* are rendered through the human face. The film's blighted other-worldliness is presented not through the motifs of the futuristic (weapons, vehicles, the architecture of the strange so beloved of science fiction design), but through its attitude to human skin as the limit of the self. As the film proceeds, any notion of human three-dimensionality – an illusion crucial to our identification, pleasure, recognition – gradually breaks down. Its narrative charts the progressive suturing of skin to self: self becomes what the skin displays. Despite Winston's dream-scape flashbacks, briefly intruding into the linear 'now' of the film's plot-time, character in *Nineteen Eighty-Four* is increasingly written blankly on the face, there is nothing beneath what we see. The politics of depersonalisation which Orwell feared and loathed has resulted in a blanking out of the concept of 'inner self', flattening difference so that all the fragments of contradictory subjectivity are gathered and synthesised into a singular, chanting, unquestioning mask-like retro-future-self. It is as if the Party's attempt at eradicating all traces of private being – individual linguistic quirks, memory, desire itself – has resulted in the most cinematically simplistic human form – one in whom what you see is what you get, fusing surface and interior.

However, the film (as well as Orwell) judges this to be a bad thing. This synthesis of (democratic) difference into (totalitarian) sameness is rendered through a palette of grey and sepia, a 'rubble film' *mise-en-scène* of cluttered frames and mildewed walls. Escape brings a more expansive sense of space, more vibrant colours. Mentally releasing himself from the horrors of torture, Winston flashes back to the open downland location of his rendezvous with Julia: sunshine and an unbroken, undulating green hillside. Dystopia is quite characteristically viewed as urban containment and overpopulation, utopia as solitary rural escape. But this recognisable world is there only to make the mask-face of Winston as dystopic non-subject accepting his prison, all the more horrific in contrast. These flashbacks precede Winston's total submission under torture, referring back to one of the film's most significant moments, a utopic glimpse which is not only Winston's fantasy, but the whole film's. Jameson's utopian moment was a flashpoint of ecstatic disturbance, but the 'disturbance' of dystopian images is not the same as this. Dystopias disturb as an effect of their displeasurable qualities, not because they interrupt. *The Oxford English Dictionary* defines disturbance as agitation, interruption, as a break or gap – displeasure only if what is being interrupted is equilibrium, calm or tranquillity. Developing Jameson's argument, we need to get away from the value-led understanding of disturbance as negative. That which 'disturbs' the dystopic terrain of *Nineteen Eight-Four* and *Brazil* is an image which offers a break from the negative.

I have read Jameson's 'hesitant' utopic moment as the subordination of narrative to still spectacle, when action, events or even history are suspended. This is an event uncannily like the woman's face, 'freez[ing] the flow of the action in moments of erotic contemplation' in Laura Mulvey's famous conception of sexual spectacle (Mulvey 1989: 14–26). Both *Nineteen Eighty-Four* and *Brazil* stunningly articulate the fusion of Jameson and Mulvey's frozen moments. In both films, the woman's face is the utopic image which does 'freeze the flow of the action' (see figure 24). Yet in *Nineteen Eighty-Four's* case, that old adage that one man's utopia is another man's dystopia comes to mind again. The key 'hesitant' image is set up thus. Julia – the active party in the development of the relationship ('I'm corrupt to the core', she says as she seduces the passive Winston) – brings to their meetings trinkets and motifs of the lost past, commodities which have been all but rationed out of existence – jam, 'proper white bread', and coffee. These made a bleak enough picnic, but the couple are grateful. At their next meeting she betters this, in an extraordinary scene in which, like some grotesque parody of postfeminism, freedom becomes the power to use cosmetics and don a pretty dress. Here, her gift to them both is the repackaged commodity of herself, as first she withdraws behind a screen, and then emerges, a proper woman, in floral print and subtle make-up. For just a moment – a moment which echoes that 'timeless' scene of memory collapsing into the present in *Vertigo* (1958), when Kim Novak's Judy remakes herself as Madeleine and appears from the bathroom – the film's time stops, *Nineteen Eighty-Four's* history is halted. Femininity in this conventional form is the agent of interruption.

Earlier I mentioned Jameson's argument, that dystopian images are often the dark renderings of anti-socialists:

Figure 24 'Utopia's female face: Kim Greist in *Brazil* (1985).
Source: Courtesy of the British Film Institute Stills, Posters and Designs

from religious arguments about the sinful hubris of an anthropocentric social order all the way to the vivid 'totalitarian' dystopias of the contemporary counterrevolutionary tradition (Dostoyevsky, Orwell, etc.), Utopia is a transparent synonym for socialism itself, and the enemies of Utopia sooner or later turn out to be the enemies of socialism.

(Jameson 1988: 76–7)

The enemies of utopia are then those who reread utopia as dystopia, by translating its key positive terms (the effacing of sexual difference, for instance) into negatives. This is nowhere clearer than in the moment when Julia masquerades as, and so becomes, a Real Woman, a refeminisation cast by the film as only the latest act in a long line of rebellions, following illegal daytrips, purloined sugar, orgasms, and subversive notes passed to Winston. Her makeover may be read as parody or performance, an active self-shaping which self-consciously constructs femininity, controlling it as well as displaying just what a construction it is. That the made-up woman offers Winston a brief glimpse of something better suggests that the film might in part be striking a bold challenge to the normative dogma of natural beauty. When Julia dresses up and makes up, is she fighting the fiction that real beauty must be natural? That this is the couple's last liaison, and that their arrest soon follows, suggests otherwise. To see such a conventional image of femininity as a bold escape from the strictures of a pseudo-communist state is a little like complimenting Soviet youth on their rebellious desire for Levis and Big Macs. Julia's is a desperate act which binds forbidden eroticism to sexual nostalgia, sealing arousal in a memory of a more gender-sure time, when Oceana's grey minions were not consigned to the social and sartorial sameness which effaced sexual difference. Underpinning all this is an insidious gender paranoia, that the result of social egalitarianism is sexual non-difference: it is not the orgasm specifically but its gender in general which is in peril.

By contrast, *Brazil's* sexual discourse is both more outrageous and less compromising. Terry Gilliam's dream girls are rather different, although Kim Griest's Jill, glimpsed swathed in ethereal gauze in Sam's dreams, may at first glance seem to be another of the elements of overlap between the two films under discussion here, constituting *Brazil's* as well as Sam's utopic escape. Gilliam lays open a wide range of feminine images to question the mutability of fashion, the malleability of flesh, the demands made of femininity. If *Nineteen Eighty-Four* accepts the image of escape from 'oppression' figured first through Julia's nakedness, then through her act of dressing up, *Brazil* sets up femininity as an escape which becomes a trap, as both the best and the worst possible visions. But one act of dressing up has particular significance for how we read the film's dystopianism.

Nineteen Eighty-Four resists the awkward questions raised by its positive presentation of Julia's desire for frills and femininity, and perhaps *Brazil* fares no better in answering the real sexual problems it poses. But what it does do is show how every positive form and image is always grounded in desire, a desire which is itself subject to the strictures of context. Sam's dream girl is *his* fantasy – the marked difference between the Jill of his dreams and Jill as she emerges in the 'real' world of the narrative, as an overall-clad truck driver, exposes the terms under which Sam desires at all. At first, Jill is only the dream girl who activates and animates Sam's internal escape-valve. She then appears as a 'real' woman, doing an active macho job, refusing to do anything but push forward the narrative. Finally, in her romance with Sam, she succumbs to Sam's dream and swaps action for spectacle. As the doomed romance proceeds, the pair exchange their respective images of what a 'dream girl' is. Sam increasingly falls for the truck driver as long as, in the end, she will drive him to the countryside to escape his urban nightmare (this is his final fantasy). But Jill goes the other way. In an extraordinary scene at Sam's mother Ida's flat (Ida Lowry is played by Katherine Helmond), Jill realises his dream, posing for him swathed in gauze in Ida's blonde wig. The dream comes alive in Sam's mother's bed. Jill disappears – from the story itself soon after this, and at this moment when she turns into his mother – and Ida takes her place. Then a little later in the film Ida disappears under the cosmetic knife, and Jill takes *her* place. In the end, Sam's mother's surgery turns her into his lover: Ida reveals that her final reconstruction has turned her into Jill. Gilliam brings this off by switching actresses: we see Ida's back – recognisable as Sam's mother – and then she turns around. Dream-girl becomes mother-lover: briefly it is Griest not Helmond who plays Sam's mother.

If this is *Brazil's* version of Julia's feminine masquerade, it twists the issue in a powerfully oedipal direction. The worst thing of all, Sam's final nightmare image, is that his mother is his dream girl. It is of course the best thing of all, too, as fulfilled oedipal fantasy briefly presents Sam's secret desire as the result of some of *Brazil's* most dystopian reconstructive practices. Hitherto the film may have focused on the unnaturalness of the surgical manipulation itself as key sign of *Brazil's* future-horror. In this final frieze, bodily manipulation becomes the process through which dystopia and utopia collapse into each other. The raw mechanism of the oedipal taboo, sharpening Sam's terminal panic as the film draws to a close, is laid bare in the wilful unfixity of the woman's face. That lover can become mother, mother lover, is the best and the worst of all possible desires. When Jill dons the wig, Sam's dreams take on flesh. When Ida turns around, he is confronted by the dream which can only bring punishment.

Bibliography

Franklin, H. Bruce (1990) 'Visions of the future in science fiction films from 1970 to 1982', in Annette Kuhn (ed.) *Alien Zone: Cultural Theory and Contemporary Science Fiction Cinema*, Verso: London.

Garrett, J.C. (1984) *Hope or Disillusion: Three Versions of Utopia: Nathaniel Hawthorne, Samuel Butler, George Orwell*, Christchurch, New Zealand: University of Canterbury Publications.

Jameson, Fredric (1986) *The Political Unconscious: Narrative as a Socially Symbolic Act*, London: Methuen.

—— (1988) *The Ideologies of Theory: Essays 1971–1986, Volume 2: The Syntax of History*, London: Routledge.

Johnson, Kim 'Howard' (1993) *Life Before and After Monty Python: The Solo Flights of the Flying Circus*, London: Plexus.

Kumar, Krishan (1987) *Utopia and Anti-Utopia in Modern Times*, Oxford: Basil Blackwell.

Levitas, Ruth (1990) *The Concept of Utopia*, Hemel Hempstead: Philip Allan.

Mathews, Jack (1987) *The Battle of Brazil*, New York: Crown Publishing.

Morgan, David (1988) 'The mad adventures of Terry Gilliam', *Sight and Sound* Autumn: 238–42

—— (1996) 'Extremities', *Sight and Sound* January 1996: 18–21.

Mulvey, Laura (1989) *Visual and Other Pleasures* London: Macmillan.

12 'No flesh shall be spared'
Richard Stanley's *Hardware*

Sue Short

From *Things to Come* (1936) onwards Britain has contributed a number of innovative but flawed exercises to a genre Hollywood has largely made its own. Lack of resources frequently precludes producing anything of real worth and originality, but occasionally a small gem is smuggled out which is more than a pale imitation of past successes, possessing a vitality that belies economic constraint, and inspiring new hope for British science fiction. *Hardware* (1990), though admittedly flawed, is one such work.

Richard Stanley first shot *Hardware* in 1983 while a film student in his native South Africa. After moving to London, he directed two award-winning shorts and went on to make pop promos for groups such as Fields of the Nephilim, Renegade Soundwave and Pop Will Eat Itself before *Hardware* was chosen to become Wicked Films' first feature. Stanley was twenty-four when he directed this sf/horror hybrid in only eight weeks in 1990, with a shoestring budget of £1 million (Finney 1996: 187–97). Although dismissed by most critics as cut-and-paste exploitation, the film became the most successful British independent production in America at the time of its release, taking £4 million in its opening fortnight (*Daily Mail* 5 October 1990: 32). Described by one critic as 'the first movie made in this country with a definite fanzine mentality' (Jones 1990: 38), it remains one of Britain's most notable forays into the science fiction genre.

Stanley's childhood spent travelling around war-torn parts of the world and his subsequent experiences in Afghanistan strongly influenced the film's image of an overpopulated future destroying itself through perpetual warfare. As Stanley perceived it, 'The way things are in the third world at the moment is a good model for what things would be like in the first world if things just slipped a notch, like they did in *Hardware*' (Dorgan 1990: 14). What causes this 'slip' is the trusty convention of a post-apocalyptic society derived from the Book of Revelation, a childhood diet of horror comics and Michael Moorcock, and the obvious influence of a lifetime of films. *Hardware*'s visual and thematic concerns place it within the select sf sub-genre of cyberpunk cinema, including *Blade Runner* (1982), *RoboCop* (1987) and *Akira* (1988), which feature violent urban dystopias and disenfranchised masses. Steve Woolley of Palace Pictures, the company that produced *Hardware*, was the first to note the commercial familiarity of the script, describing it as being 'like *Mad Max* meets Judge Dredd' of *2000 AD* comic (Board 1990: 66). This is ironic in light of the lawsuit subsequently brought against the film by Fleetway Comics, which contended that it had substantially plagiarised 'SHOK!', a comic-strip story published in the 1981 annual edition of *2000 AD*, home to Judge Dredd and the post-apocalyptic future of Megacity One (Finney 1996: 194–5).

Both 'SHOK!' and *Hardware* share the same initial premise: a war droid's remains are brought from the cursed Earth/Outer Zone into the home of a metalwork sculptress, where it re-assembles, plugs itself into the electricity supply, and traps her within the apartment. The film also includes a key scene in which a fridge is used to fool the droid's heat-sensors. However, there is more to *Hardware* than these similarities suggest and its eclectic borrowing cannot be credited to just one source. General comic-strip influences are also evident in *Hardware*'s visual style, which crams each scene with detail, as well as in its black humour, off-the-wall dialogue and relentless narrative pace. The rapid cuts, unusual camera angles and colour tints also reveal Stanley's apprenticeship in music videos, which enabled him to make the most of limited resources. Belated acknowledgement was given to Fleetway and the writers of 'SHOK!' in the final credits, yet despite the debt to comics and sf films like *Mad Max* (1979), *Alien* (1979) and *The Terminator* (1984), *Hardware* is considerably more than the sum of its parts.

An anonymous nomad (played by Fields of the Nephilim frontman, Carl McCoy) finds the helmet and torso of an android in the desert wastes of the Outer Zone and takes these to a scrap-dealer called Alvy. Soldier Mo (Dylan McDermott) drops by on his return from space to buy his girlfriend Jill (Stacy Travis) a last-minute Christmas present (see figure 25). As he makes his way to her apartment with the droid's remains and his side-kick Shades (John Lynch), we are given a view of a shanty town futureworld complete with goats, fires and medieval costumes. A river boat cabbie, played by Lemmy of Motorhead, comments on the declining neighbourhood: 'It used to be all right with brass knuckles, a piece of pipe or wood. Nowadays you need a gun all the time.' We are familiar with this territory, yet Stanley plays with our knowledge of previous post-apocalyptic futures, employing various subcultural icons and images along the way. Iggy Pop supplies the voice of DJ Angry Bob ('the man with the industrial dick') sneering the bad news on W.A.R. Radio: 'Rise and shine folks, it's a beautiful day. Just look at that sky' – cut to industrial landscape bathed in red – 'It's a work of art! Nature never knew colour like that.' This is our mordant introduction to the consequences of fatally tampering with nature, a theme explored throughout the narrative with the same mixed response of wonder and dread.

As Mo and Shades make their way past a crowded slum dwelling, Mo remarks, 'Somebody ought to help these people. Or clear them out.' It's the latter option the government has decided on in the form of the Mark 13, the android Mo unwittingly carries with him. The Mark 13 is a multi-limbed metal nightmare with a humanoid skull, developed to implement the government's

Figure 25 Post-punk apocalypse: Dylan McDermott as Mo in *Hardware* (1990).
Source: Courtesy of the British Cinema and Television Research Group archive

'Emergency Population Control Bill' – the next stage of a 'voluntary' sterilisa-
tion programme described by the President as 'a clean break with
procreation'. The pollution caused by a 'constant war state' has taken its toll on
humanity, and the government's solution is fascistic and final. Radiation
poisoning has led to genetic mutations like Alvy, a deformed midget whose
'mom got a dose in the Big One'. Shades advises Mo that dying in space
would be preferable to 'waiting for your first cancer cells to show, or your kids
to be born blind and blue because you've had one trip too many and have
come up snake-eyes in the genetic crap game'. Mo takes his chances, but his
girlfriend Jill is unwilling to take such a risk.

   Shut away in high-tech security solitude from the masses, she greets visitors with a Geiger counter and makes metalwork sculptures that no one ever
sees or buys. The world is brought to her via the TV and radio, the food
parcels she orders and the welfare cheques sent to her apartment. She has a
job on the side 'customising consoles for up-towners', with chainsaw and
blowtorch functioning as the tools of her trade and her craft. Jill uses technology as both self-expression and self-defence, to protect herself from the
outside world and to comment on it. As she says of her latest sculpture, 'I've
been basing my work more on organic forms, but sometimes by the time
they're finished it's hard to tell. It's like I'm fighting with the metal and, so far,
the metal's winning.'

This assessment underlies the film's repeated motif of a doomed humanity trapped by monstrous technology. The world has sown the seeds of its own destruction and created a future fit only for machines. Genetic mutation anticipates the ultimate death of the species and the obsolescence of flesh, as symbolised by the Mark 13, whose fangs drip with cell-destroying toxins. The droid can be seen as a literal war machine, combining paramilitary technology such as heat-seeking weapons and chemical warfare. As Stanley comments in *Hardware*'s production notes, 'The Mark 13 is very much a mechanical creature trying to be alive. But it's also representative of the worst of technology gone haywire.' Jill's apartment functions as a technologised womb within which the Mark 13 gestates. It lies in a jumbled heap waiting to be reborn.

Jill and Mo's love-making marks an act that no longer signifies. Invaded by technology via pervert neighbour Lincoln's infra-red telescope, Jill's image is appropriated by photographs taken with a gloved hand: the epitome of private space rendered obscene and pornographic. It is at this point that the eyes of the Mark 13 are first triggered, as if witnessing a primal scene and recognising its purpose and prey. It bides its time as Jill, inspired by the spectacle of war and violence on her TV set, sets about the shattered fragments of the android with blowtorch and chainsaw, welding together her latest creation. The metal skull of the Mark 13, sprayed with stars and stripes and surrounded by burnt plastic dolls, is her response to the Population Control Bill and a world where reproduction is 'stupid and sadistic and suicidal'. Jill and Mo argue over the implications of the Bill, with Mo maintaining that, 'It'll never work. It's our nature to reproduce, to live on through our children.' Yet as Jill points out, 'nature' is no longer a fixed term, but a relative one: 'Mankind's always gone against his nature. It used to be natural to die of old age before you were thirty.' In refusing to have children she takes maternal responsibility for creation, unaware that this role is about to be superseded by the 'sculpture' she tinkers with. Mo doesn't think beyond his own place in the evolutionary stakes, convinced that 'things will get worse before they get better' and looking forward to proving himself 'one of the fittest'. He is himself a cyborg, fitted with a prosthetic mechanical arm and filled with a confident machismo that seriously underestimates the true purpose of the Mark 13, itself a physical embodiment of Mo's philosophy and Jill's nightmare vision of the world.

Christmas Day marks the advent of a new 'messiah' as the droid reconstructs itself from the various pieces of hardware in the apartment. Its relative superiority in terms of self-reproduction, adaptability and assimilation announce the arrival of the ultimate combat model intent on rendering both Mo and Jill obsolete. Mo – named after Moses, the Old Testament prophet and patriarch – reads aloud from the Bible of the 'birth pains' humanity must endure in the Final Judgement: 'The earth will shake, rattle and roll. The masses will go hungry, their bellies bloat. These are the birth pains. No flesh shall be spared.' (Mo also experiences an earlier moment of prophecy when he wakes from a dream that foretells what is to come and the final solution: 'I could hear the rain, and the glass,' he tells Jill, his hand almost touching the window she will finally go through.)

Satanic references to the Mark 13 are scattered throughout the film, such as the 'BAAL' access code, the pentangle at the centre of its circuit diagram, and its demonic red eyes. Yet though all are indications of an infernal power, the Mark 13 is man-made evil, created and programmed by the latest weapons technology, and designed to absorb information from the humans it comes into contact with. As such it is no more mechanical and no less human than the predatory society that has created it: 'The Mark 13 does not transgress the boundary between human and machine so much as it denies that boundary's existence, its intelligence is performative, assimilating voices and programs from its victims' (Fuchs 1995: 295).

That the droid is gendered as male appears to be a given. It waits until Jill is alone before trapping her in the apartment. After its eyes meet his across the surveillance, Lincoln arrives at the door intending to actualise fantasy into action: a sick twist on the slasher's male 'helper' tradition. This provides a 'double monster' dilemma, with Lincoln's attempts to override the security system delaying the rape for narrative tension. Yet his conceit fatally underestimates the Mark 13 and by way of poetic justice he is stabbed through the eyes while attempting to open the blinds. The threat he posed, however, is merely increased by the droid. As in *Saturn 3* (1980) a British sf film directed by Stanley Donen, and an acknowledged influence on *Hardware*, a malevolent droid assimilates the illicit desire of a dysfunctional male character. The Mark 13 subjects Jill to more than a quick kill, attempting to fulfil Lincoln's misogynistic lust through the ultimate means of displaying male power. A disturbing simulated rape sequence, in which a drill moves between Jill's forcibly opened legs, combines elements of *Demon Seed* (1977) and the worst of the 'stalk and slash' tradition. Another stock horror cliché follows as Jill is saved in the nick of time by Mo, who blasts the Mark 13 out of the window. Seeing the world outside her broken window (rather than through a monitor or TV screen) her relative isolation is made clear as Jill gasps: 'Jesus, it's beautiful.' The shot is like a spell being broken and a rite of passage. Only now does she understand the purpose of the droid and its implications for humanity, wryly commenting that: 'It doesn't care who it kills. It's the first useful thing they've given us.' Yet crucially she also affirms, 'I want to live', before being pulled out of the windows by her relentless adversary.

Technology again separates Jill from Mo as she clings to an electrified pole outside her apartment, forming a deadly unbreakable circuit between them. Unable to hold on, she falls crashing into the apartment below. Inside, the Mark 13 injects Mo with a deadly narcotic. His drug-fuelled outrage and disbelief echo Tony Montana in the climax of *Scarface* (1982) as he protests, 'You can't fuck with me. You can't fuck with Mo. I'm divinely protected, asshole.' Rendered defunct by the latest technology, his mechanical hand takes a knife and slashes his human wrist as his last thoughts are recorded by the Mark 13: a haunting image of the man/machine interface taken to its ultimate conclusion.

At this point the film undergoes an interesting gender reversal as Jill is resurrected from her fall and returns upstairs with a baseball bat. Like the 'Final Girl' of the slasher film, it is Jill rather than Mo who displays the courage and resourcefulness of a true survivor, realising the need to fight to stay alive (Clover 1992: 35–41). As Stanley put it, 'I wanted to give a thumbs-up for essential human savagery' (Dorgan 1990: 14) and it is significant that Jill finds the strength to face the enemy. Facing the enemy is synonymous with naming it, and Jill understands not only the purpose of the droid but why she is a threat to it, shouting, 'Why don't you come after me, you fucking power junkie? You're scared.' Her threat to the Mark 13 is implicit. Able to kill male characters with ridiculous ease, the Mark 13's pursuit of her is difficult and prolonged. Although capable of perpetual rebirth, it is unable to compete with the human female's ability to generate new life, and sets out to destroy it at source. This fear of the female as the site of reproduction is also evident in *Alien* (1979), with its depiction of monstrous fecundity, as well as *Inseminoid* (1980) and *Xtro* (1982) (see Wright, this volume). Vivian Sobchack has lamented sf's tendency to obscure the realities of reproduction and the female role within this (Sobchack 1990: 108–9). *Hardware* makes a significant contribution to redressing the balance, with reproduction as a central theme.

Jill's technological environment has contributed to her entrapment in the apartment: her surveillance system is turned against her, the metal doorway malfunctions, and there is the Mark 13 itself. (The film works on one level as a parody of female domestication, with the kitchen as a battleground and Jill armed at one point with an electric carving knife.) Yet humanity wins out against technology when Jill learns to use it against itself and gains access to the Mark 13's programme via her computer console. She turns the tables on the Mark 13 through this mental assault: 'Yeah, you can feel me now, mother-fucker. I'm right inside your mind.' Mo is but a ghost in the machine during this software/hardware interface, a disembodied voice possessing the vital clue to the Mark 13's fatal flaw. Hearing Mo's dream of rain played back through the terminal, Jill grasps its significance for the first time: it indicates a defect in the droid's moisture insulation. Water, symbol of goodness and purity, is the droid's Achilles' heel, as it is for the Wicked Witch of the West. Jill lures the Mark 13 into the shower in a parodic reversal of the murder in *Psycho* (1960) and smashes it to smithereens.

In winning the battle and slaying the beast, Jill not only confirms her will to survive but stakes a claim in the future. Yet victory is only temporary. The final image shows Jill looking at the droid's remains as we hear that the Mark 13 is about to go into production. Like the only survivor of *Westworld* (1973), or Sarah Connor facing the approaching storm at the end of *The Terminator*, Jill knows that humanity doesn't seem to have a hope in hell, but at least she knows what's coming. Suzanne Moore has criticised the negative fatalism of this conclusion as emblematic of 'Left pessimism' and what Fredric Jameson called the 'atrophy of the utopian imagination' – the cultural inability to conceive of any alternative to capitalism (*New Statesman and Society* 5 October 1990).

As Moore says, 'The attitude in *Hardware* is one of resignation – the world is fucked up and we can do nothing to change it.' Stanley admits to this pessimistic streak in his work, citing the strong influence of the seventies cycle of post-holocaust sf, which had a similarly ominous view of society's fate: 'It does tend to say that the world's going to hell very quickly and there's not a lot anyone can do' (Board 1990: 66). Despite criticising war and industrial capitalism, the film falls short of any solutions and lapses instead into nihilistic despair. The repetition of PiL's insistent refrain of 'This is what you want, this is what you get' in the final reels appears to be a wake-up call to cynicism and complacency, but *Hardware* strongly implies that it may already be too late for change. Despite the film's lack of solutions, it remains an essentially *critical* dystopia in placing its concerns within the context of an extreme but believable world. In this sense *Hardware* is a political film played for entertainment.

Like *The Terminator* and countless other scenarios, *Hardware* hinges on the fear that we will be superseded by our machines, warning against the danger of creating a mechanical weapon that can no longer distinguish between the 'enemy' and ourselves. However, *Hardware* goes one political step further in having the government deliberately programme machines to wipe out humanity, or at least those parts of it deemed undesirable. The implication is that a none too subtle form of eugenics is being carried out by the Mark 13. Its victims are all imperfect in terms of reproduction: Alvy is genetically deformed, Lincoln is bloated and monstrous, and numerous references are made to the levels of radiation to which Mo has been exposed in the Outer Zone. Within this context Fuchs considers the colour of the two security guards who also die to be significant, and claims that people of colour have been selectively targeted: 'Their connection to Miles Dyson [of *Terminator 2: Judgment Day* (1992)] who also dies to save a white woman and the future, cannot be overlooked' (Fuchs 1995: 297). Described by Stanley as 'A psychedelic neo-fascist entertainment spiked for the Nineties', the film is a cynical commentary on the state of the world today and the tendency of history to repeat itself: 'I've included Auschwitz references, genocide and other nastiness to underline how these things won't mean anything to 21st century people. I'm moving punk from vinyl to film' (Jones 1990: 28).

Concerned with the level of complicity that occurs within oppressive societies, Stanley aimed to make the film both relevant and recognisable to contemporary audiences. That the source of the problem is governmental rather than corporate locates the film's concerns firmly within the present, implicating Thatcherism in the cynical self-interest exhibited by Mo and Jill. As Stanley explains:

> There are a number of elements that are not so much science-fiction as a much more insane version of now. Jill is basically living on welfare and cheating on the side, by customising and selling consoles. The right-wing government, too, is faintly recognisable. I wanted to have a situation in which the government was totally right-wing, almost fascistic, but where

all the characters have come to assume that their extreme policies are the best ones under the circumstances. Basically, in order to survive, they have had to buy into the machine, the monster, and what it represents, even though they know that it's killing them.

(Floyd 1990: 21)

This investment is literalised by the Mark 13 going into production. Disguised as job creation for the unemployed, the assembly-line that produces the Mark 13 is designed for mechanical and not human reproduction, its workers literally about to be transformed into dead labour. This concept recalls *Metropolis* (1926), in which the masses shuffle into the mouth of Moloch and humanity is sacrificed to the machine. As Fuchs notes, 'Jill's art, Mo's scavenging, even Lincoln's voyeuristic thrills serve to reproduce technoculture instead of bodies' (Fuchs 1995: 296).

Of course, *Hardware* is as guilty of reproducing 'technoculture' as any of the film's characters. The film itself, like Jill's art, is a postmodern assemblage of found objects and reflections of popular culture. As well as allusions to other films (including spaghetti westerns, Hitchcock's *Rear Window* (1954), and the copious use of red-filtered lighting borrowed from Italian horror director, Dario Argento), *Hardware* also refers to the cyberpunk performance art of Survival Research Laboratories in the clips of SRL videos seen on Jill's TV and in the Mark 13 itself. As Mark Dery contends (1996: 128), 'The renegade combat droid is undeniably patterned after SRL's robots.' (SRL founder Mark Pauline has described his shows as 'a satire of kill technology, an absurd parody of the military-industrial complex', which could equally describe both *Hardware* and its monster (Dery 1996: 119).) The inclusion of numerous horror motifs are a deliberate pastiche of generic convention, while the soundtrack, which combines Rossini's *Stabat Mater* and Ministry's industrial rock, is a postmodern conflation of high and low culture. The film is also highly self-reflexive, not only identifying itself with both Jill's art and the Mark 13, but also implicating itself and the audience with Lincoln's voyeurism. Yet perhaps *Hardware*'s most significant postmodern trait is its overwhelming pessimism. Evoking Baudrillard's cynical vision of a future that is 'more a survival among the remnants than anything else' (Kellner 1989: 25), a scrap metaphor is used throughout the film, its characters forced to scavenge a living and humanity itself seen as the disposable waste product of an exploitative system.

Like the resurrected Mark 13, *Hardware* is assembled from reconstituted parts, a salvage operation made necessary by lack of funding and the prevailing punk ethos of its makers. Costumes were cobbled together from material left behind from fringe theatrical productions at the Roundhouse Theatre, while designer Joseph Bennett raided aircraft scrapyards for the retrotech setting. As Stanley stated, 'It's cyberpunk combined with an Italian sensibility and my personal obsessions' (Jones 1990: 30). Cyberpunk motifs include prosthetics, urban waste, eroded high tech, drugs and industrial music as well as the subcultural references to *2000 AD* and SRL. Yet the film also rejects cyber-punk's central ethos that humanity must ultimately become refigured in technological terms if it is to survive, arguing instead that it will merely be superseded. The Mark 13 is a fatal embodiment of technological rationalism, and Mo's renegade robot arm is proof that any attempt at fusion with the machine can only result in suicide.

Stanley has claimed that *Saturn 3* was the film's biggest inspiration, further arguing that the writers of 'SHOK!' had used the same film as their artistic springboard (Landon 1991: 27). Similarities certainly exist between the malfunctioning droid Hector in *Saturn 3* and the Mark 13, most obviously in the extent to which both droids assimilate the 'programming' of their imper-fect male role models and then set about terrorising young women. Religious significance is equally implied through Hector's being labelled the 'first of the demi-god series', and the Mark 13's demonic status (see figure 26). Moreover, both droids are designed to replace human functions. Of the two competing males in *Saturn 3* both are inferior to Hector, with Benson (Harvey Keitel) being mentally defective and the Major (Kirk Douglas) old and 'obsolete'. The Major, who represents an outmoded value system, regrets that he is 'not update enough for murder' and dies in the battle against the machine. But whereas Alex (Farrah Fawcett, the object of three-fold desire) is passive and child-like and relies on the Major's sacrifice to be saved, Jill is clearly a modern heroine and knows that she must save herself if she is to survive.

What *Hardware* has taken from *Saturn 3* it clearly improves upon, with one interesting exception. An exchange between the two security guards in *Hardware* is lifted almost wholesale from *Saturn 3*. While playing chess, Chief cites the Sicilian Manoeuvre as the only way to beat a computer: 'Machines don't understand sacrifice. Neither do morons.' In *Saturn 3* the Major beats Hector at chess with the same method, admonishing Benson for not having taught the droid enough: 'Sacrifice. It's the one thing you can't teach them, Captain.' But while the Major emphasises the narrative weight of this line by sacrificing himself for Alex, the security men's deaths in *Hardware* are effec-tively rendered meaningless, played for laughs rather than pathos. Mo's death too is also utterly futile, ironically reinforcing his philosophy of the 'survival of the fittest', and perhaps indicating that *Hardware* is deliberately, as one critic put it, 'miles of surface without an inch of depth' (Landon 1991: 24). *Saturn 3*, in turn, exemplifies the worst tendency of postmodern film to borrow from sources without contributing anything of its own. In contrast to the vitality of *Hardware*, it is a lacklustre exercise in genre film-making. Opening with a shot from *Star Wars* (1977) and concluding with a spaceship scene reminiscent of *2001: A Space Odyssey* (1968), it borrows from numerous sf texts including Harlan Ellison's short story 'I Have No Mouth, and I Must Scream' (1967), *Forbidden Planet* (1956) in the near incestuous relationship between the Major and Alex, and *Alien*'s claustrophobic setting. The film remains a relatively poor example of British sf compromising artistry and originality in a bid to sell itself.

Figure 26 *Hardware*'s 'biggest inspiration': killer droid Hector and Alex (Farrah
          Fawcett) in *Saturn 3* (1980).
Source: Courtesy of the British Cinema and Television Research Group archive

The same economic imperative also applied to *Hardware* yet yielded far
different results. Part horror flick, part science fiction, part pop promo, with
influences culled from American mainstream and European arthouse cinema,
Hardware is emphatically hybrid. Made in England by a South African
director, and cast in Hollywood with American leads, the film shows the signs
of a product clearly tailored for an American market. The script was revised

four times and the resulting Americanisation of terminology, with giros renamed 'welfare cheques' and the Prime Minister termed the 'President', indicate cultural references easily lost in translation yet still apparent within the film. What survives of British culture reveals itself in the film's dour atmosphere, location shots around the Thames, and Jill's lifestyle on the dole. As Stanley commented, 'I'd have loved to have taken over a council estate and used that as the main setting. It would have been ideal, because the whole idea basically grew out of all the maniacs I knew living on the dole, customising their council flats into something that was eventually worse than the outside world' (Board 1990: 67). What might have resulted with this in mind is an intriguing idea. Nevertheless contemporary British themes – an underlying pessimism about Anglo–US relations, unemployment as a scrapheap existence, and the dangers of individual collusion – are all hinted at in the text. Although nominally set in the United States, location shots around London remain recognisable signifiers of national identity disguised in an attempt at commercial acceptability. Part of *Hardware*'s charm is the extent to which it reveals more than it conceals in terms of the expectations and constraints placed upon it.

Since *Star Wars* gave the sf genre new legitimacy, each commercial success has inspired a series of imitations, with plots, iconography, stars and directors endlessly recycled. *Hardware* is as guilty of this as any other sf film but opts for a mode of enunciation that openly plays on a collective 'knowing-ness'. Freely trading on its derivative qualities, the video release was even marketed as a copy – 'A Terminator for the Nineties' – a cynical strategy that negates *Hardware*'s own innate qualities. The plot may be familiar and the allusions all too easy to spot, yet the film possesses an integrity, witty self-reflexivity and an assured visual style that raise it above mere imitation or scrapbook film-making.

At the time of its release, Stanley claimed that the problem with the British film industry was that it no longer made good cheap exploitation movies of the Hammer and Carry On variety (Freedman 1990: 65). *Hardware* was designed to be just such a film. As Anne Billson admiringly remarked, these kind of 'cheap, cheerful stories in which people are chopped in half and gush blood are *precisely* the sort of entertainment the British Film Industry should be turning out if it wants to survive' (*Sunday Correspondent* 7 October 1990: 37). Two years after its completion, Stanley was ambiguous about the film, stating that '*Hardware* is like a monster child to me. I don't know whether to be proud of it or reject it' (Kermode 1992: 14). He remains equally ambivalent about it today, stating, 'It gives people what they want. I'm still fond of the beast but hope to get a few more ideas in' (personal interview 1998). Plans to direct a sequel, updating and extending his original aims, are currently in development. Having turned down a lucrative offer to direct an adaptation of *Judge Dredd*, Stanley returned to hybrid film-making in his next feature, *Dust Devil* (1992) – a horror/road movie/Western set in South Africa that further demonstrated his versatility and political awareness. A Marillion video in 1994 was followed by a screenwriting credit on the ill-fated re-make of *The Island of Dr Moreau* (1996) and there has since been a notable silence from a talent that should not go to waste.

What *Hardware* proves above all, with its sheer style and energy, is that lack of money is not always a barrier to innovative film-making, and that resourcefulness and determination can go a long way – without necessarily having to buy into the machine.

Bibliography

Board, Steve (1990) 'Killing machine', *The Face* September: 66–7.

Clover, Carol J. (1992) *Men, Women and Chainsaws: Gender in the Modern Horror Film*, London: British Film Institute.

Dery, Mark (1996) *Escape Velocity: Cyberculture at the End of the Century*, London: Hodder and Stoughton.

Dorgan, George (1990) 'See androids fighting', *Independent* August 31: 14.

Finney, Angus (1996) *The Egos Have Landed: The Rise and Fall of Palace Pictures*, London: Heinemann.

Floyd, Nigel (1990) 'Cheap thrills', *Time Out* 26 September: 20–2.

Freedman, Peter (1990) 'Richard Stanley: film director', *ES Magazine* January: 65.

Fuchs, Cynthia (1995) 'Death is irrelevant: cyborgs, reproduction, and the future of male hysteria', in Chris Hables Gray (ed.) *The Cyborg Handbook*, London: Routledge.

Jones, Alan (1990) 'Hardcore *Hardware*', *Starburst* September: 28–30.

Kellner, Douglas (1989) *Jean Baudrillard – from Marxism to Postmodernism and Beyond*, London: Polity.

Kermode, Mark (1992) 'Blow up a storm: the making of *Dust Devil*', *Sight and Sound* September: 14–17.

Landon, Brooks (1991) 'Cyberpunk on a shoestring', *Cinefantastique* April: 21–4.

Sobchack, Vivian (1990) 'The virginity of astronauts', in Annette Kuhn (ed.) *Alien Zone: Cultural Theory and Contemporary Science Fiction Cinema*, London: Verso.

Filmography of British science fiction films of the sound era

I. Q. Hunter

This is a chronological filmography of British sound movies over sixty minutes in length with significant but not necessarily dominant science fiction elements.

As noted in the Introduction, science fiction is very much a hybridised genre and sf films frequently overlap with both fantasy and horror. In fact many of the films on this list might equally be assigned to the horror genre, since their primary intention is to terrify rather than to extrapolate imaginatively from current scientific knowledge. For the purposes of this filmography, I have assumed that if a film's horrors have an innovative rational basis rather than a magical or supernatural one, then it can be ushered into the science fiction genre. Thus movies about mad scientists like Frankenstein and Dr Jekyll and Mr Hyde are included, though strictly speaking such films belong to the hyphenated category of 'sf-horror', which accounts in fact for the majority of British sf films.

This filmography does not strain to include all films that touch on science fiction, or needlessly to claim for the genre films that the original audience would have categorised in very different ways. It lists films that involve distinctive sf themes such as time-travel, futuristic space flight, aliens and so on, but not those in which the sf element is limited to McGuffins like atom bombs and laser beams. The Bond films and its imitators are left off for that reason, with the exception of *Moonraker* (1979), and so are the Bulldog Drummond films of the 1930s and 1940s. It makes more sense to regard these as fantastical spy thrillers. Comedies are included, except for three sex comedies of the 1970s, *She'll Follow You Anywhere* (1971), *The Love Pill* (1972) and *I'm Not Feeling Myself Tonight* (1975), whose plots turn on the invention of infallible aphrodisiacs and in which the sf element is minimal.

From the 1970s onwards it is often difficult to pin down the nationality of a film. For example, reference sources often class *Alien* (1979) and *Outland* (1981) as American rather than British movies. This confusion simply reflects the complex nature of internationally funded co-production as well as the changing formulae that determine a film's national identity. In ambiguous cases I have generally followed the recommendation of the *Monthly Film Bulletin* and the British Film Institute's SIFT database.

This is a speculative rather than definitive filmography, and readers will doubtless want to add and subtract titles. There is no attempt to construct a pure or uncluttered list, but rather to indicate the breadth of sf-related production and the persistence of sf themes across a range of genres and periods.

Films are listed chronologically by their British release title. Alternative and American variations are shown in brackets. The date shown is that of registration as a British film rather than the date of first release. It is noted when these dates differ significantly. Running times refer to the original cinema release in Britain; variations are given when they occur.

Abbreviations used

US   American title

orig   the original, usually pre-release running time

bw   black and white

col   colour. Details are given of special widescreen/anamorphic processes with aspect ratios over 1:1.85.

pc   production company (distributors are not given)

d   director

prod   producer (executive and associate producers are not shown)

sc   author of screenplay

story   original story by. A source novel, play, TV serial, short story etc. is specified as such, with its title given if different from the film's. More unusual writing credits are given in full as they appear on the screen.

cast   four leading players

High Treason

1929 95, 69m bw; *pc* Gaumont; *d* Maurice Elvey; *sc* L'Estrange Fawcett; *play* Noel Pemberton-Billing; *cast* Benita Hume, Jameson Thomas, Basil Gill, Humberston Wright.

Elstree Calling

1930 95m bw/Pathécolour; *pc* British International Pictures; *d* Adrian Brunel, Alfred Hitchcock, Jack Hulbert, André Charlot, Paul Murray; *prod* John Maxwell; *sc* Adrian Brunel, Walter C. Mycroft, Val Valentine; *cast* Jack Hulbert, Cicely Courtneidge, Anna May Wong.

Once in a New Moon

1934 63m bw; *pc* Fox British; *d, sc* Anthony Kimmins; *novel* Owen Rutter; *cast* René Ray, Morton Selten, Wally Patch, John Clements.

The Tunnel (US: Transatlantic Tunnel)

1935 94m bw; *pc* Gaumont; *d* Maurice Elvey; *prod* Michael Balcon; *sc* Kurt Siodmak, L. Du Garde Peach, Clemence Dane; *novel Der Tunnel* by Bernhard Kellermann; *cast* Richard Dix, Leslie Banks, Madge Evans, Helen Vinson, C. Aubrey Smith.

The Man Who Changed His Mind (US: The Man Who Lived Again)

1936 68m bw; *pc* Gainsborough; *d* Robert Stevenson; *prod* Michael Balcon; *sc* L. du Garde Peach, Sidney Gilliat, John L. Balderstone; *cast* Boris Karloff, Anna Lee, John Loder, Frank Cellier.

The Man Who Could Work Miracles

1936 82m bw; *pc* London; *d* Lothar Mendes; *prod* Alexander Korda; *sc* H.G. Wells, Lajos Biró (uncredited); *short story* Wells; *cast* Roland Young, Joan Gardner, Ralph Richardson, Ernest Thesiger.

Things to Come

1936 113m bw; *pc* London; *d* William Cameron Menzies; *prod* Alexander Korda; *sc* H.G. Wells, Lajos Biró (uncredited); *novel The Shape of Things to Come* by Wells; *cast* Raymond Massey, Cedric Hardwicke, Margaretta Scott, Ralph Richardson.

Midnight Menace (US: Bombs over London)

1937 78m bw; *pc* Grosvenor; *d* Sinclair Hill; *prod* Harcourt Templeman; *sc* G.H. Moresby-White; *cast* Charles Farrell, Fritz Kortner, Margaret Vyner, Danny Green.

Non Stop New York

1937 71m bw; *pc* Gaumont; *d* Robert Stevenson; *prod* Michael Balcon; *sc* Curt Siodmak, Roland Pertwee, J.O.C. Orton, Derek Twist; *novel Sky Steward* by Ken Attiwill; *cast* John Loder, Anna Lee, Francis L. Sullivan, Frank Cellier.

Q Planes (US: Clouds over Europe)

1939 82m bw; *pc* London; *d* Tim Whelan; *prod* Irving Asher; *sc* Ian Dalrymple; *orig story* Brock Williams, Jack Whittingham, Arthur Wimperis; *cast* Laurence Olivier, Valerie Hobson, Ralph Richardson, George Merritt.

Give Us the Moon

1944 95m bw; *pc* Gainsborough; *d, sc* Val Guest; *prod* Edward Black; *novel* *The Elephant is White* by Caryl Brahms, S.J. Simon; *cast* Margaret Lockwood, Vic Olivier, Peter Graves, Jean Simmons.

Time Flies

1944 88m bw; *pc* Gainsborough; *d* Walter Forde; *prod* Edward Black; *sc* J.O.C. Orton, Ted Kavanaugh, Howard Irving Young; *cast* Tommy Handley, Felix Aylmer, Evelyn Dall, George Moon.

Counterblast (US: The Devil's Plot)

1948 99m bw; *pc* British National; *d* Paul Stein; *prod* Louis H. Jackson; *sc* Jack Whittingham; *story* Guy Morgan; *cast* Marvyn Johns, Robert Beatty, Nora Pilbeam, Margaretta Scott.

The Perfect Woman

1949 89m bw; *pc* Two Cities; *d* Bernard Knowles; *prod, adaptation* George Black; *dialogue* Knowles, J.B. Boothroyd; *play* Wallace Geoffrey, Basil Mitchell; *cast* Patricia Roc, Nigel Patrick, Stanley Holloway, Miles Malleson.

Mr Drake's Duck

1950 85m bw; *pc* Douglas Fairbanks Jnr Productions; *d, sc* Val Guest; *prod* Daniel M. Angel; *radio play* Ian Messiter; *cast* Douglas Fairbanks Jnr, Yolande Donlan, Wilfred Hyde-White, A.E. Matthews.

The Man in the White Suit

1951 81m bw; *pc* Ealing; *d* Alexander Mackendrick; *prod* Sidney Cole; *sc* Roger MacDougall, John Dighton, Mackendrick; *cast* Alec Guinness, Joan Greenwood, Cecil Parker, Ernest Thesiger.

Four Sided Triangle

1952 81m bw; *pc* Hammer; *d* Terence Fisher; *prod* Michael Carreras, Alexander Paal; *sc* Paul Tabori, Fisher; *novel* William F. Temple; *cast* Barbara Payton, Stephen Murray, James Hayter, John Van Eyssen.

The Sound Barrier (US: Breaking the Sound Barrier)

1952 118m bw; *pc* London; *d, prod* David Lean; *sc* Terence Rattigan; *cast* Ralph Richardson, Nigel Patrick, Ann Todd, John Justin.

The Net

1953 86m bw; *pc* Two Cities; *d* Anthony Asquith; *prod* Anthony Darnborough; *sc* William Fairchild; *novel* John Pudney; *cast* Phylis Calvert, Noel Willman, Herbert Lom, James Donald.

Spaceways

1953 76m bw; *pc* Hammer; *d* Terence Fisher; *prod* Michael Carreras; *sc* Paul Tabori, Richard Landau; *radio play* Charles Eric Maine; *cast* Howard Duff, Eva Bartok, Alan Wheatley, Philip Leaver.

Devil Girl from Mars

1954 76m bw; *pc* Danzigers; *d* David Macdonald; *prod* Edward J. Danziger, Harry Lee Danziger; *sc, play* John C. Mather, James Eastwood; *cast* Patricia Laffan, Hugh McDermott, Hazel Court, Adrienne Corri.

Stranger from Venus (US: Immediate Disaster)

1954 75m bw; *pc* Rich and Rich/Princess; *d* Burt Balaban; *prod* Balaban, Gene Martel; *sc* Hans Jacoby; *story* Desmond Leslie; *cast* Helmut Dantine, Patricia Neal, Derek Bond, Cyril Luckham.

The Quatermass Experiment (aka The Quatermass Xperiment, US: The Creeping Unknown)

1955 82m (US: 78m) bw; *pc* Hammer; *d* Val Guest; *prod* Anthony Hinds; *sc* Richard Landau, Guest; *TV serial* Nigel Kneale; *cast* Brian Donlevy, Richard Wordsworth, Jack Warner, Margia Dean.

Fire Maidens from Outer Space

1956 80m bw; *pc* Criterion; *d, sc* Cy Roth; *prod* George Fowler; *cast* Anthony Dexter, Susan Shaw, Harry Fowler, Paul Carpenter.

The Gamma People

1956 79m (US: 76m) bw; *pc* Warwick; *d* John Gilling; *prod* John Gossage; *sc* Gilling, Gossage; *story* Louis Pollock; *cast* Paul Douglas, Eva Bartok, Leslie Phillips, Walter Rilla.

1984

1956 91m bw; *pc* Holiday; *d* Michael Anderson; *prod* N. Peter Rathvon; *sc* William P. Templeton, Ralph Bettinson; *novel* George Orwell; *cast* Edmond O'Brien, Jan Sterling, Michael Redgrave, David Kossoff.

Satellite in the Sky

1956 85m col Cinemascope; *pc* Tridelta; *d* Paul Dickson; *prod* Edward J. Danziger, Harry Lee Danziger; *sc* John Mather, Lois Maxwell, Donald Wolfit, Bryan Forbes.

Timeslip (US: The Atomic Man)

1956 93m (US: 76m) bw; *pc* Merton Park; *d* Ken Hughes; *prod* Alec C. Snowden; *sc* Charles Eric Maine; *novel The Isotope Man* by Maine; *cast* Gene Nelson, Faith Domergue, Joseph Tomelty, Peter Arne.

X the Unknown

1956 78m bw; *pc* Hammer; *d* Leslie Norman, Joseph Walton; *prod* Anthony Hinds; *sc* Jimmy Sangster; *cast* Dean Jagger, Leo McKern, William Lucas, Edward Chapman.

The Abominable Snowman (US: The Abominable Snowman of the Himalayas)

1957 91m (US: 85m) bw Regalscope; *pc* Hammer; *d* Val Guest; *prod* Aubrey Baring; *sc* Nigel Kneale; *TV play The Creature* by Kneale; *cast* Forrest Tucker, Peter Cushing, Maureen Connell, Richard Wattis. (See figure 27.)

The Curse of Frankenstein

1957 83m col; *pc* Hammer; *d* Terence Fisher; *prod* Anthony Hinds; *sc* Jimmy Sangster; *cast* Peter Cushing, Robert Urquhart, Hazel Court, Christopher Lee.

Figure 27 The Belgian poster for *The Abominable Snowman* (1957).
Source: Courtesy of the British Cinema and Television Research Group archive

Escapement (US: The Electronic Monster)

1957 76m bw; *pc* Merton Park; *d* Montgomery Tully; *prod* Alec C. Snowden; *sc* Charles Eric Maine, J. MacLaren Ross; *novel* Maine; *cast* Paul Cameron, Mary Murphy, Meredith Edwards, Peter Illing.

Fiend without a Face

1957 74m bw; *pc* Producers Associates; *d* Arthur Crabtree; *prod* John Croydon; *sc* Herbert J. Leder; *short story* 'The Thought Monster' by Amelia Reynolds Long; *cast* Marshall Thompson, Kim Parker, Kynaston Reeves, Stanley Maxted.

The Man without a Body

1957 80m bw; *pc* Filmplays; *d* W. Lee Wilder, Charles Saunders; *prod* Guido Coen; *sc* William Grote; *cast* Robert Hutton, George Coulouris, Julie Arnall, Nadja Regin.

Quatermass II (US: Enemy from Space)

1957 85m bw; *pc* Hammer; *d* Val Guest; *sc* Nigel Kneale, Guest; *TV serial* Kneale; *cast* Brian Donlevy, John Longden, William Franklyn, Tom Chatto.

The Strange World of Planet X (US: The Cosmic Monster, The Crawling Terror)

1957 75m bw; *pc* DCA; *d* Gilbert Gunn; *prod* George Maynard; *sc* Paul Ryder; *novel* René Ray; *cast* Forrest Tucker, Gaby André, Martin Benson, Wyndham Goldie.

Womaneater

1957 71m bw; *pc* Fortress; *d* Charles Saunders; *prod* Guido Coen; *sc* Brandon Fleming; *cast* George Coulouris, Vera Day, Joy Webster, Pater Wayn.

First Man into Space

1958 77m bw; *pc* Amalgamated; *d* Robert Day; *prod* John Croydon, Charles Vetter Jr; *sc* John C. Cooper, Lance Z. Hargreaves; *story* Wyatt Ordung; *cast* Marshall Thompson, Marla Landi, Robert Ayres, Bill Nagy.

The Revenge of Frankenstein

1958 91m col; *pc* Hammer; *d* Terence Fisher; *prod* Anthony Hinds; *sc* Jimmy Sangster; *cast* Peter Cushing, Michael Gwynn, Francis Matthews, Eunice Grayson.

The Trollenberg Terror (US: The Crawling Eye)

1958 84m bw; *pc* Tempean; *d* Quentin Lawrence; *prod* Robert S. Baker, Monty Berman; *sc* Jimmy Sangster; *TV serial* Peter Keys; *cast* Forrest Tucker, Laurence Payne, Janet Munro, Warren Mitchell.

Behemoth the Sea Monster (US: The Giant Behemoth)

1959 72m (US: 79m) bw; *pc* Allied Artists; *d* Douglas Hickox, Eugène Lourié; *prod* David Diamond, Ted Lloyd; *sc* Lourié; *story* Robert Abel, Allen Adler; *cast* Gene Evans, André Morrell, Leigh Madison, John Turner.

The Man Who Could Cheat Death

1959 83m col; *pc* Hammer; *d* Terence Fisher; *prod* Anthony Hinds; *sc* Jimmy Sangster; *play The Man in Half Moon Street* by Barré Lyndon; *cast* Anton Diffring, Hazel Court, Christopher Lee, Arnold Marle.

Konga

1960 90m col Spectamation; *pc* Merton Park – Herman Cohen; *d* John Lemont; *prod* Herman Cohen; *sc* Albert Kondel, Cohen; *cast* Michael Gough, Mayo Johns, Claire Gordon, Jess Conrad.

Man in the Moon

1960 98m bw; *pc* Excalibur/Allied Film Makers; *d* Basil Dearden; *prod* Michael Relph; *sc* Relph, Bryan Forbes; *cast* Kenneth More, Shirley Anne Field, Norman Bird, Michael Hordern.

The Two Faces of Dr Jekyll (US: House of Fright, Jekyll's Inferno)

1960 78, 88m (US: 80m) bw; *pc* Hammer; *d* Terence Fisher; *prod* Michael Carreras; *sc* Wolf Mankowitz; *novel The Strange Case of Dr Jekyll and Mr Hyde* by Robert Louis Stevenson; *cast* Paul Massie, Dawn Addams, Christopher Lee, David Kossoff.

Village of the Damned

1960 78m bw; *pc* MGM; *d* Wolf Rilla; *prod* Ronald Kinnoch; *sc* Stirling Sillphant, Wolf Rilla, George Barclay (Kinnoch); *novel The Midwich Cuckoos* by John Wyndham; *cast* George Sanders, Barbara Shelley, Martin Stephens, Michael Gwynn.

The Damned (US: These Are the Damned)

1961 87m (US: 96m) bw Hammerscope; *pc* Hammer-Swallow; *d* Joseph Losey; *prod* Anthony Hinds; *sc* Evan Jones; *novel The Children of Light* by H.L. Lawrence; *cast* Macdonald Carey, Shirley Anne Field, Vivieca Lindfors, Oliver Reed. (See figure 28.)

The Day the Earth Caught Fire

1961 99m bw (some prints partly tinted) Dyaliscope; *pc* Melina/British Lion; *d, prod* Val Guest; *sc* Wolf Mankowitz, Guest; *cast* Edward Judd, Janet Munro, Leo McKern, Arthur Christiansen.

Gorgo

1961 78m col; *pc* King Brothers; *d* Eugène Lourié; *sc* John Loring, Daniel Hyatt; *story* Lourié, Hyatt; *cast* Bill Travers, William Sylvester, Vincent Winter, Bruce Setton.

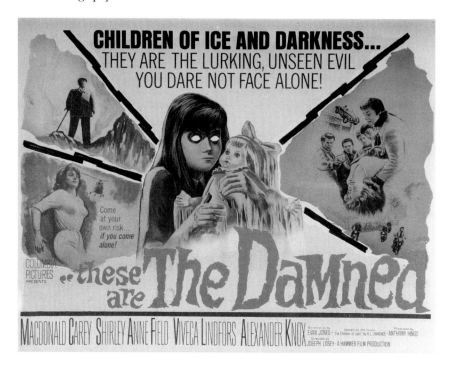

Figure 28 The American poster for Joseph Losey's *The Damned* (1961).
Source: Courtesy of the British Cinema and Television Research Group archive

Mysterious Island

1961 GB/US 101m col; *pc* Ameran; *d* Cy Endfield; *prod* Charles H. Schneer; *sc*
John Prebble, Daniel Ullman, Crane Wilbur; *novel L'Ile mystérieuse* by Jules
Verne; *cast* Michael Craig, Joan Greenwood, Herbert Lom, Gary Merrill.

What a Whopper!

1961 89m bw; *pc* Viscount; *d* Gilbert Gunn; *prod* Teddy Joseph; *sc* Terry
Nation; *cast* Adam Faith, Sidney James, Carole Lesley, Terence Longdon.

Paradisio

1962 82m bw 3D; *pc* Dramatis Personae/Tonylyn; *prod* Jacques Henrici; *sc*
Lawrence Zeitlin, Henri Halle, Henrici; *cast* Arthur Howard, Eva Waegner.

Road to Hong Kong

1962 91m bw; *pc* Melnor; *d* Norman Panama; *prod* Melvin Frank; *sc* Panama,
Frank; *cast* Bob Hope, Bing Crosby, Dorothy Lamour, Joan Collins.

Vengeance (US: The Brain)

1962 GB/West Germany 83m bw; *pc* CCC/Governor; *d* Freddie Francis; *prod* Raymond Stross; *sc* Philip Mackie, Robert Stewart; *novel Donovan's Brain* by Curt Siodmak; *cast* Peter Van Eyck, Anne Heywood, Cecil Parker, Bernard Lee.

Children of the Damned

1963 90m bw; *pc* MGM; *d* Anton M. Leader; *prod* Ben Arbeid; *sc* Jack Briley; *cast* Ian Hendry, Alan Badel, Barbara Ferris, Alfred Burke.

The Day of the Triffids

1963 95m col Cinemascope; *pc* Philip Yordan; *d* Steve Sekely, Freddie Francis (uncredited); *prod* George Pitcher; *sc* Yordan; *novel* John Wyndham; *cast* Howard Keel, Nicole Maurey, Janette Scott, Kieron Moore.

The Evil of Frankenstein

1963 84m col; *pc* Hammer; *d* Freddie Francis; *prod* Anthony Hinds; *sc* John Elder (Hinds); *cast* Peter Cushing, Kiwi Kingston, Sandor Eles, Peter Woodthorpe.

It Happened Here

1963 99m bw; *d, prod, sc* Kevin Brownlow, Andrew Mollo; *cast* Sebastian Shaw, Pauline Murray, Fiona Leland, Honor Fehrson.

Lord of the Flies

1963 91m bw; *pc* Allen Hogdon/Two Arts; *d, sc* Peter Brook; *prod* Lewis M. Allen; *novel* William Golding; *cast* James Aubrey, Tom Chapin, Hugh Edwards, Roger Elwin.

The Mind Benders

1963 113m bw; *pc* Novus; *d* Basil Dearden; *prod* Michael Relph; *sc* James Kennaway; *cast* Dirk Bogarde, Mary Ure, John Clements, Michael Bryant.

The Mouse on the Moon

1963 85m col; *pc* Walter Shenson; *d* Richard Lester; *prod* Walter Shenson; *sc* Michael Pertwee; *novel* Leonard Wibberley; *cast* Margaret Rutherford, Bernard Cribbins, Terry-Thomas, Ron Moody.

Unearthly Stranger

1963 75m bw; *pc* Independent Artists/Julian Wintel–Leslie Parkyn; *d* John Krish; *prod* Albert Fennell; *sc* Rex Carlton; *cast* John Neville, Gabriella Licudi, Philip Stone, Jean Marsh.

Doctor Strangelove, or How I Learnt to Stop Worrying and Love the Bomb

1964 93m bw; *pc* Hawk Films; *d, prod* Stanley Kubrick; *sc* Kubrick, Terry Southern, Peter George; *novel Red Alert* by George; *cast* Peter Sellers, George C. Scott, Keenan Wynn, Sterling Hayden.

The Earth Dies Screaming

1964 62m bw; *pc* Lippert; *d* Terence Fisher; *prod* Robert L. Lippert, Jack Parsons; *sc* Henry Cross; *cast* Willard Parker, Virginia Field, Dennis Price, Thorley Walters.

First Men in the Moon

1964 103m col Panavision; *pc* Ameran; *d* Nathan Juran; *prod* Charles H. Schneer; *sc* Nigel Kneale, Jan Read; *novel* H.G. Wells; *cast* Lionel Jeffries, Edward Judd, Martha Hyer, Miles Malleson.

City Under the Sea (US: War Gods of the Deep)

1965 84m col Colorscope; *pc* AIP; *d* Jacques Tourneur; *prod* Daniel Haller; *sc* Charles Bennett, Louis M. Heyward; *cast* Vincent Price, Tab Hunter, David Tomlinson, Susan Hart.

The Curse of the Fly

1965 86m bw Cinemascope; *pc* Lippert; *d* Don Sharp; *prod* Robert L. Lippert, Jack Parsons; *sc* Harry Spalding; *cast* Brian Donlevy, George Barker, Carole Gray, Michael Graham.

Doctor Who and the Daleks

1965 83m col Techniscope; *pc* Aaru; *d* Gordon Flemyng; *prod* Milton Subotsky, Max J. Rosenberg; *sc* Subotsky; *TV serial* Terry Nation; *cast* Peter Cushing, Roy Castle, Jennie Linden, Roberta Tovey.

The Night Caller (US: Blood Beast from Outer Space, The Night Caller from Outer Space)

1965 84m bw; *pc* Armitage; *d* John Gilling; *prod* Ronald Liles; *sc* Jim O'Connolly; *novel The Night Callers* by Frank Crisp; *cast* John Saxon, Maurice Denham, Patricia Haines, Alfred Burke.

Spaceflight IC-1

1965 65m bw; *pc* Lippert; *d* Bernard Knowles; *prod* Robert L. Lippert, Jack Parsons; *sc* Harry Spaulding; *cast* Bill Williams, Norma West, John Cairney, Linda Marlowe.

Daleks – Invasion Earth 2150 AD

1966 84m col Techniscope; *pc* Aaru; *d* Gordon Flemyng; *prod* Max J. Rosenberg, Milton Subotsky; *sc* Subotsky; *cast* Peter Cushing, Bernard Cribbins, Ray Brooks, Andrew Keir.

The Deadly Bees

1966 83m (orig 123m) col; *pc* Amicus; *d* Freddie Francis; *prod* Max J. Rosenberg, Milton Subotsky; *sc* Robert Bloch, Anthony Marriott; *novel A Taste of Honey* by H.F. Heard; *cast* Frank Finlay, Guy Doleman, Suzanna Leigh, Catherine Finn.

Fahrenheit 451

1966 112m col; *pc* Vineyard; *d* François Truffaut; *prod* Lewis M. Allen; *sc* Truffaut, Jean-Louis Richard; *novel* Ray Bradbury; *cast* Julie Christie, Oskar Werner, Cyril Cusack, Anton Diffring.

Frankenstein Created Woman

1966 86m col; *pc* Hammer/Warner Seven Arts; *d* Terence Fisher; *prod* Anthony Nelson Keys; *sc* John Elder (Anthony Hinds); *cast* Peter Cushing, Susan Denberg, Robert Morris, Thorley Walters.

The Frozen Dead

1966 95m col; *pc* Goldstar/Seven Arts; *d, prod, sc* Herbert J. Leder; *cast* Dana Andrews, Anna Palk, Philip Gilbert, Karel Stepanek.

Invasion

1966 82m bw; *pc* Merton Park; *d* Alan Bridges; *prod* Jack Greenwood; *sc* Roger Marshall; *story* Robert Holmes; *cast* Edward Judd, Valerie Gearon, Yoko Tani, Lyndon Brook.

Island of Terror

1966 89m col; *pc* Planet; *d* Terence Fisher; *prod* Tom Blakeley; *sc* Edward Andrew Mann, Alan Ramsen; *cast* Peter Cushing, Edward Judd, Carole Gray, Eddie Byrne.

It!

1966 97m col; *pc* Goldstar/Seven Arts; *d, prod, sc* Herbert J. Leder; *cast* Roddy McDowell, Jill Haworth, Paul Maxwell, Aubrey Richards.

One Million Years BC

1966 100m (US: 96m) col; *pc* Hammer; *d* Don Chaffey; *prod* Michael Carreras; *sc* Michael Carreras based on the screenplay of *One Million BC* by Mickell Novak, George Baker, Joseph Frickert; *cast* Raquel Welch, John Richardson, Robert Brown, Martine Beswick.

The Projected Man

1966 90m (US: 77m) col Techniscope; *pc* MLC; *d* Ian Curteis; *prod* John Croydon, Maurice Fisher; *sc* John C. Cooper, Peter Bryan; *story* Frank Quattrocchi; *cast* Bryan Halliday, Mary Peach, Norman Woolland, Roland Allen.

Thunderbirds Are Go

1966 94m col Techniscope; *pc* AP Films/Century 21; *d* David Lane; *prod* Sylvia Anderson; *sc* Gerry Anderson, Sylvia Anderson.

The Vulture

1966 91m bw; *pc* Homeric/Illiad/Film Finance; *d, prod, sc* Lawrence Huntington; *cast* Robert Hutton, Akim Tamiroff, Broderick Crawford, Diane Clare.

Battle Beneath the Earth

1967 92m col; *pc* Reynolds Vetter; *d* Montgomery Tully; *prod* Charles Reynolds; *sc* L.Z. Hargreaves; *cast* Kerwin Matthews, Viviane Ventura, Robert Ayres, Peter Arne.

The Blood Beast Terror (aka The Vampire Beast Craves Blood)

1967 83m col; *pc* Tigon British; *d* Vernon Sewell; *prod* Arnold L. Miller; *sc* Peter Bryan; *cast* Peter Cushing, Robert Flemyng, Wanda Ventham, Vanessa Howard.

The Day the Fish Came Out

1967 GB/Greece 109m col; *pc* Michael Cacoyannis Productions; *d, prod, sc* Michael Cacoyannis; *cast* Tom Courtenay, Sam Wanamaker, Colin Blakely, Candice Bergen,

Jules Verne's Rocket to the Moon (aka Those Fantastic Flying Fools, Blast Off)

1967 95m col Panavision; *pc* Jules Verne Films; *d* Don Sharp; *prod* Harry Alan Towers; *sc* Dave Freeman; *story* Peter Welbeck (Towers) based on the writings of Jules Verne; *cast* Burl Ives, Troy Donahue, Gert Frobe, Hermione Gingold.

Night of the Big Heat (US: Island of the Burning Damned, Island of the Burning Doomed)

1967 94m col; *pc* Planet; *d* Terence Fisher; *prod* Tom Blakeley; *sc* Ronald Liles *add dialogue* Pip Baker, Jane Baker; *novel* John Lymington; *cast* Christopher Lee, Peter Cushing, Patrick Allen, Sarah Lawson.

Privilege

1967 103m col; *pc* World Film Services/Memorial Enterprises; *d* Peter Watkins; *prod* John Heyman; *sc* Norman Bogner; *story* Johnny Speight; *cast* Paul Jones, Jean Shrimpton, Mark London, Max Bacon.

Quatermass and the Pit (US: Five Million Miles to Earth)

1967 97m col; *pc* Hammer; *d* Roy Ward Baker; *prod* Anthony Nelson Keys; *sc* Nigel Kneale; *TV serial* Kneale; *cast* Andrew Keir, James Donald, Barbara Shelley, Julian Glover.

The Sorcerers

1967 85m col; *pc* Tigon/Curtwel/Global; *d* Michael Reeves; *prod* Patrick Curtis, Tony Tenser; *sc* Reeves, Tom Baker based on an original idea by John Burke; *cast* Boris Karloff, Catherine Lacey, Ian Ogilvy, Elizabeth Grey.

The Terrornauts

1967 75, 62m col; *pc* Amicus; *d* Montgomery Tully; *prod* Max J. Rosenberg; *sc* John Brunner; *novel The Wailing Asteroid* by Murray Leinster; *cast* Simon Oates, Zena Marshall, Charles Hawtrey, Patricia Hayes.

They Came from Beyond Space

1967 85m col; *pc* Amicus; *d* Freddie Francis; *prod* Max J. Rosenberg, Milton Subotsky; *sc* Subotsky; *novel The Gods Hate Kansas* by Joseph Millard; *cast* Robert Hutton, Jennifer Jayne, Zia Mohyeddin, Michael Gough. (See figure 29.)

Figure 29   An American lobby card for *They Came from Beyond Space* (1967).
Source: Courtesy of the British Cinema and Television Research Group archive

The Lost Continent

1968 98m col; *pc* Hammer; *d, prod* Michael Carreras; *sc* Michael Nash (Carreras); *novel Uncharted Seas* by Dennis Wheatley; *cast* Eric Porter, Hildegarde Neff, Suzanna Leigh, Tony Beckley.

Popdown

1968 98, 54m col; *pc* Fremar; *d, prod, sc* Fred Marshall; *cast* Diane Keen, Jane Bates, Zoot Money, Carol Rachell.

Slave Girls (US: Prehistoric Women)

1968 (made in 1966) 74m (US: 95m) col Cinemascope; *pc* Hammer; *d, prod* Michael Carreras; *sc* Henry Younger (Carreras); *cast* Michael Latimer, Martine Beswick, Edina Ronay, Carol White.

Thunderbird 6

1968 90m col Techniscope; *pc* AP Films/Century 21; *d* David Lane; *prod* Sylvia Anderson; *sc* Gerry Anderson, Sylvia Anderson.

2001: A Space Odyssey

1968 141m (orig 160m) col Super Panavision/Cinerama; *pc* MGM/Stanley Kubrick; *d, prod* Stanley Kubrick; *sc* Kubrick, Arthur C. Clarke; *short story* 'The Sentinel' by Clarke; *cast* Keir Dullea, Gary Lockwood, William Sylvester, Douglas Rain.

Work is a Four Letter Word

1968 93m col; *pc* Cavalcade; *d* Peter Hall; *prod* Thomas Clyde; *sc* Jeremy Brooks; *play Eh?* by Henry Livings; *cast* David Warner, Cilla Black, Elizabeth Spriggs, Zia Mohyeddin.

The Bed Sitting Room

1969 91m col; *pc* Oscar Lewenstein; *d, prod* Richard Lester; *sc* John Antrobus; *play* Antrobus, Spike Milligan; *cast* Ralph Richardson, Rita Tushingham, Michael Hordern, Arthur Lowe.

The Body Stealers (US: Thin Air, Invasion of the Body Stealers)

1969 91m col; *pc* Tigon British/Sagittarius; *d* Gerry Levy; *prod* Tony Tenser; *story and script* Mike St Clair; *revised screenplay* Peter Marcus; *cast* George Sanders, Maurice Evans, Patrick Allen, Neil Connery.

Captain Nemo and the Underwater City

1969 106m col Panavision; *pc* Omnia; *d* James Hill; *prod* Bertram Ostrer, Steven Pallos; *sc* Pip Baker, Jane Baker; *cast* Robert Ryan, Chuck Connors, Nanette Newman, Bill Fraser.

Doppelganger (aka Journey to the Far Side of the Sun)

1969 99m col; *pc* Century 21; *d* Robert Parrish; *prod, sc* Gerry Anderson, Sylvia Anderson; *cast* Ian Hendry, Roy Thinnes, Herbert Lom, Lynn Loring.

Frankenstein Must Be Destroyed

1969 96m col; *pc* Hammer; *d* Terence Fisher; *prod* Anthony Nelson Keys; *sc* Bert Batt; *story* Batt, Keys; *cast* Peter Cushing, Simon Ward, Veronica Carlson, Freddie Jones.

The Mind of Mr Soames

1969 98m col; *pc* Amicus; *d* Alan Cooke; *prod* Max J. Rosenberg, Milton Subotsky; *sc* John Hale, Edward Simpson; *novel* Charles Eric Maine; *cast* Terence Stamp, Robert Vaughn, Nigel Davenport, Donal Donnelly.

Moon Zero Two

1969 100m col; *pc* Hammer/Warner Bros; *d* Roy Ward Baker; *prod, sc* Michael Carreras; *story* Gavin Lyall, Frank Hardman, Martin Davidson; *cast* James Olson, Catherina von Schell, Warren Mitchell, Adrienne Corri.

Nine Ages of Nakedness

1969 95m col; *pc* Token; *d, prod, sc* George Harrison Marks; *cast* Marks, Max Wall, Max Bacon, Julian Orchard.

Scream and Scream Again

1969 95m col; *pc* Amicus; *d* Gordon Hessler; *prod* Milton Subotsky, Max J. Rosenberg; *sc* Christopher Wicking; *novel The Disorientated Man* by Peter Saxon; *cast* Vincent Price, Christopher Lee, Peter Cushing, Michael Gothard.

Zeta One (US: Alien Women, The Love Factor)

1969 84m col; *pc* Tigon; *d* Michael Cort; *prod* George Maynard; *sc* Cort, Alastair McKenzie based on a story from *Zeta* magazine; *cast* Robin Hawdon, Yutte Stensgaard, James Robertson Justice, Charles Hawtrey.

Horror of Frankenstein

1970 95m col; *pc* Hammer; *d, prod* Jimmy Sangster; *sc* Sangster, Jeremy Burnham; *cast* Ralph Bates, Kate O'Mara, Graham James, Veronica Carlson.

I, Monster

1970 75m col; *pc* Amicus; *d* Stephen Weeks; *prod* Max J. Rosenberg, Milton Subotsky; *sc* Subotsky; *cast* Christopher Lee, Peter Cushing, Richard Hurndall, George Merritt.

No Blade of Grass

1970 97m col Panavision; *pc* MGM; *d, prod* Cornel Wilde; *sc* Sean Forestal, Jefferson Pascal; *novel The Death of Grass* by John Christopher; *cast* Nigel Davenport, Jean Wallace, Anthony May, Lynne Frederick.

Toomorrow

1970 95m col; *pc* Sweet Music/Lowndes; *d, sc* Val Guest; *prod* Harry Saltzman, Don Kirshner; *cast* Olivia Newton-John, Benny Thomas, Vic Cooper, Karl Chambers.

Trog

1970 91m col; *pc* Herman Cohen/Warner; *d* Freddie Francis; *prod* Herman Cohen; *sc* Aben Kandel; *story* Peter Bryan, John Gilling; *cast* Joan Crawford, Michael Gough, Bernard Kay, David Griffin.

When Dinosaurs Ruled the Earth

1970 100m (US: 96m) col; *pc* Hammer; *d* Val Guest; *prod* Aida Young; *sc* Guest from screen treatment by J.G. [J.D. in credits] Ballard; *cast* Victoria Vetri, Patrick Allen, Robin Hawdon, Imogen Hassell.

A Clockwork Orange

1971 136m col; *pc* Polaris/Warner Bros; *d, prod, sc* Stanley Kubrick; *novel* Anthony Burgess; *cast* Malcolm McDowell, Patrick Magee, Michael Bates, Adrienne Corri.

Percy

1971 103m col; *pc* Anglo-EMI/Welbeck; *d* Ralph Thomas; *prod* Betty E. Box; *sc* Hugh Leonard; *novel* Raymond Hitchcock; *cast* Hywel Bennett, Elke Sommer, Denholm Elliott, Britt Ekland.

Quest for Love

1971 90m col; *pc* Peter Rogers; *d* Ralph Thomas; *prod* Peter Eton; *sc* Terence Feely; *short story* 'Random Quest' by John Wyndham; *cast* Tom Bell, Joan Collins, Denholm Elliott, Laurence Naismith.

The Creeping Flesh

1972 91m col; *pc* Tigon British/World Film Services; *d* Freddie Francis; *prod* Michael Redbourn; *sc* Peter Spenceley, Jonathan Rumbold; *cast* Christopher Lee, Peter Cushing, Lorna Heilbron, George Benson.

Death Line (US: Raw Meat)

1972 87m col; *pc* K-L; *d, story* Gary Sherman; *prod* Paul Maslansky; *sc* Ceri Jones; *cast* Donald Pleasance, Norman Rossington, Christopher Lee, Hugh Armstrong.

Doomwatch

1972 92m col; *pc* Tigon; *d* Peter Sasdy; *prod* Tony Tenser; *sc* Clive Exton; *cast* Ian Bannen, Judy Geeson, John Paul, Simon Oates.

Dr Phibes Rises Again

1972 89m col; *pc* AIP; *d* Robert Fuest; *prod* Louis M. Heyward; *sc* Fuest, Robert Blees based on characters created by James Whitton, William Goldstein; *cast* Vincent Price, Robert Quarry, Valli Kemp, Peter Cushing.

Horror Express (aka Panic on the Transiberian Express)

1972 GB/Spain 88m (orig 90m) col; *pc* Granada/Benmar; *d* Gene Martin;

prod Bernard Gordon; *sc* Arnaud d'Usseau, Julian Halevy; *story* Eugenio Martin; *cast* Christopher Lee, Peter Cushing, Telly Savalas, Silvia Tortosa.

Digby – the Biggest Dog in the World

1973 88m col; *pc* Walter Shenson; *d* Joseph McGrath; *prod* Walter Shenson; *sc* Michael Pertwee; *cast* Jim Dale, Spike Milligan, Angela Douglas, Milo O'Shea.

The Final Programme (US: Last Days of Man on Earth)

1973 89m col; *pc* Goodtimes/Gladiole; *d, sc* Robert Fuest; *prod* John Goldstone, Sanford Lieberson; *novel* Michael Moorcock; *cast* Jon Finch, Jenny Runacre, Sterling Hayden, Patrick Magee.

Frankenstein and the Monster from Hell

1973 99m col; *pc* Hammer; *d* Terence Fisher; *prod* Roy Skeggs; *sc* John Elder (Anthony Hinds); *cast* Peter Cushing, Shane Briant, Madeleine Smith, John Stratton.

Horror Hospital

1973 91m col; *pc* Noteworthy; *d, sc* Anthony Balch; *prod* Richard Gordon; *cast* Michael Gough, Robin Askwith, Vanessa Shaw, Dennis Price.

The Mutations (US: The Freakmaker)

1973 92m col; *pc* Getty Picture Corp.; *d* Jack Cardiff; *prod* Robert D. Weinbach; *sc* Weinbach, Edward Mann; *cast* Donald Pleasance, Tom Baker, Brad Harris, Julie Ege.

Phase IV

1973 84m col; *pc* Alced/Paramount/PBR; *d* Saul Bass; *prod* Paul B. Radin; *sc* May Simon; *cast* Nigel Davenport, Lynne Frederick, Michael Murphy, Alan Gifford.

Zardoz

1973 104m (orig 105m) col Panavision; *pc* John Boorman/20th Century Fox; *d, prod, sc* John Boorman; *cast* Sean Connery, Charlotte Rampling, Sara Kestleman, John Alderton.

The Land that Time Forgot

1974 91m col; *pc* Amicus; *d* Kevin Connor; *prod* John Dark; *sc* James Cawthorne, Michael Moorcock; *novel* Edgar Rice Burroughs; *cast* Doug McClure, John McEnery, Susan Penhaligon, Keith Barron.

Percy's Progress (US: It's Not the Size that Counts)

1974 101m col; *pc* Betty E. Box–Ralph Thomas; *d* Ralph Thomas; *prod* Betty E. Box; *sc* Sid Colin inspired by the novel *Percy* by Raymond Hitchcock; *cast* Leigh Lawson, Elke Sommer, Denholm Elliott, Judy Geeson.

Who? (US: The Man in the Steel Mask, Robo Man)

1974 (rel 1979) 93m col; *pc* Lion International/Hemisphere; *d* Jack Gold; *prod* Barry Levinson; *sc* John Gould (Gold); *novel* Algis Budrys; *cast* Elliott Gould, Trevor Howard, Joseph Bova, Ed Grover.

The Rocky Horror Picture Show

1975 100m (US: 95m) col; *pc* 20th Century Fox; *d* Jim Sharman; *prod* Michael White; *sc* Richard O'Brien, Sharman; *play* O'Brien; *cast* Tim Curry, Susan Sarandon, Barry Bostick, Richard O'Brien.

The Sexplorer (US: The Girl from Starship Venus)

1975 85m col; *pc* Meadway; *d, sc* Derek Ford; *prod* Morton Lewis; *cast* Monika Ringwald, Andrew Grant, Mark Jones, Tanya Ferova.

At the Earth's Core

1976 90m col; *pc* Amicus; *d* Kevin Connor; *prod* John Dark; *sc* Milton Subotsky; *novel* Edgar Rice Burroughs; *cast* Doug McClure, Peter Cushing, Caroline Munro, Cy Grant.

The Man Who Fell to Earth

1976 138m (US: 118m) col Panavision; *pc* British Lion; *d* Nicolas Roeg; *prod* Michael Deeley, Barry Spikings; *sc* Paul Mayersberg; *novel* Walter Tevis; *cast* David Bowie, Rip Torn, Candy Clark, Buck Henry.

The People That Time Forgot

1977 90m col; *pc* Amicus/AIP; *d* Kevin Connor; *prod* John Dark; *sc* Patrick Tilley; *novel* Edgar Rice Burroughs; *cast* Patrick Wayne, Sarah Douglas, Dana Gillespie, Doug McClure.

Prey (US: Alien Prey)

1977 83, 75m (orig 85m) col; *pc* Tymar; *d* Norman J. Warren; *prod* Terence Marcel, David Wimbury; *sc* Max Cuff; *story* Quinn Donoghue based on a story by Wimbury, Marcel; *cast* Sally Faulkner, Barry Stokes, Glory Annan, Sandy Chinn.

Jubilee

1978 104m col; *pc* Whaley-Malin/Megalovision; *d, sc* Derek Jarman; *cast* Jenny Runacre, Toyah Willcox, Jordan, Little Nell.

Superman

1978 143m col Panavision; *pc* Dovemead/International; *d* Richard Donner; *prod* Alexander Salkind, Pierre Spengler; *sc* Mario Puzo, David Newman, Robert Benton, Leslie Newman; *cast* Christopher Reeve, Margot Kidder, Marlon Brando, Gene Hackman.

Warlords of Atlantis

1978 96m col; *pc* EMI; *d* Kevin Connor; *prod* John Dark; *sc* Brian Hayles; *cast* Doug McClure, Peter Gilmore, Shane Rimmer, Lea Brodie.

Alien

1979 GB/US 117m col Panavision; *pc* 20th Century Fox/Brandywine; *d* Ridley Scott; *prod* Gordon Carroll, David Giler, Walter Hill; *sc* Dan O'Bannon; *story* O'Bannon, Ronald Shussett; *cast* Tom Skerritt, Sigourney Weaver, John Hurt, Ian Holm.

Moonraker

1979 GB/France 126m col Panavision; *pc* Eon/Les Productions Artistes Associés; *d* Lewis Gilbert; *prod* Albert R. Broccoli; *sc* Christopher Wood; *novel* Ian Fleming; *cast* Roger Moore, Lois Chiles, Michael Lonsdale, Richard Kiel.

Outer Touch (US: Spaced Out)

1979 78m (US: 84m) col; *pc* Three-Six-Two; *d* Norman J. Warren; *prod* David Speechley; *sc* Andrew Payne from an idea by Speechley; *cast* Barry Stokes, Tony Maiden, Glory Annen, Michael Rowlatt.

Flash Gordon

1980 115m col Panavision; *pc* Famous/Sterling; *d* Michael Hodges; *prod* Dino De Laurentiis; *sc* Lorenzo Semple Jnr from characters created by Alex Raymond; *cast* Sam Jones, Melody Anderson, Topol, Max Von Sydow.

Inseminoid (US: Horror Planet)

1980 92m col J-D-C Scope; *pc* Jupiter; *d* Norman J. Warren; *prod* Richard Gordon, David Speechley; *sc* Nick Maley, Gloria Maley; *cast* Judy Geeson, Robin Clarke, Jennifer Ashley, Stephanie Beacham.

Saturn 3

1980 86m (orig 87m) col; *pc* Transcontinental; *d, prod* Stanley Donen; *sc* Martin Amis; *story* John Barry; *cast* Kirk Douglas, Farrah Fawcett, Harvey Keitel, Ed Bishop.

Superman 2

1980 127m col Panavision; *pc* Dovemead/International; *d* Richard Lester; *prod* Pierre Spengler; *sc* Mario Puzo, David Newman, Leslie Newman; *cast* Christopher Reeve, Gene Hackman, Ned Beatty, Margot Kidder.

Memoirs of a Survivor

1981 115m col; *pc* Memorial; *d* David Gladwell; *prod* Michael Medwin, Penny Clark; *sc* Kerry Crabbe, Gladwell; *novel* Doris Lessing; *cast* Julie Christie, Christopher Guard, Leonie Mellinger, Debbie Hutchings.

Outland

1981 109m col Panavision; *pc* The Ladd Company; *d, sc* Peter Hyams; *prod* Richard A. Roth; *cast* Sean Connery, Peter Boyle, Frances Sternhagen, James B. Sikking.

Time Bandits

1981 113m col; *pc* Handmade; *d, prod* Terry Gilliam sc Michael Palin, Gilliam; *cast* John Cleese, David Rappaport, Kenny Baker, Sean Connery.

Xtro

1982 86m col; *pc* Ashley-Amalgamated; *d* Harry Bromley Davenport; *prod* Mark Forstater; *sc* Iain Cassie, Robert Smith from an original screenplay by Michael Parry, Davenport; *add dialogue* Jo Ann Kaplan; *cast* Bernice Stegers, Philip Sayers, Maryam D'Abo, Danny Brainin.

Krull

1983 121m col; *pc* Columbia/Ted Mann-Ron Silverman; *d* Peter Yates; *prod* Ron Silverman; *sc* Stanford Sherman; *cast* Ken Marshall, Lysette Anthony, Freddie Jones, Francesca Annis.

Prisoners of the Lost Universe

1983 US/GB 90m (orig 91m) col; *pc* Marcel-Robertson; *d, sc* Terry Marcel; *prod* John Hardy; *cast* Richard Hatch, Kay Lenz, John Saxon, Peter O'Farrell.

Superman 3

1983 125m col Panavision; *d* Richard Lester; *prod* Pierre Spengler; *sc* David Newman, Leslie Newman; *cast* Christopher Reeve, Richard Pryor, Annette O'Toole, Robert Vaughn.

Dark Enemy

1984 97m col (16mm); *d* Colin Finbow; *pc, sc* Children's Film Unit; *cast* David Haig, Douglas Storm, Martin Laing, Chris Chescoe.

Electric Dreams

1984 GB/US 112m col; *pc* Virgin/MGM/UA; *d* Steve Barron; *prod* Rusty Lemorande, Larry De Waay; *sc* Lemorande; *cast* Lenny Von Dohlen, Virginia Madsen, Maxwell Caulfield, Bud Cort.

Nineteen Eighty-Four

1984 110m col; *pc* Umbrella-Rosenbloom/Virgin; *d, sc* Michael Radford; *prod* Simon Perry; *novel* George Orwell; *cast* John Hurt, Richard Burton, Suzanna Hamilton, Cyril Cusack.

Supergirl

1984 124m col Panavision; *pc* Artistry/Cantharus; *d* Jeannot Swarc; *prod* Timothy Burrill; *sc* David Odell; *cast* Helen Slater, Faye Dunaway, Peter O'Toole, Mia Farrow.

Brazil

1985 142m (US: 131m) col; *pc* Brazil Productions; *d* Terry Gilliam; *prod* Arnon Michan; *sc* Gilliam, Tom Stoppard, Charles McKeown; *cast* Jonathan Pryce, Robert De Niro, Michael Palin, Kim Greist.

D.A.R.Y.L.

1985 99m col; *pc* Paramount; *d* Simon Wincer; *prod* John Heyman; *sc* David Ambrose, Allan Scott, Jeffrey Ellis; *cast* Mary Beth Hurt, Michael McKean, Barett Oliver, Kathryn Walker.

Lifeforce

1985 101, 116m col Cinemascope; *pc* London Cannon; *d* Tobe Hooper; *prod* Menahem Golan, Yoram Globus; *sc* Dan O'Bannon, Don Jakoby; *novel The Space Vampires* by Colin Wilson; *cast* Steve Railsback, Peter Firth, Frank Finlay, Mathilda May.

Lorca and the Outlaws (US: Starship)

1985 100m col; *pc* Lorca Films; *d* Roger Christian; *prod* Michael Guest; *sc* Christian, Matthew Jacobs; *cast* John Tarrant, Donogh Rees, Deep Roy, Ralph Cottrell.

Morons from Outer Space

1985 91m col; *pc* Thorn EMI; *d* Mike Hodges; *prod* Barry Hanson; *sc* Griff Rhys Jones, Mel Smith; *cast* Smith, Jones, Paul Bown, Joanne Pearce.

Underworld (aka Transmutations)

1985 103, 100, 84m col; *pc* Green Man; *d* George Pavlou; *prod* Kevin Attew, Don Hawkins, Al Burgess; *sc* Clive Barker, James Caplin; *cast* Denholm Elliott, Steven Berkoff, Larry Lamb, Miranda Richardson.

Biggles (US: Biggles: Adventures in Time)

1986 92m col; *pc* Compact Yellowbill/Tambarle; *d* John Hough; *prod* Kent Walwin, Pom Olivier; *sc* John Groves, Walwin based on characters created by Captain W.E. Johns; *cast* Neil Dickson, Alex Hyde-White, Peter Cushing, Fiona Hutchison.

When the Wind Blows

1986 84m col (animation); *pc* Meltdown/British Screen/Film Four International TVC London/Penguin Books; *d* Jimmy T. Murakami; *prod* Joan Coates; *sc, book* Raymond Briggs *voices* John Mills, Peggy Ashcroft, Robin Houston.

Whoops Apocalypse!

1986 91m col; *pc* ITC; *d* Tom Bussmann; *prod* Brian Eastman; *sc* Andrew Marshall, David Renwick; *cast* Loretta Swit, Peter Cook, Rik Mayall, Ian Richardson.

Friendship's Death

1987 78m col; *pc* Modelmark/BFI; *d, sc, short story* Peter Wollen; *prod* Colin McCabe; *cast* Bill Paterson, Tilda Swinton, Patrick Bauchau, Ruby Baker.

Slipstream

1989 102m col; *pc* Entertainment Film Productions; *d* Stephen M. Lisberger; *prod* Gary Kurtz; *sc* Tony Kayden based on story material by Bill Bauer, Charles Edward Pogue; *cast* Mark Hamill, Bob Peck, Bill Paxton, Kitty Aldridge.

Hardware

1990 GB/USA 94m col; *pc* Palace/Millimeter/British Screen/Wicked; *d, sc* Richard Stanley; *prod* Joanne Sellar, Paul Trybits; *story* 'SHOK!' by Steve McManus, Kevin O'Neill in *2000 AD*; *cast* Dylan McDermott, Stacey Travis, John Lynch, William Hootkins.

Split Second

1991 90m col; *pc* Challenge/Muse; *d* Tony Maylam; *prod* Laura Gregory; *sc* Garry Scott Thompson; *cast* Rutger Hauer, Kim Cattrall, Neil Duncan, Michael J. Pollard.

The Lawnmower Man

1992 GB/USA 108m ('director's cut' 142m) col; *pc* Allied Vision/Lane Pringle/Fuji Eight; *d* Brett Leonard; *prod* Gimel Everett; *sc* Leonard, Everett; *story* Stephen King; *cast* Jeff Fahey, Pierce Brosnan, Jenny Wright, Geoffrey Lewis.

Death Machine

1993 GB/Japan 98m col; *pc* Fugitive/Entertainment/Victor; *d, sc* Stephen Norrington; *prod* Dominic Anciano; *cast* Ely Pouget, Brad Dourif, William Hootkins, John Sharian.

Shopping

1993 107m col; *pc* Impact/Channel Four/Polygram/Kuzui Enterprises/WMG; *d, sc* Paul Anderson; *prod* Jeremy Bolt; *cast* Sadie Frost, Jude Law, Sean Pertwee, Marianne Faithfull.

U.F.O.

1993 79m col; *pc* Polygram/George Foster; *d* Tony Dow; *prod* Simon Wright; *sc* Richard Hall, Wright, Roy 'Chubby' Brown; *cast* Brown, Sara Stockbridge, Amanda Symons, Roger Lloyd Pack.

Welcome II the Terrordome

1994 94m col; *pc* Non Aligned/Channel Four/Metro Tartan; *d, sc* Ngozi Onwurah; *cast* Suzette Llewellyn, Saffron Burrows, Felix Joseph, Valentine Nonyela.

Loch Ness

1994 101m col; *pc* Working Title/Stephen Ujlaki; *d* John Henderson; *prod* Tim Bevan; *sc* John Fusco; *cast* Ted Danson, Joely Richardson, Ian Holm, Harris Yulin.

Event Horizon

1997 GB/USA 96m col Panavision; *pc* Paramount/Golar/Impact; *d* Paul Anderson; *sc* Philip Eisner; *cast* Laurence Fishburne, Sam Neill, Kathleen Quinlan, Joely Richardson.

Index